VOCATIONAL STEWARDSHIP
FOR THE COMMON GOOD

KINGDOM
CALLING

Amy L. Sherman

Foreword by Reggie McNeal
Afterword by Steven Garber

IVP Books

An imprint of InterVarsity Press
Downers Grove, Illinois

InterVarsity Press
P.O. Box 1400, Downers Grove, IL 60515-1426
World Wide Web: www.ivpress.com
E-mail: email@ivpress.com

InterVarsity Press® is the book-publishing division of InterVarsity Christian Fellowship/USA®, a movement of
students and faculty active on campus at hundreds of universities, colleges and schools of nursing in the United States
of America, and a member movement of the International Fellowship of Evangelical Students. For information
about local and regional activities, write Public Relations Dept., InterVarsity Christian Fellowship/USA, 6400
Schroeder Rd., P.O. Box 7895, Madison, WI 53707-7895, or visit the IVCF website at <www.intervarsity.org>.

While all stories in this book are true, some names and identifying information in this book have been changed to
protect the privacy of the individuals involved.

Design: Cindy Kiple

ISBN 978-0-8308-3809-7

Printed in the United States of America ∞

Library of Congress Cataloging-in-Publication Data

Sherman, Amy L., 1965-
  Kingdom calling: vocational stewardship for the common good / Amy
L. Sherman.
    p. cm.
  Includes bibliographical references and index.
  ISBN 978-0-8308-3809-7 (pbk.: alk. paper)
  1. Work—Religious aspects—Christianity. 2. Employees—Religious
life. 3. Christian stewardship. 4. Righteousness—Biblical teaching.
5. Bible. O.T. Proverbs XI, 10—Criticism, interpretation, etc.
I. Title.
  BV4593.S54 2011
  306.3'613—dc23

2011032887

P	19	18	17	16	15	14	13	12	11	10	9	8	7	6	5	4	3	2	1
Y	27	26	25	24	23	22	21	20	19	18	17	16	15	14	13	12	11			

May the favor of the Lord our God rest upon us;
establish the work of our hands for us—yes,
establish the work of our hands.

Psalm 90:17

For Jay Hein,

a genuine servant-leader,
a man of vision and humility,
a tsaddiq.

How blessed I am to colabor with you.

Contents

Foreword by Reggie McNeal 11

Acknowledgments 13

Introduction
The Glorious Vision of Proverbs 11:10 15

PART 1: Theological Foundations

1. What Does a Rejoiced City Look Like? 27

2. What Do the Righteous Look Like? 45

3. Why We Aren't the *Tsaddiqim* 64

4. How the Gospel of the Kingdom Nurtures
the *Tsaddiqim*. 77

PART 2: Discipling for Vocational Stewardship

5. Integrating Faith and Work 91
The Status Quo Is Inadequate

6. Inspiration 101

7. Discovery. 116

8. Formation 129

PART 3: Pathways of Vocational Stewardship

9. Deploying Vocational Power 143
Four Pathways

10. Pathway 1 151
Bloom Where You're Planted

11. Pathway 2 169
    Donate Your Skills

12. Pathway 3 183
    Launch Your Own Social Enterprise

13. Pathway 4 199
    Participate in Your Church's Targeted Initiative

Conclusion 223
Rejoicing the City

Afterword by Steven Garber 232

Appendix A 235
Key Theological Themes Undergirding Vocational Stewardship

Appendix B 242
A Discussion Guide for Congregational Small Groups

Appendix C 245
For Further Information

Appendix D 246
Index of Profiles by Vocation

Notes 248

About the Author 272

Foreword

Two recent personal conversations tell the story inside the story of this book. The first one took place over dinner in my home with my older daughter. "I don't need the church coming up with anything else for me to do in order to be missional," she said. "I feel missional five days a week." Working as a Licensed Master Social Worker (LMSW) in a local hospital, she is exposed to the dark underbelly of our culture, helping people each day sort through a series of health-care options that will shape the next chapter of their lives. Lots of times none of the options are good, and people are devastated. Often she is the only person who can speak a word of hope in the situation. She is living out her faith in a place and in a way that really counts. Right where life (and death) is happening.

The second conversation took place half a continent away from me. A pastor relayed to one of our Leadership Network researchers a comment made by one of his team members after they had participated in our Missional Renaissance Leadership Community. The multiple teams involved in this leadership community include both church leaders and community leaders who figure out ways to fast-forward the church's missional engagement in their respective communities. This particular team had brought their city's mayor to a recent gathering in Dallas. On the flight back home from the experience the mayor commented to the pastor, "I have never thought of my job as mayor as a ministry—until now." I suspect no church committee assignment could compare in terms of community impact with what this guy does every single day.

My daughter and the mayor represent a growing number of people who share an awareness that kingdom assignments typically involve venues beyond local church real estate and programming. Kingdom callings take us into schools, hospitals, businesses and art studios, as well as homeless shelters, AIDs clinics and battered-women's homes. Kingdom callings are lived out as neighbors, friends, spouses, parents, employees and students, as well as community volunteers, school mentors, Little League coaches and, yes, church workers. In other words, kingdom callings play out in all of life, because that's where life plays out!

For centuries we have focused on church-centric activities as the primary arena for exercising our calling as followers of Jesus. The missional perspective of the church does not shrinkwrap the kingdom down to this limited scope of activity. Missional thinkers see the church in its full-blown kingdom capacity—deployed across all domains of our culture. We are the "called out" people of God for sure. But we have been "called out" to be "sent back"! We are sent back as viral agents of the King to partner in his redemptive mission *in the world*.

In this thoughtful volume Amy Sherman shares with us her conviction that "vocational stewardship"—the intentional deployment of our workplace knowledge, skills, platforms and networks—provides us a way to advance the kingdom for community transformation. Amy's work goes beyond the typical discussion of faith/work integration. Not only does she help us see the potential for promoting a kingdom agenda at work, she gives us suggestions for how congregations and church leaders can equip their members to pull it off. If you are thinking this book primarily will help church people learn how to start Bible studies at work, then your thinking is far too restricted. Amy has nothing less than changing your city in mind!

Imagine architects serving the kingdom as architects and bankers promoting kingdom values as bankers, all directing their efforts into community development to help people experience the abundant life Jesus talked about. Now imagine having a resource so people who "get" this can "get on" with it. Imagine no longer.

Just turn the page.

Reggie McNeal
Missional Leadership Specialist, Leadership Network, Dallas, Texas
Author of *Missional Renaissance* and *Missional Communities*

Acknowledgments

Many individuals participated in this project, and I owe them a debt of gratitude that I cannot convey in mere words. Nonetheless, these thanks are heartfelt. My intellectual debt to Rev. Tim Keller of Redeemer Presbyterian Church, New York City, will be readily evident in the pages ahead. Tim, your work and words have enriched my life beyond measure. Andy Crouch generously shared his time with me and steered me ably in the early days of the project. Andy, your encouragement has been precious, and your writing has taught me much. Steve Garber's insights and counsel have been invaluable. Steve, how pleased I am to be colaboring with you in this vineyard where you have been faithful over so many years!

My pastor, Greg Thompson, and Rev. Scott Seaton of Emmanuel Presbyterian, Arlington, Virginia, read a draft of my manuscript with great care and offered suggestions that significantly improved the final product. Thanks so much, brothers. A number of other church leaders, including Andy Rittenhouse, Sean Radke, Drue Warner, Wade Bradshaw, Sue Mallory, Don Simmons, Tom Nelson and Dana Preusch, have also offered generous encouragement and useful commentary along the way.

My thanks also go to Gary MacPhee of Engineering Ministries International, Gordon Murphy of The Barnabas Group, Lloyd Reeb of Halftime, Bill Wellons of Fellowship Associates, and Mark Stearns and Dale Bowen of Lincoln Village Ministries for connecting me to several of the individuals profiled in the book.

My friends from Mariners Church in Irvine, California, particularly Robin Riley, Laurie Beshore and Matt Olthoff, made possible my "testing out" of some of the concepts of the book in a real-life congregational context. Thanks so much to each of you for that amazing opportunity. My young research assistants from the past few years—Reynolds Chapman, Becca Saunders, Rose Merritt, Mary Grace Edwards, Sally Carlson and Kelly Givens—helped faithfully with research, interviewing and endless transcribing. Their good humor and genuine enthusiasm for the project were a source of encouragement throughout.

I'm very grateful as well to my dear friends Barb Armacost, Anne McLain Brown and Ellen Merry for the many conversations we've shared about this material and the numerous suggestions they made that have strengthened the book. Thanks are also due to Ken Myers, Jerry Moll, Steve Hayner, Mark Labberton, Arloa Sutter, Nate Ledbetter and Jason Adkins for useful comments along the way. I'm grateful as well for on-site visits to Crossroads Church in Cincinnati and particularly to Don Gerrod and Andrew Peters for their help and hospitality.

My visit to Mavuno Church in Nairobi under the kind and generous hospitality of pastors Murithii Wanjau and Linda Ochola-Adolwa and Murithii's able assistant, Frank Ondere, was the highlight of the project. Mavuno's example continues to inspire me, and I pray that it will do so for many other American Christians through this book. Warm thanks to Emily Masloff for accompanying me as my cheerful and helpful assistant on the Nairobi trip. I hope we get to do this again sometime.

I am also deeply grateful to every person who agreed to be interviewed for and profiled in this book. Without your stories, it would not have life, inspiration and instruction.

Finally, my best thanks go to my boss and friend, Jay Hein, without whose tremendous support this book would not have been possible.

Introduction

THE GLORIOUS VISION OF PROVERBS 11:10

I wept when I read the book—and felt a bit embarrassed. After all, it was a nonfiction text—a sociologist's tome assigned in a friend's graduate religion class. It wasn't exactly a tearjerker. But cry I did while reading Michael Lindsay's *Faith in the Halls of Power*.

It's a work of fine scholarship. Lindsay spent three years interviewing some 360 evangelicals who had achieved substantive positions in their various fields—business, politics, the academy, media and entertainment. The book's animating question concerns how these successful individuals integrate their faith and work. After his exhaustive research, Lindsay concluded:

> As these leaders have climbed the professional ladder, they have not jettisoned their religious identity. Actually, according to many, the journey has deepened their faith. Yes, the leaders I interviewed fall into the same pits as their secular peers. They are susceptible to materialism and overweening pride. Yet on the whole, they remain very different from other leaders, and the reason is their faith.[1]

That doesn't sound like something that would inspire tears. But Lindsay's research suggests his conclusion is too generous; there is little evidence provided in *Faith in the Halls of Power* of how these evangelical leaders' lifestyles differ from those of their secular peers.

Concerning business leaders, for example, Lindsay found that "evangelical executives tend to accept the material accoutrements of an affluent lifestyle without question."[2] To his surprise and dismay, almost none of his interviewees raised the issue of exorbitant CEO pay. Less than half of the business executives reported that their faith influences how they invest their money. One CEO of a giant company admitted he never prayed over business deals. Several of the male business executives, when asked how their faith affected their work, pointed to plaques in their offices that signaled their Christian beliefs. Meanwhile, the females reported they deliberately wore crosses.

With regard to evangelicals in influential positions in Hollywood, Lindsay wrote that they "differ little from others in the entertainment industry. They drive luxury cars, live in exclusive communities, and worry that their fame and talent will evaporate overnight."[3]

More than 60 percent of Lindsay's interviewees were not involved in a local church. Very few were members of accountability groups that could help them wrestle with the temptations of power, privilege and wealth.

There were exceptions, of course, and these bright spots in the book can be inspiring.[4] Phil Anschutz, a billionaire movie producer, has used his influence and money to bring to the big screen such greats as *Amazing Grace* and the Narnia tales. And Max De Pree, former CEO of Herman Miller, pursued justice in his firm by deliberately capping his salary at no more than twenty times the earnings of his lowest-paid worker.

On the whole, though, Lindsay's careful research showed that the vast majority of evangelicals perched atop their career ladders in various social sectors displayed a profoundly anemic vision for what they could accomplish for the kingdom of God. And *that* made me cry, because just before reading Lindsay's book, I'd been deeply moved by a sermon given by Rev. Tim Keller of Redeemer Presbyterian in New York City. In it, Keller spoke briefly about Proverbs 11:10: "When the righteous prosper, the city rejoices."[5]

Keller explained that the "righteous" (Hebrew *tsaddiqim*) are the just, the people who follow God's heart and ways and who see everything they have as gifts from God to be stewarded for his purposes. Keller wrote, "The righteous in the book of Proverbs are by definition those who are willing to disadvantage themselves for the community while the wicked are those who put their own economic, social, and personal needs ahead of the needs of the community."[6]

This definition of the righteous is what makes the verse sensible. Otherwise, it would be counterintuitive. After all, the text tells us that there is a particular group of people in the city who are prospering—flourishing in their jobs, their health, their finances. This fortunate group has power, wealth and standing; they are, as Keller put it, "at the top." And as they continue to thrive, the entire city—including those at the bottom—celebrates.

That's a bit strange, given human nature. One could easily imagine a more plausible scenario marked by jealousy and resentment, where those at the bottom complain, "The rich keep getting richer while the poor just get poorer."

Instead, the flourishing of the righteous is a cause for rejoicing. (And not just any sort of rejoicing, as we will see in a minute.) Because the *tsaddiqim* view their prosperity not as a means of self-enrichment or self-aggrandizement, but rather as a vehicle for blessing others, *everyone* benefits from their success. As the *tsaddiqim* prosper, they steward everything—their money, vocational position and expertise, assets, resources, opportunities, education, relationships, social position, entrée and networks—for the *common* good, for the advancing of God's justice and shalom.[7] And when the people "at the top" act like this, the whole community cheers. When the righteous prosper, their prosperity makes life better for all.

A Dancing-in-the-Streets Rejoicing

The word *rejoice* in Proverbs 11:10 is very important. A unique term, used only one other time in the Old Testament, it carries almost military connotations. It describes ecstatic joy, the exultation and triumph that people express in celebration when they have been delivered from the hand of their oppressors.

So *rejoice* here is a big, robust word. This is deep, passionate rejoicing—not the "happy, happy" rejoicing of a birthday party but VE-Day–type rejoicing—"the war is over and we won" rejoicing. This is soul-soaring exultation.

By this we realize that the righteous, in their prospering, must be making a remarkably positive difference in their city. They must be stewarding their power, wealth, skills and influence for the common good to bring about noticeable, significant transformation in the city. Otherwise, what would be prompting the residents there to go crazy with gladness and gratitude? Clearly the *tsaddiqim*'s stewardship is not simply taking their used clothes over to the Salvation Army Thrift Store and poor people finding them there and being pleased to get a hundred-dollar dress for five dollars. No, this dancing-in-the-streets rejoicing occurs when the *tsad-diqim* advance justice and shalom in the city in such ways that vulnerable people at the bottom stop being oppressed, start having genuine opportunity and begin to enjoy spiritual and physical health, economic sufficiency and security.

Indeed, what the text teaches is that by the intentional stewardship of their time, talent and treasure, the *tsaddiqim* bring nothing less than *foretastes of the kingdom of God* into reality.

VE-Day–type celebrations occur at those places where King Jesus is about his grand, sweeping work of restoration. They occur at the intersections where Jesus is pushing back the kingdom of darkness and pushing in the kingdom of light. His life was one of offering foretastes of the coming kingdom's shalom; his death conquered all sin and evil that could oppose the kingdom's full realization. He came to begin the work of "making all things new." He saves us from our sins to call us into that work with him.

JESUS' KINGDOM MISSION

Jesus made his kingdom mission abundantly clear. He announced it in his inaugural address in Luke 4:16-21. Reading that prophetic passage about the time to come when the good news will be preached to the poor, the blind healed and the oppressed set free, he announced that in him, this text was "fulfilled." Jesus' central teaching theme was the kingdom. His Sermon on the Mount was about the ethics of the kingdom. He offered parables to give people windows into the kingdom's ways and virtues.

Jesus' evangelistic invitation was "Come, enter my kingdom." And he interpreted his miracles in kingdom language. For example, he cast out a demon in a suffering man, and the Pharisees were critical of it. They accused him of being in sync with Beelzebub. But Jesus responded, "If I drive out demons by the finger of God, then the kingdom of God has come upon you" (Lk 11:20). When he healed the lepers, it is as though he was reaching into the new heavens and new earth, where there will be no disease, and yanking a foretaste of that back into the present.[8]

Our King wants us realize that the kingdom of God has begun to break into our time and space.[9] His work was about offering foretastes of kingdom realities—and this is the life and mission he calls us, his followers, into. The *tsaddiqim* gladly join King Jesus in that glorious mission.

Prospering, but Not the *Tsaddiqim*

The jarring discrepancy between this noble, inspiring vision of the *tsaddiqim* and the anemic vision of so many of the evangelical professionals Lindsay interviewed really got under my skin. How tragic that so many believers who bear the name "the prospering" could not also lay claim to the title "the *tsaddiqim*." Why was this happening? Apparently the Christian communities that Lindsay's interviewees were part of failed to disciple them to become people who thought well and deeply about using their vocational power to advance the kingdom. I wondered, How widespread is this problem throughout evangelicalism? More importantly, what can be done in our churches to change it? And are there any congregations of the *tsaddiqim* out there that we can learn from?

Because of my own sense of vocational calling, I couldn't let go of these questions. For nearly twenty years, I've been trying to help churches grow in loving their neighbors near and far—especially their vulnerable, lower-income neighbors. My life's work is to help churches live out Micah 6:8: "He has shown you, O man, what is good. And what does the LORD require of you? To act justly and to love mercy and to walk humbly with your God." Toward that end, I've served on my own church's staff, founding and running a Christian community-development nonprofit serving one lower-income neighborhood in Charlottesville, Virginia. I've trained ministry leaders in mapping their community's needs and assets, designing effective responses and evaluating progress. I've written books and how-to manuals to aid congregational leaders in mobilizing and deploying their people in holistic community ministries.

Keller's vision of the *tsaddiqim* completely entranced me. Proverbs 11:10 gave some new, exciting language to my work. I realized that what I'd been trying to do all those years is help churches "rejoice" their cities—whether those churches were in little cities like my hometown of Charlottesville, or in megatropolises like Miami, or in communities abroad like Nairobi or Guatemala City. I also realized that the glorious vision of Proverbs 11:10, coupled with the sad evidence from *Faith in the Halls of Power*, meant that accomplishing that "rejoicing" requires at least two big things.

First, it means that many churches need to have a more robust, comprehensive view of what they should be aiming at missionally. If we're going to actually "rejoice" our cities, we need to candidly assess what we're doing.

Are we engaged in efforts that are relevant to the groans of creation and the cries of the poor? Are we producing disciples whose work is contributing to profound transformations that set people to dancing in the streets? Have we joined King Jesus on his grand, sweeping mission of restoration? In cooperation with him, are we bringing foretastes of justice and shalom—or are we largely engaged in mere charity?

Second, it means that churches need to take vocation much more seriously. Proverbs 11:10 tells us what our prosperity is for. Most middle- and upper-middle-class American evangelicals can be labeled "the prospering." True, we're not Bill Gates or Donald Trump. But compared with many of our neighbors and with the billions of poor all over the world, we are indeed privileged and wealthy.

A vital part of that prosperity is our vocational power. Unlike so many in the world, we have choices about what work to do. We are well educated and skilled. We have networks to draw on, platforms to use, knowledge to share. Many of us are working in institutions—schools, media, government agencies, corporations—that significantly influence the quality of life in our nation. God has lavished all this on us for a reason: that we would use it for the common good, not for individual gain.

Clearly, learning how to steward our vocational power is a major component of growing as the *tsaddiqim* who rejoice our cities. By vocational stewardship, I mean *the intentional and strategic deployment of our vocational power—knowledge, platform, networks, position, influence, skills and reputation—to advance foretastes of God's kingdom.* For missional congregations that desire to rejoice their cities, vocational stewardship is an essential strategy. To accomplish their big vision, they need to capitalize intentionally on the vocational power of their members.

I decided to try to write a book to help missional leaders do just that.

INTENDED AUDIENCE

I've never known of a church that doesn't encourage its people to serve God with their "time, talent and treasure." Nonetheless, very few congregations—even those sold out to the *missio Dei*—are actually facilitating "serving God with your talent" in an intentional, sustained, practical and strategic way that pays attention to members' vocational gifts, passions and power.

Dr. Don Simmons has been assisting churches with their "equipping" ministries for decades. Based on observations of scores of congregations, he reports,

> There are very few churches that have strong, intentional systems for deploying their people's time and their talent. Churches would not consider doing a stewardship campaign for money and not having systems in place to be able to gather it in, to disseminate it, to report how it's being used, and report back to the people that were giving it. But they don't think of people's service of their time and use of their talent in the same way.[10]

Congregants in our pews need to know that they should—and can—connect their workaday world and their faith. So often they feel that God is just a Sunday God. Sometimes we as church leaders exhort our people to "live for Christ's kingdom" but fail to explain adequately what that means for their lives Monday through Friday, nine to five. We must do a better job of inspiring our members about the role they can play in the mission of God and equipping them to live missionally *through their vocation*.

Based on what I've learned about congregations that are doing this, it is clear that vocational stewardship produces exciting results. Congregants experience newfound joy, meaning and intimacy with Christ. Simultaneously, the church significantly improves its effectiveness in bringing to neighbors near and far a greater foretaste of shalom.

This is a book primarily for pastors and ministry leaders—particularly those already committed to leading missional churches (that is, churches that seek to follow King Jesus on his mission of making all things new). I also hope pastors will hand it out to individual congregants who are struggling to integrate their faith and work. Hopefully believers who want to understand better how to advance kingdom purposes through their vocations—whether they've got fifty years on the job or are just starting out—will find this book helpful. I also pray that readers still in college or graduate school find some relevant wisdom in these pages about their future work.

OVERVIEW OF THE BOOK

Part one, "Theological Foundations," provides the biblical underpinning for both the "foretaste-bringing" mission of the church and the strategy of vocational stewardship. Based on a study of the "preview" passages in Scripture that describe the new heavens and new earth, I argue in chapter one that a "rejoiced" city is a place where ever-increasing foretastes of justice and shalom are experienced realities. I explore several specific dimensions of justice and shalom, and I describe how Christians today are advancing those kingdom values through their work. Nurturing a rejoiced city is a glorious and daunting task.

Chapter two describes the *tsaddiqim* who try to undertake this labor. They are utterly humble, God-dependent, spiritually mature people who seek to live righteously in and through their work. Chapter three examines the obstacles that have kept many Christians from living as the *tsaddiqim*, and chapter four discusses how churches can respond to those obstacles.

Part two, "Discipling for Vocational Stewardship," provides practical how-to guidance for church leaders. It begins in chapter five with a look at the current state of evangelical thinking on faith/work integration—and the shortcomings therein. Then I outline three key tasks necessary for equipping parishioners to become people who steward their vocational power intentionally as the *tsaddiqim*.

Chapter six, "Inspiration," offers a concise biblical theology of work that should undergird any vocational stewardship initiative. Chapter seven examines the task of discovery—helping congregants to identify their passions, "holy discontents"[11] and the dimensions of their vocational power. Chapter eight then addresses the critical task of formation—that is, the necessary shaping of congregants' inner life that enables them to be effective, humble and wise stewards of their vocational power.

Part three gets into the meat of vocational stewardship. First, I offer a brief introduction to four pathways for deploying congregants in the stewardship of their vocations: (1) blooming where we are planted by strategically stewarding our current job; (2) donating our vocational skills as a volunteer; (3) launching a new social enterprise; and (4) participating in a targeted initiative of our congregation aimed at transforming a particular community or solving a specific social problem. Here I also talk briefly about the temptations inherent in each pathway—potential stumbling blocks for which church leaders must prepare their members.

Chapters nine through twelve take up one pathway each. Each shows what vocational stewardship looks like in the lives of actual believers and gives examples of specific churches that have learned lessons in how to equip and deploy their members along that pathway.[12]

The Pink Spoon

Several years ago, Rev. Jeff White from Harlem New Song Church taught a workshop at my church. He talked about the work of King Jesus in bringing restoration and held up one of those tiny pink taste-test spoons from Baskin-Robbins. You know, the spoons that offer you a foretaste of the ice cream to come. Jeff challenged attendees to see themselves as such spoons, for our role in the world is about offering foretastes of the kingdom to our neighbors near and far.

Missional church leaders call their people to live as pink spoons. But they need to *show them* what that actually looks like. I wrote this book because, to a significant degree, being pink spoons means stewarding our vocational power for the common good.

American workers, on average, spend forty-five hours a week at work.[13] That's about 40 percent of our waking hours each week—a huge amount of time. If church leaders don't help parishioners discern how to live missionally through that work, they miss a major—in some instances *the* major—avenue believers have for learning to live as foretastes.

PART 1

Theological Foundations

What Does a
Rejoiced City Look Like?

*The citizens of God's city are the
best possible citizens of their earthly cities.*

REV. TIM KELLER

If the missional call of the church is to "rejoice" our cities by offering our neighbors foretastes of kingdom realities, we need to understand what the Scriptures tell us about the coming kingdom. Congregational leaders need to know the marks of the kingdom—its characteristics, features, purposes and virtues. Then they need to preach and teach on these kingdom marks, helping their congregants catch a vision for what a rejoiced city looks like. Church members then have direction for strategically deploying their God-given vocational power to advance those kingdom expressions.

One helpful way of identifying these kingdom features is to examine closely the "preview" passages in the Bible. Pop a movie into your DVD player, and you'll first see previews of coming attractions. Similarly, throughout the Bible are previews of the coming "feature film": the kingdom of God in all its consummated fullness. These texts offer us glimpses into what life will be like in the new heavens and new earth.

Jesus used a preview passage (Is 61:1-2) when he stood up in a Nazarene synagogue and announced his mission on earth. Many believers are familiar with preview passages like Isaiah 11:6 ("the wolf will live with the lamb") and Micah 4:3 ("they will beat their swords into plowshares") because these are commonly read during Advent. Many other preview passages, however, are less familiar.

A comprehensive study of all the preview passages is beyond the scope of this book. However, we can launch an initial excavation based on a collection of preview passages.[1] These offer us a clear view of the characteristics of the consummated kingdom. Preeminently, the preview passages reveal that the consummated kingdom is marked by two major, closely related features: justice and shalom. A rejoiced city, therefore, is one where ever-greater tastes of justice and shalom are made real.

Both concepts are massive. Using a couple of shorthand organizing schemes, I'll examine several specific dimensions of justice and shalom. Along the way, we'll meet Christians who are nurturing those aspects of justice and shalom through their work. My hope is that this material provides fodder for sermons and illustrations as church leaders seek to inspire their flock to catch a vision of being the *tsaddiqim* who rejoice the city.

JUSTICE

The latter half of Proverbs 11:10 draws our attention to the vital place of justice in rejoicing the city. The full verse reads, "When the righteous prosper, the city rejoices; when the wicked perish, there are shouts of joy."

Readers familiar with Old Testament study recognize a structure here common to much Hebrew poetry: parallelism. Essentially, the poet says the same thing twice in a verse, using two slightly different constructions. In Proverbs 11:10, there is a connection between the "righteous prospering" on the one hand, and the "wicked perishing" on the other. Notice that both events—the righteous prospering and the wicked perishing—produce the same reaction: wild rejoicing. Jubilation arises when the wicked—who are described over and over in the Old Testament as doers of injustice and inequity—are cast down and replaced by the *tsaddiqim*, the doers of justice.

When the righteous prosper, justice prevails. The *tsaddiqim* seek to bring into reality three dimensions of justice that mark the consummated kingdom.[2] These are presented in figure 1.1. We'll look at each in turn.

Rescue. The consummated kingdom is marked by the end of all oppression. In it, the poor, the innocent and the helpless will be rescued from all the grim realities they face at the hands of violent oppressors. Psalm 10

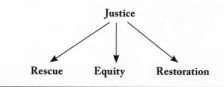

Figure 1.1. Three dimensions of justice

paints a terrifying picture of these realities, noting how the wicked person "hunts down the weak" and "lies in wait like a lion in cover" to attack and drag off the poor. The prophet laments in Isaiah 5:23 that the wicked "acquit the guilty for a bribe but deny justice to the innocent" and that they are "swift to shed innocent blood" (Is 59:7). Under the wicked, the social order is bankrupt and the people feel hopeless: "Justice is far from us, and righteousness does not reach us. We look for light, but all is darkness; for brightness, but we walk in deep shadows" (Is 59:9).

The work of rescue is about remedying these sorts of violent injustice. It involves identifying, exposing and transforming situations where there is an abuse of power, typically perpetuated through coercion and deception. It means bringing about the kinds of foretastes of justice celebrated in Isaiah 62:8-9 (ending bonded labor) and Isaiah 61:1 (freeing the illegally detained from their dark prisons).[3]

British solicitor Matthew Price has deployed his vocational talents to affect these kinds of rescue. For two years, Matthew and his wife and baby boy made their home Kampala, Uganda, serving the cause of justice on a short-term assignment through a British mission agency, BMS World Mission. There Matthew came alongside the Ugandan Christian Law Fellowship (UCLF), mentoring paralegals and law-school students to train them in "maintain[ing] justice in the courts" (Amos 5:15). Under his supervision, the students reached out to prisoners, many of whom were victims of illegal detention. They were not served due process of law and had languished in overcrowded jails for months, not even knowing what crimes they were charged with.

Matthew and his team visited police stations and jail cells to advise prisoners of their rights under Ugandan law. By the end of his first year, Matthew and the UCLF lawyers had offered representation to more than 260 prisoners, and nearly two hundred of their cases were completed. He explains, "Through the intervention of Christian lawyers these prisoners

have finally tasted justice in their case, whether by way of an acquittal and
release or conviction and a defined term of sentence."[4]

Equity. The second dimension of justice we see in the preview passages
is equity. Isaiah 11:4 celebrates the time to come when the King will righteously "judge the poor, and decide with equity for the meek of the earth"
(ASV). Jeremiah looks forward with similar anticipation: "'The days are
coming,' declares the LORD, 'when I will grow a righteous branch for
David. He will be a king who will rule wisely. He will do what is fair and
right in the land'" (Jer 23:5 God's Word Translation).

Other prophets also celebrate the equitable relations that will character-
ize life in the new heavens and new earth. In Isaiah we learn no more scoun-
drels will be in power, defrauding the needy (Is 32:5-8). Ezekiel prophesies
that there will be no one who plunders the weak (Ezek 34:17-22).

Equity is not a simple word to define. It denotes fairness and impartial-
ity. Equity is about ensuring that the poor and weak are not disproportion-
ately burdened by society's common problems. It is about promoting public
policies that do not favor the rich over the poor but treat people equally. It
is about avoiding policies that unfairly burden the poor and weak.

Equity is somewhat easier to describe than to define. Consider, for example, the process of seeking equitable solutions to the challenge of providing affordable housing in a community. Such housing has to be constructed,
and that requires money. Decisions have to be made about where to locate
the units. Those decisions entail costs. To oversimplify for the purposes of
illustration, in light of this societal challenge, two possible paths could be
pursued. One involves concentrating the building and placement of affordable housing in poor, politically weak communities such as inner-city
neighborhoods. We might label this approach "concentrating the burden."
The other path involves distributing the cost of building the housing over a
wide region and spreading those units across many different neighborhoods. We might label this approach "sharing the burden."

In many cities, the first path is taken—largely as a result of NIMBYism
("Not In My Back Yard"). Better-off citizens in suburban municipalities
don't want such housing to be built in their neighborhoods, out of fears
about crime or depressed property values. Since the economically well off
are typically also well connected politically, affordable housing often gets
built only in already depressed areas of an inner city. This creates what

scholars call "concentrated poverty neighborhoods."[5] And that brings attendant problems such as overwhelmed schools, higher crime rates and social isolation. These social problems have economic costs (for example, it is harder to start businesses in concentrated poverty neighborhoods). This approach also financially squeezes the municipalities where concentrated poverty neighborhoods exist. They have to spend more money on law enforcement and social welfare programs while having less revenue from property and business taxes.

The second path is the more equitable approach. In this scenario, the costs for constructing housing are shared across a metropolitan region, and the housing units are scattered throughout the area to avoid creating concentrated poverty neighborhoods. This is a more difficult approach to put into practice politically, but it has been implemented in places where persevering citizens demanded it.

Lobbyist Rich Nymoen played a role in a successful faith-based campaign to pursue just this approach to the affordable housing issue in the Twin Cities area of Minnesota back in the mid-1990s.[6] He was a new attorney from the University of Minnesota Law School. His decision to get involved in the effort was prompted in part by his embrace of the concept of metropolitan equity. He'd learned of this idea through an adjunct professor at the university, Myron Orfield, who was also a state legislator at the time.[7]

Orfield was pushing a variety of legislative initiatives, including one called "fair share" housing. The approach was attractive to Nymoen as it emphasized that "we're all in this together." It called for a regional approach to share the costs of constructing affordable housing.

Nymoen began working with a coalition of congregations and nonprofits that eventually was named ISAIAH. It first led a successful campaign to heavily increase state funding for affordable housing. Then it began promoting the idea of inclusionary housing—scattering affordable housing in mixed-income developments to avoid the problems of concentrated poverty.

This battle to promote equity wasn't easy, and it took three years. In the end, decisions about affordable housing were placed into the hands of a seven-county metropolitan council. The council members negotiate housing goals (such as the number of units to build and where they would be located). Each county contributes financially to the regional housing fund, instead of that burden being borne by the city of Minneapolis alone.

Restoration. The third dimension of biblical justice we see in the grand story of creation/Fall/redemption/consummation concerns restoration.

In the Bible, justice is a relational concept, not simply an abstract legal concept. That is to say, biblical justice is not solely concerned with the punishment of wrongdoing, but with the healing of wrongdoers and their restoration to the community. Justice and salvation are linked concepts. As one scholar put it, "The justice of God is all about restoring wholeness in relationships—with God and with other human beings."[8]

Much of Zechariah 8 is a preview passage, and two verses speak of God's restorative justice (Zech 8:16-17). The Israelites have committed grave offenses against God. They have acted unjustly, failing to render just judgments in the courts, swearing falsely and plotting evil against their neighbors. God's response is not only punitive but also corrective. The text recalls God's judgment, but God promises forgiveness and a restoration of the relationship, and then reminds the people not to repeat their former sins.

In a rejoiced city, the criminal justice system includes this notion of restorative justice, as opposed to focusing exclusively on retributive justice. Certainly it calls offenders to account, yet it also seeks to address the *harm* of the crime, not just the legal offense against the state. It takes the victim seriously and seeks the reinstatement of the offender into the social fabric when possible. Recognizing that crime is about harm to human relationships, it seeks reconciliation of those relationships to the greatest degree possible.[9]

The restorative justice movement has had some success in infiltrating criminal justice systems in the United States and abroad. The system in Genesee County, New York, is one of them. There a sheriff named Doug Call and a longtime public servant named Dennis Wittman worked together to incorporate key principles of restorative justice into the way the county prosecuted nonviolent offenders. The initiative became known as Genesee Justice.

By the late 1970s, Call had deepened his faith by attending seminary and become convinced that true justice was not always served under the prevailing system. He recalled a case in which a young woman lost both legs in an accident caused by a twenty-year-old man. The young man was sentenced to one year in jail. At the end of the year, he moved to nearby Rochester and took a good-paying job. The victim, meanwhile, was left legless and in debt because of medical bills.

"The system broke down in her case," says Call. "We didn't make him [the offender] constructively responsible for his crime."[10] Call felt it was time to try a different approach. The more he talked about it, the more his friends urged him to run for the office of county sheriff. He did, winning that post in 1980.

Early on, Sheriff Call hired former fellow seminarian Dennis Wittman, who was then serving as a town supervisor in the area. Call asked Wittman to establish a new sentencing program requiring community service for nonviolent offenders. Call wanted offenders to do some good for the community rather than just sit in jail, being a drain on taxpayer dollars. Over the next twenty-five years, Wittman tirelessly implemented the program. When he retired in 2006, nearly five thousand offenders had performed more than 350,000 hours of unpaid work in Genesee County.

The two men were pleased with the program but felt Genesee Justice also needed to do more to attend to crime victims. Over the years, they implemented several new initiatives. One involved partnering with the local faith community to provide practical assistance to victims, such as home repairs in cases of robbery. Another brought changes to sentencing procedures whereby victims were permitted to offer "impact statements" about the harm they had suffered. A third was a reconciliation program bringing victims and offenders together face-to-face in mediated conversations. Wittman says, "Wherever there was a gap in the justice system we tried to fill it."[11]

SHALOM

A rejoiced city is marked by the three dimensions of justice noted above: rescue, equity and restoration. It is also a place where justice's twin sister, shalom, is evident in increasing measure.

Theologian Cornelius Plantinga Jr. defines *shalom* as "the webbing together of God, humans, and all creation in justice, fulfillment, and delight. . . . We call it peace, but it means far more than mere peace of mind or cease-fire among enemies. In the Bible shalom means *universal flourish-ing, wholeness, and delight.*"[12]

The consummated kingdom is characterized by shalom in the four fundamental relationships of life: peace with God, peace with self, peace with others and peace with the creation. Several of the characteristic marks of the kingdom can be loosely organized under those four headings, as depicted in table 1.2.[13] I say "loosely" organized because some kingdom values, such as beauty or wholeness, could fit under more than one heading. But this schematic offers us a starting point for constructing a robust understanding of the dimensions of shalom. Let's look at each in detail.

Table 1.2. Marks of the Consummated Kingdom

Peace with God	*Peace with Self*
Intimacy with God	Health/Wholeness
Beauty	Hope
	Comfort
Peace with Others	*Peace with the Creation*
Unity	Economic flourishing
Security/Lack of Violence	Sustainability

PEACE WITH GOD

Intimacy with God. At the center of our joy in the consummated kingdom will be our intimate relationship with God. As Zephaniah exulted, we will "sing," "shout aloud" and "be glad" because the Lord will be *with* us. The awesome Creator of all will "rejoice over [us] with singing" and "take great delight" in us (Zeph 3:14-20). We will see him "face to face" (1 Cor 13:12).

With this great hope before us, an essential part of our mission now is introducing people to a personal relationship with God. Evangelism that leads people to follow Jesus offers new believers a foretaste of the intimacy with God they will one day experience for eternity. Many of us have opportunities to do evangelism through our work-based relationships.

Stanley Tam is an excellent example. He's been running thriving businesses since the 1930s. He legally incorporated one firm, United States Plastic Corporation, so that God was a 51-percent shareholder. The company has made over 120 million dollars. Tam sends millions of that to support evangelistic ministries worldwide. He reports that through such groups, some 140,000 people have made decisions for Christ.

But Tam doesn't just write checks so others can do the work. He's an evangelist himself. He "retired" a few years back and opened a small furniture-making store. On its front door, he hung a sign: "Are you seeking peace? Come in for a free Bible." It has led to many interesting conversations.

Heisman trophy winner Danny Wuerffel seized opportunities he had to share his faith during his first "real" job after college—as a professional football player for the New Orleans Saints. He recalls expecting to be ridiculed in the locker room for his faith, but he found that the opposite happened. In the highly competitive and stressful world of professional sports, Danny's pastoral heart and manner were attractive. The environment "created a lot of ministry opportunities where people actually came to me asking some really neat questions," he explains.[14]

Additionally, in his first year with the Saints, Danny and a fellow team member started an *Our Daily Bread* club:

> We'd challenge people to read *Our Daily Bread* [a monthly devotional booklet with short, daily readings] each morning, and you had to remember what it was about. And if anyone asked you and you didn't know, you had to put a dollar in the pot. And I thought we'd get maybe five or six guys, but we ended up with fifty-six players and coaches that year.

Danny established similar clubs in the other pro teams he played on. His years as a quarterback offered, as he says, "a pretty great opportunity to share who I was and to share my faith and how that could connect in the world of the NFL."

Beauty. In the new earth, nature's comeliness will reach its pinnacle; the wilderness itself will burst into blossom, and streams will gush in the desert (Is 35). To complement all this natural beauty, human culture will flourish. All the great creativity of humankind—artistry in music, dance, painting, woodcrafts, sculpture, architecture and more—will be brought into the New Jerusalem (Is 60).

God is the source of all beauty and creativity. Artists, musicians, sculptors, writers, actors and dancers can lead people into worship of this God. Artistic talent can connect us to that transcendent beauty; it has a "vertical" purpose.[15]

Artists Jessie Nilo and Lisa Marten from Boise Vineyard Church in Idaho have brought beauty to many. Jessie, a graphic designer and illustrator, launched VineArts at the church in 2004. Her group of twenty professional and emerging artists deployed their talents to create spaces in the church building for worship prompted by beauty. Jessie felt there had been nothing "visually moving" at the church facility to complement the Vineyard's spiritually rich teaching. So VineArts painted murals on the walls. It also created a gallery at the church, with artwork from a variety of media, where congregants could spend quiet time. "I really wanted it to be about worship and contemplation," Jessie explains.[16]

One day the Vineyard's missions pastor suggested to Jessie the possibility of an arts-oriented short-term mission trip abroad. He'd told his Ecuadorian pastor friend about how VineArts was enriching the worship life of the Boise congregation, and that pastor asked if some artists would come to his church. In June 2010, five artists from Boise Vineyard traveled to Quito to serve Iglesia la Viña.

The highlight of the trip was a special morning of worship and arts facilitated by the team. In the worship room, they set up several large canvases alongside small tables with paint supplies. "The pastor explained to them that this was a morning where all forms of worship, including our creativity, would be brought," Lisa says.[17] While the musicians played worship songs, congregants could get up and paint on the canvases to express their hearts to God. "It seemed to involve all the senses at once," Jessie recalls. "They came up with some beautiful imagery—around themes of redemption and transformation and living water." On that Sunday morning, God met his worshipers in a moving way as they spoke to him through a new, visual language, thanks to artists using their vocation for the kingdom.

PEACE WITH SELF

Health/wholeness. How wonderful it will be in the age to come when we enjoy freedom from the decay of our bodies. In the consummated kingdom, there will be no more blindness or deafness (Is 32:3-4). The "lame will leap like the deer" (Is 35:6). There will be no more sickness of body or mind or spirit (Is 65:19).

Jesus' earthly ministry showed him ever attentive to the sick. Time and again, he snatched foretastes of the coming kingdom and granted sufferers healing and relief. Today we continue to represent him as we build medical clinics and hospitals, create new distribution channels to get prescription medicines where they are needed, advocate for adequate access to health care for all who need it and conduct research into new health-care technologies.

As a primary care physician in a small private practice, Dr. Andy Macfarlan reports that his faith motivates him to take a very holistic approach to patient care. He believes that God has created human beings in such a way that the spiritual, emotional and physical all intertwine. When doctors attend to patients with resources for all these arenas, he says, the patient gets the best possible care. To him, this is what it looks like to advance the kingdom value of wholeness.

This approach requires a deep commitment to relationships. Andy's conviction that "the purpose of life is about love relationships with God, self, others and the environment" motivated his desire to go into primary care medicine.[18] He also never wanted to work in a big practice, because time with patients might be compromised. Andy measures success in terms of not only providing the most excellent and competent health care, but also delivering it in a way that deeply respects patients. For him, a huge part of the definition of success is having patients "go out of [here] saying, 'I was listened to; I was given enough time. They respected me.'"

Out of respect for his elderly patients, Andy has sponsored special luncheons in his home for those over age seventy. "I want to celebrate the gifts they have given me in my practice over the years," he explains. His relationships with his senior patients have deepened his spiritual life. "These are the people who have a long-term perspective on what it means to have a relationship with God and know where God is in their life and how important that is over time," he says.

Andy's desire for patients to be served with dignity through a long-lasting relationship with a primary doctor has motivated him to launch a new initiative in his city. A free clinic there serves the working poor who lack health insurance, but they rarely see the same doctor. So Andy founded the Physicians Partnership Network (PPN). Through it, doctors coordinate pro bono care for patients who meet certain eligibility requirements. Each doctor agrees to take on a certain number of patients through PPN and serve them at their own offices. The free clinic then handles paperwork and provides liability coverage for participating doctors. Although PPN began in late 2010, Andy had already recruited thirty-six doctors who were seeing about 250 patients through the program as of early 2011.

Hope. There is a way in which all the preview passages are about hope. All make promises about what the glorious future life in the new heavens and new earth will be like. They speak to us in the midst of our pain and assure us that none who hope in the Lord will be disappointed. We learn that God will set "the lonely in families" (Ps 68:6), and he will heal the barren (Ps 113:9). Because of God's goodness, faithfulness and justice, the islands will put their hope in his law (Is 42:3-4). In the new creation, all our hopes—for change, for healing, for renewal, for reunion, for resurrection—will be fulfilled.

Offering hope to those who feel hopeless is kingdom work. Through their work as urban gardeners, Mark and Courtney Williams are nurturing hope in their distressed neighborhood in inner-city Pittsburgh.

Courtney grew up in rural Kentucky, where farming was "very much a part of the culture I knew," she says.[19] After graduating from Wheaton College, she worked at Grow Pittsburgh, "an urban agricultural organization that grew vegetables for high-end restaurants and worked with teenagers from troubled neighborhoods." There she honed her gardening skills and gained knowledge in health and nutrition. When her husband's nonprofit employer decided to launch a summer urban-gardening initiative, they hired Courtney as coordinator. The program was such a hit that the job became full time.

Today she and Mark oversee the three Lots of Hope gardens. One emerged from a long-standing community eyesore: an abandoned baseball field that had been "waist-high with weeds and bushes and garbage." Middle-school students of the neighborhood cleaned up the trash, turned the sod and planted seeds. The theme verse for the project, Mark explains, is Genesis 2:15: "The Lord God took the man and put him in the Garden of Eden to work it and take care of it."[20]

Life isn't the way it ought to be for these kids, Mark says. They suffer because of abuse, family members with addictions, discrimination and poverty. But as they work to turn the vacant lot into a thing of beauty and health, they accomplish "one small step towards making this neighborhood like it's supposed to be."[21]

The Lots of Hope name came about because of the transformation

Courtney and Mark witnessed among the middle-school students involved in the program. As Mark reports:

> The pre- and post-test was just a one-question survey. We said, "Do you believe it's possible for our neighborhood to change?" Without fail, all the kids said no. At the end of our semester, [the survey] said, "Do you believe it's possible for our neighborhood to change?" All of them said yes.[22]

Comfort. God cares about the wounded in spirit. Rich in compassion, he comes with "comfort speedy."[23] His comfort is expressed in multiple metaphors in Isaiah 54—of those rejected and abandoned who experience embrace; of the disgraced and humiliated who receive new dignity and healing; of the widow who experiences the Lord himself as husband.

Presence with the grieving, counseling for the afflicted—these are kingdom works. Our efforts to uncover the mysteries of mental illness, our therapy programs to heal the sexually abused and emotionally traumatized, our work in all kinds of counseling centers and rehabilitation camps, and our faithful visitation ministries to shut-ins and those in nursing homes—all these are expressions of kingdom priorities.

Nurse Susan Beeney works daily to bring comfort to the grieving through New Hope Grief Support. New Hope runs some thirty weekly grief groups, provides grief counselors in public schools and partners with the U.S. military in reaching out to grieving families of soldiers killed in action. Most uniquely, in 2003 Beeney's organization created New Hope Kids Camp—the only camp of its kind in the nation. Each camp provides fifteen grieving children between the ages of five and eighteen with the priceless gift of time away, listening ears, group therapy sessions, art, games, pet therapy, a mobile marine museum and nature activities. "The camps are small in number, but they are huge in the effect," Beeney reports.[24]

PEACE WITH OTHERS

Unity. In the consummated kingdom, we will experience deeper, richer, more satisfying community with other people. Isaiah 25:6-9 paints a picture of the great feast God himself will prepare for "all peoples." In the new earth, we will experience peace and harmony as members from every "nation, tribe, people and language" join in common worship of King Jesus (Rev 7:9-20).

Today our efforts to encourage racial reconciliation and build diversity and crosscultural sensitivity advance this kingdom foretaste of unity. In the multiracial village of South Holland, Illinois, Mayor Don De Graff has made the promotion of unity a major theme throughout his many years on the job.

Fifty years ago, South Holland was a mostly white, historically Dutch community. In 1990, the population was 86 percent white.[25] Today De Graff reports that the town is 72 percent African Americans, 23 to 24 percent Caucasians, 3 to 4 percent Hispanics and 1 to 2 percent Asians.[26]

To break down the barriers among these diverse groups, De Graff has promoted CommUNITY dinners. As the Village of South Holland website explains, "The main goal of CommUNITY Dinners is to foster positive discussions between people with differences in a relaxed and enjoyable setting. This helps members of the community get to know one another in a positive setting."[27] Several dinners are sponsored throughout the year. "The churches, the business association and the schools all promote these community dinners," De Graff reports. "At these meetings [we have] opportunity to talk about this broader concept of 'How do we live in a community together? What makes us tick? What makes us special and unique?'"

The mayor also strongly encourages neighborhoods to hold block parties. "We provided resources for that, which include food, fire engines, police, park benches . . . all in an effort to try and bring people together." He's found that such social events can jump-start new friendships between neighbors and catalyze the development of new neighborhood associations.

In a multiethnic community, there is a risk of prejudice between racial groups, prejudices that can be expressed in housing discrimination. De Graff works intentionally with the local realtors association to "keep close tabs on our housing situation." The association provides him with "stats as to the length of time it [takes] to sell a house, the average prices, and [we watch for] abuses or red-lining, or any illegal, unethical activities."

In South Holland, De Graff says proudly, "we have virtually broken down the walls that typically divide people. And the reason is because we make an honest and intentional intent, day in and day out, month in and month out, to address those head on. We are very proactive."

Security/lack of violence. One day, God will cause all wars to cease (Ps 46:9). In the new heavens and new earth, swords will be remade into plowshares (Mic 4:3). Nations will no longer take up arms against one another. The day of violence will be eternally ended, and God's people will enjoy perfect security. As Ezekiel put it beautifully, we will be secure in our land and live in safety, and no one will make us afraid (Ezek 34:27-28).

Today diplomacy to prevent and end warfare, and efforts to protect public safety, to nurture forgiveness and healing between former enemies and to reduce violence (for example, through educational programs, mentoring or therapy) all help to nurture foretastes of the peace that awaits us in the age to come.

In Uganda, God has used a veterinarian to promote a foretaste of security. Dr. Val Shean, a member of Christian Veterinary Mission, has been serving in the Karamoja region of northeastern Uganda since 1992. Tribes there have a decades-long legacy of warring over cattle. Things intensified in the late 1970s with the introduction of automatic weapons to the region. "Since 1979 we have had fighting, fighting, fighting in this land, from one corner to the next," Shean says.[28] A small cattle raid by one side leads to retaliation, and then the violence escalates. "Sometimes hundreds of people would come with machine guns, descending upon small villages," she says.

In spring 2009, though, a small miracle unfolded. More than six thousand Karamojong people were peacefully resettled in over sixty villages. These were members of the Pian and Bokora subtribes who had been killing each other. The peace accord was a direct result of Shean's labors.

Among the "cattle-obsessed" Karamojong people, Shean was highly regarded. Her professional prowess as a veterinarian earned her respect and friendships with leaders on both the Pian and Bokora sides. Having gained their trust, she used her influence to urge them to stop the bloodshed. She convinced leaders to study biblical principles of reconciliation.

Drawing on her networks, Shean brought a team of mature Christian men from Oregon to Uganda to teach on reconciliation using Ken Sande's book *The Peacemaker.* In winter 2007, she and this team spent two weeks teaching sixty influential elders and pastors, warriors and women from each subtribe. Though they needed to adapt Sande's book to the African context, the biblical principles of peacemaking took hold, bringing revival and repentance among the people.[29] In subsequent months, more than 2,500 people from the Pian and Bokoro groups completed the training.[30] In November 2007, representatives from each tribe met for a breakthrough peace council.

PEACE WITH THE CREATION

Economic flourishing. The new heaven and new earth will be a place of economic bounty. All people will have access to the resources needed for their economic well-being. Every person will rest secure under his or her own vine and fig tree (Mic 4:4) and enjoy the fruits of his or her labors (Is 65:22). All will have shelter (Is 65:21). Prosperity will reign as God lavishly provides food: "In that day the mountains will drip new wine, and the hills will flow with milk" (Joel 3:18). Hunger will be no more (Is 49:10).

Believers advance foretastes of the kingdom when they devote themselves to the great work of relief and development; to hunger alleviation; to microenterprise; to sustainable agriculture; to efforts to find new ways to provide everyone with adequate shelter and clean water; and to advocacy for the rule of law so that just, free enterprise can flourish.

Diversified Conveyors Inc. (DCI), owned by Tom and Beth Phillips, is bringing unique economic benefits to Memphis—and beyond. The company has become a leading manufacturer of conveyor systems for such giants as UPS and FedEx. It employs thirty-five individuals in the Memphis headquarters and many more in field offices.

From the beginning, the Phillipses envisioned their firm as a "beyond-profit" company. "Because of what Christ has done for us, how can we not bless others?" they reason.[31] DCI partners with Advance Memphis, a Christian nonprofit that runs job training classes for residents of the Cleaborn/Foote neighborhood (the nation's third-poorest ZIP code). Residents graduating from Advance Memphis have secured jobs at DCI. The Phillipses have also created scholarship funds out of the company's profits that assist residents of Cleaborn/Foote to enroll in a vocational training school or earn a bachelor's degree in college.[32]

Not only this, but the Phillipses recently hired a full-time missions coordinator.[33] Their company may be the only for-profit corporation in the country with such a position. But with the number of partnerships DCI forms with ministries, and the significant amount of profits it earmarks for charitable giving, wise stewardship required a full-time person in the role. Locally, DCI supports urban renewal projects, literacy initiatives, prison outreach and more. Internationally, it funds ministries doing everything from health care to microloans, with partners in Nepal, Burma, Poland, Peru, Brazil and several other far-flung nations.

Sustainability. So many of the preview passages speak of the healing of the creation itself as God restores what was once barren. Isaiah 51:3 is representative: "He will make her deserts like Eden, her wastelands like the garden of the LORD." God will bring streams to the desert, making the burning sands a pool and bedecking the wilderness with blooms (Is 35:1-2, 7). God loves the earth he created. He will one day set it free from its groaning. Meanwhile, we show forth his goodness and his future intentions by stewarding the creation with care.

Today human efforts to respond effectively to industrial accidents such as oil spills, to conserve rare animal species, to reclaim polluted streams and to better steward the natural world through green technologies and buildings all participate in bringing foretastes of the new earth.

Oceanographer Jorge Vazquez says he still remembers long walks with his father along the beach when he was a youngster. His dad would point out different organisms and creation's beauty. "Those long walks instilled in me a love for understanding our planet, and more importantly, the desire to make sure we are good stewards of the precious gift we call planet Earth," he says.[34] Today as a scientist with NASA's Jet Propulsion Laboratory in California, Vazquez works to improve the quality of sea-surface temperature data, an important element in the quest to understand and monitor global warming.[35]

CONCLUSION: TEACHING THE PREVIEW PASSAGES

The preview passages we've examined here are beautiful, inspiring and hopeful. Missional leaders can use them to cast vision powerfully among their congregants for the work of rejoicing the city through vocational stewardship. In closing, though, note that it is important to help congregants avoid two extremes as they listen to this sort of preaching.

On the one hand, some parishioners might wrongly assume that they (or the church) can "just do it." That is, they may vastly underestimate what it takes to usher in these foretastes of justice and shalom. They may fail to rely sufficiently on Jesus and the Spirit. While the preview passages permit us a big God-sized vision for our labors and our hopes, there is a danger of them encouraging Utopianism. The kingdom of justice and shalom will arrive in its fullness only at the return of the King. And only in the King's power—and by *his* wisdom and guidance—will we make progress in transforming our communities.

On the other hand, we must not allow parishioners to believe that, because the *full* vision of the preview passages won't by realized until the "age to come," we don't need to do anything now. It's certainly true that we are waiting for the kingdom's full consummation at Jesus' return. But while we wait, it is the task of the church—Christ's body—to enact and embody foretastes of the coming realities of that kingdom. We as Jesus' disciples have the amazing privilege of participating in his work of restoration. Indeed, joining him in this work constitutes the very center of our redeemed lives.

To put it succinctly, we need to remember that the kingdom of God is both *now* and *not yet*.

Preaching on the preview passages directs believers' gaze toward the "life of the world to come." That phrase is from the final sentence of the Nicene Creed, which many Christians recite weekly in their congregations.[36] Despite such creedal recitations—and the frequent injunctions of the New Testament to fix our eyes on that which is eternal[37]—many churchgoers are not regularly looking in that direction. Many believers are distracted easily by the cares, temptations and idols of this world. Few have a clear vision for enacting and embodying kingdom foretastes. Consequently, parishioners need regular reminders about the beautiful world that is to come as well as exhortations to live *now* in ways that correspond to those hopes. Preaching the preview passages enables pastors to remind congregants that Jesus is on the move to enact these realities—and is calling us all to join him in his works of restoration.

Such preaching must then offer practical applications of what this looks like. My hope is that the pictures painted here of Christians working to advance tastes of justice and shalom help us to see what is possible and plausible in this time when Christ's kingdom is mysteriously both *now* and *not yet*.

What Do the Righteous Look Like?

When the righteous [tsaddiqim]
prosper, the city rejoices.

PROVERBS 11:10

A central premise of this book is that the average middle-class (or wealthier) Christian in America has been blessed with much from God—skills, wealth, opportunity, vocational position, education, influence, networks. We are, in short, the prospering. The purpose of all these blessings is simple to state and difficult to live: we are blessed to be a blessing. Our generous heavenly Father desires us to deploy our time, talents and treasure to offer others foretastes of the coming kingdom. Those who do so are called the *tsaddiqim*, the righteous. What we saw from examples in Michael Lindsay's book, though, is that it is possible to be the prospering without being the *tsaddiqim*.

Clearly, living as the *tsaddiqim* isn't easy. It requires tremendous effort and intentionality. More importantly, it requires power from God's Holy Spirit. It also requires understanding what a *tsaddiq* looks like.

But it *is* possible.

In this chapter, we'll examine the characteristics of the righteousness of the *tsaddiqim*.[1] And, since this book is mainly about our work lives, we'll focus especially on what it means to be the *tsaddiqim* in the context of our vocations.

THE *TSADDIQIM*

The Hebrew word *tsaddiq* ("righteous") and its plural, *tsaddiqim*, are used two hundred times in the Old Testament.[2] They appear frequently in Psalms (fifty times) and Proverbs (sixty-six times). Bible translators try to capture their meanings by offering the English words *just* and *lawful*, and by referring to varying kinds of righteousness—in government, in one's conduct and character, and in the justice of one's cause. Theologian N. T. Wright said, "The basic meaning of 'righteousness' . . . denotes not so much the abstract idea of justice or virtue, as right standing and consequent right behaviour, within a community."[3]

While these are handles for beginning to grasp what God means by *righteous*, they can feel a bit abstract. In studying the biblical scholarship on this concept, I've found that it is helpful to see righteousness as expressing itself in three dimensions or directions: up, in and out (see table 2.1 below).

Table 2.1. What Righteousness Looks Like at Work

Dimension of Righteousness	Characteristics	Work Implications
UP	Godward orientation	*Work for God's glory, not self-fulfillment *Eschew workaholism *Set boundaries on institutional loyalty
	Humility	*Embrace functional, daily dependence on the Spirit
	Eternal perspective	*Recognize God as the audience *Value today's work as participating in the new creation
IN	Personal holiness	*Not cheating, stealing, lying *Sexual purity with coworkers
	Fruit of the Spirit	*Grace-based relationships
	Openhandedness	*Generosity toward others; eschewing materialism and self-indulgence
	Gut-level compassion for the hurting	*Proactive "seeing" of others' needs
OUT	Social justice	*Bettering conditions for workers *Promoting just relations with customers, suppliers and shareholders *Being a good corporate neighbor/citizen *Encouraging transformation within one's institution *Encouraging social reform within one's field

By *up* I mean that "vertical" dimension of righteousness that involves our reverent worship of and humble dependence on God. By *in* I mean the state of our hearts: the internal characteristics of righteousness captured by the phrase "purity in heart" and expressed through personal righteousness (what the wisdom literature calls "clean hands"). By *out* I mean the social dimensions of righteousness, that part of righteousness involving our interactions with our neighbors near and far. This *comprehensive* expression of righteousness marks the *tsaddiqim*. As Tim Keller explained,

> Biblical righteousness is inevitably social, because it is about relationships. When most modern people see the word "righteousness" in the Bible, they tend to think of it in terms of private morality, such as sexual chastity or diligence in prayer and Bible study. But in the Bible *tzadeqah* refers to day-to-day living in which a person conducts *all* relationships in family and society with fairness, generosity, and equity.[4]

UP

The *tsaddiqim* live Godward. That is, the central orientation of their life is toward God. They eschew every idolatry, always seeking to give God (and nothing and no one else) his rightful place. And their Godward stance makes them people of prayer, because "being near to God is what the righteous seek more than anything else."[5]

The *tsaddiqim* are deeply humble. They look "up" and affirm that God is the Creator and they are the creatures. They acknowledge him as the source of all life and breath, not kidding themselves that they have "made it" themselves by their own efforts. They join the psalmist in singing, "It is He who has made us, and not we ourselves" (Ps 100:3 NASB). They recognize that they belong to God, not to themselves (1 Cor 6:19-20). Their fundamental orientation in life is not toward self-fulfillment, but toward God's glory.

The Godward orientation of the *tsaddiqim* also means that they have an eternal perspective. They seek first the kingdom of God (Mt 6:33). Their time horizon includes both this age and the age to come.

Applications to our work lives. This aspect of righteousness suggests several implications for vocational stewardship. First, this "vertical" righteousness means that we affirm that the purpose of life is glorifying God, not self. That is enormously relevant, practical and countercultural in our workaday world, since at the very core of most modern "career counseling" is devotion to self-fulfillment. For the Christ-follower, self-fulfillment is not the ultimate goal. Instead, as scholar Douglas Schuurman explained, "Vocation is first of all about serving God through serving the neighbor."[6] This does not mean, as we will see in future chapters, that God is indifferent to our joy at work. Nor does it mean that it is illegitimate to explore how God has uniquely made us as we choose a career. It does mean that we are called to resist the modern assumption that personal happiness and satisfaction are the highest and most important criteria when considering vocational decisions.

Second, a Godward orientation means that in stewarding their vocations, the *tsaddiqim* do not fall into idolizing their jobs or the organizations they work for. Perhaps the most visible expression of this is that the *tsaddiqim* are not workaholics. They seek to draw their primary identity not from their work, but from their relationship with God. Their Godward orientation helps them remember to be faithful to *all* the various callings he has placed on their lives in addition to their work, such as family relationships, parenting responsibilities, service roles within the church, and duties to community and nation.

Not idolizing work also means that the *tsaddiqim* seek discernment about the limits of their loyalties to their employer. When their organizations order them to pursue actions that exclusively benefit the firm to the harm of others, they pause. In our very complex modern economic system built on competition, navigating these waters is undoubtedly very difficult. Consider these situations:

- the engineer who is asked to "cut corners" to save the firm money—and he realizes that doing so could bring harm to consumers or the firm's own workers

- the company litigator who is asked to sue a competitor, but knows that the suit is based on biased or incomplete information about the other firm

- the accountant who is pressured to "massage the numbers" in ways that make the company's performance appear better than it is—and realizes that this will mislead investors

In each of these examples, the employee is asked to put the employer's interest above all other interests, breaking the foundational law of love of neighbor. In such circumstances, loyalty to God and his law must prevail over institutional loyalty.

Third, this vertical dimension of righteousness means that we seek to do our work in active, functional, daily reliance on the indwelling power of the Holy Spirit. The *tsaddiqim* practice God's presence in the midst of their labors. They are humble. They admit their creaturely limitations and thus seek regularly to invite the Father's heavenly wisdom and the Spirit's guidance. They understand the folly of leaning on their own understanding and look instead to the instruction of God's Word (Prov 3:5). They believe that Christ is alive and risen and working in the world, and say to him, "Lord, please use me through my work for your purposes. Let me know what you would have me do, and grant me the courage and strength to do it."

Relatedly, the *tsaddiqim* do their work "heartily, as for the Lord rather than for men" (Col 3:23 NASB). That is, they know their audience. They offer up their work—whatever it involves, whether great tasks or small—in worship to God. They resist slavish devotion to people-pleasing. They can handle the pain of being passed over for rightful recognition, because they are focused primarily on their heavenly Father's affirmation, not their boss's.

Finally, because the righteous are fundamentally Godward in their orientation, they view their work in eschatological terms. We will examine this idea in greater depth in chapter four. For now, suffice it to say that the *tsaddiqim* have an eternal perspective. They are confident in God's promise to make everything new (Rev 21:5). They trust that in their work they participate in the new creation, even if that very glorious idea is somewhat mysterious to them. Theologian Miroslav Volf refers to this as a pneumatological theology of work. In *Work in the Spirit: Toward a Theology of Work*, he writes, "Through the Spirit, God is already working in history, using human actions to create provisional states of affairs that anticipate the new creation in a real way."[7]

The *tsaddiqim* trust that their labors are not in vain, because they believe that there is continuity between the present and future eschatological eras (even while they admit that the nature of this continuity is often inscrutable). They embrace what Volf calls the *transformatio mundi* paradigm—the belief that the final judgment is a refining fire, transforming

but not completely destroying the present creation. From this eschatological paradigm, they celebrate the significance of human work and see it as
a matter of "cooperation with God."[8]

In

The second aspect of righteousness concerns the state of our own hearts.
This aspect involves both right personal conduct and, importantly, holy
motivations and dispositions. The righteous seek not only to *act* rightly but
also to *be* right inside. Scholar Jerome Creach points to Psalms 15 and 24
in this regard. These texts convey the idea of righteousness as a matter of
both "clean hands" and a "pure heart."[9]

The God to whom we are directed is the One who commands us, "Be
holy as I am holy." This holiness takes a variety of expressions. For example, the righteous hate all that is false (Prov 13:5). They have a "blameless"
walk, speak the truth from their hearts and fear the Lord (Ps 15). They
delight in God's law (Ps 1:2). They keep themselves sexually pure (Ezek
18:6). They do not swear deceitfully (Ps 24:4). They maintain just weights
and balances; they do not defraud (Lev 19:36).

Personal righteousness also involves the zealous pursuit of "putting off"
the old self and "putting on" the new self that is spoken of in Colossians 3.
The *tsaddiqim* seek to walk in the Spirit and yield themselves to the Spirit's
work (Rom 8). They ask God to nurture within them the fruit of the Spirit:
love, joy, peace, patience, kindness, goodness, faithfulness, gentleness and
self-control (Gal 5:22-23). They seek to put to death the misdeeds of the
old self—to mortify the flesh with its greed, pride, lust and selfishness.

The righteous are also deeply grateful people who understand that all
they are and all they have comes from God. They affirm his ownership
over all things and know that only from the Father comes breath itself
and everything needful for life. Their hearts are not full of pride rooted
in their own accomplishments or their own hard work. They realize that
the wealth they've accumulated or the successes they've achieved have
largely resulted from God's providence. Nor is there a grasping orientation in their hearts. Instead, they recognize that they own nothing; rather,
they are stewards of God's resources. Consequently, they are joyfully
openhanded.

The internal dimension of righteousness also involves the disposition of our hearts toward compassion and mercy. Many Pharisees in Jesus' day were considered righteous by their fellow citizens because of the multiple disciplines they followed. The Pharisees sought to be honest, faithful to religious requirements and ethical. Yet sometimes Jesus found their personal righteousness lacking because their hearts were cold. To be pure in heart, from Jesus' perspective, is not only to be a person who "keeps her nose clean." The pure in heart have *warm* hearts, ready to feel others' pain and to respond with compassion.

This compassion is described well in Proverbs 29:7: "The righteous *care about* justice for the poor, but the wicked have no such concern" (emphasis added). This "caring about" the poor is actually a radical commitment not well captured by English translations, which tend to weaken and mask the true import of the statement. In the original Hebrew, the verb translated "care about" is *ya-vah*, and it is intense. The same term is translated in Genesis as "to know"—as in "Adam knew Eve" and Eve became pregnant. So, when the righteous "care about" justice for the poor, it means they are intensely passionate to see justice done for the poor. Their concern is deep, intimate and heartfelt.

Jesus displays this kind of intense caring about the poor in the feeding of the five thousand. In the accounts of this miracle in Matthew 14 and Mark 6, we are told that when Jesus sees the crowd, he "has compassion" on them because they are like sheep without a shepherd. He proceeds to both heal them and feed them.

The words translated into English as "felt compassion" or "had pity" don't quite do justice to the original language. The Greek word for "felt compassion" is *splagchnizomai*, meaning "to have the bowels yearn" with pity. *Splagchnizomai* refers to "innards" or "guts." As Jesus looks out at the hungry crowds, he experiences "gut-wrenching" compassion. This Greek word is used twelve times in the New Testament. Eleven of them refer to Jesus being "moved with compassion" and then feeding or healing or teaching. The twelfth usage is from the parable of the prodigal son and is used of the father, who sees his son a long way off, "is moved with compassion," and starts running toward him.

The Hebrew term that matches up with *splagchnizomai*'s notion of "guts" or "innards" is *qereb*. It is found in Leviticus where God describes how the Israelites are to make the various animal sacrifices. Without getting into too many gory details, suffice it to say that the priests followed various instructions concerning what to do with the different parts of the animals—heads, tails and "inwards" (or entrails or guts). For our purposes here, the main point is this: it's the guts that are put on the altar as the sacrifice.

A preacher once offered this formula for describing Jesus' caring ministry: Jesus sees suffering and is punched in his guts with deep compassion, and this provokes him to make a sacrificial offering.

To be the *tsaddiqim*, then, means to care about justice for the poor—to care with a deep, gut-level compassion that energizes personal, sacrificial commitment.

Applications to our work lives. Most of the teaching on the integration of faith and work emphasizes the importance of cultivating personal righteousness in the context of our daily labor. That's understandable given the considerable ethical perils of the contemporary workplace. The Fall has affected both our work itself and the environment in which we do it. Because of the Fall, work has become toilsome and sometimes feels futile. Because of the Fall, both we Christians and our nonbelieving coworkers are sinners. The modern workplace, as authors Doug Sherman and William Hendricks write in *Your Work Matters to God*, "is a jungle."[10]

God has called us into the world, including the fallen world of work. There, the wheat and the tares are growing up together (Mt 13:25). Christians sometimes find themselves confronted by coworkers whose lives are dissipated or bosses who are dishonest. They may face pressure to lie to customers or vendors or shareholders. They may work in an environment where everyone cheats on their expense reports. They may face sexual temptations from handsome coworkers.

In this setting, the *tsaddiqim* seek to heed the apostle Paul's call to "shine like stars in the universe" through their intentional, diligent, prayerful pursuit of holiness (Phil 2:15). The righteous ask God to help them maintain "clean hands" on the job by refusing to lie, cheat, steal or engage in a workplace sexual affair.

Congregational leaders need to recognize the jungle that their members confront and encourage their flock by reminding them of God's redemptive power. Through his death and resurrection, Christ has defeated both the guilt and the power of sin. His indwelling Spirit makes possible growth in personal righteousness. Pastors need to remind their people that they can indeed, though Christ's power, be different kinds of workers than the nonbelievers around them.

Sometimes coworkers or supervisors are hostile to faith. Believers face ridicule or persecution on the job. Other times believers simply work with people whose failings may include gossiping, laziness or mean-spiritedness. In such a context, the righteous cry out to God to display the fruit of his Spirit in them. They ask God to impart in them gentleness, patience, kindness and self-control. They seek to return good for evil and to offer grace to difficult coworkers.

Other times, the greatest challenges on the job relate less to persecution and trial than to the temptations that follow success. As believers enjoy promotions, the worldly rewards of labor increase. Salaries go up. Titles and offices become more prestigious. Such earthly joys can beguile congregants' hearts, dulling resistance to pride, consumerism and self-indulgence. Congregational leaders must warn their flock of these dangers.

Indeed, pastors should remind their people that believers who face hostility on the job because of their faith may actually have it easier than those who enjoy promotions and success. The former are well aware of how the atmosphere around them is dangerous and how it requires countercultural behavior and attitudes. In the midst of their trials and distresses, they likely find it easy to remember to pray, study Scripture and seek the intercessions of others. After all, they have a sense of their desperate need of these means of grace.

The latter, by contrast, may be lulled into complacency. Success, recognition, privileges, financial rewards—the Christian who receives all this at work may be easily enchanted. Such pleasurable things get a hold on us, and we don't want to lose them. We begin justifying moral compromises that enable us to retain the goodies to which we've grown accustomed. Pastors should remind their members that professionals enjoying success on the job may need an even greater discipline than those who are persecuted at work.

We've seen that the call of personal righteousness involves not only a pure heart, but also a warm heart. Cultivating a heart marked by *splagchnizomai*—that gut-wrenching compassion for those in need—involves much prayer. Believers need to look to the Spirit to grow them in this area just as he grows them in honesty or sexual purity. In addition to prayer, though, the *tsaddiqim* seek to nurture this kind of heart by intentionally seeking exposure to people in need.

Many middle- and upper-middle-class Christians live in economically homogenous neighborhoods, worship at churches with little class or ethnic diversity, and work most closely with people from the same class. Without some exposure and engagement with the oppressed, the hungry or the impoverished, we can easily lack the heartfelt, *splagchnizomai* compassion of Jesus. Culturally distanced from the poor, we become emotionally distant as well. And sometimes we're not even conscious of it.

The *tsaddiqim*, by contrast, pursue the common good out of a keen awareness of the cries of those at the bottom. Knowing God is the true owner of all they possess, they are willing to share their resources and talents for the rejoicing of the whole community. They take intentional steps to acquaint themselves with the needs of their neighbors. Some of those neighbors may be people within their workplaces, such as the nighttime janitor who's struggling to make it as a single mom with three kids and two minimum-wage jobs. Other times neighbors in need may be people affected by the *tsaddiq*'s employer (such as families living close to a company factory that is polluting the environment or poor people in the developing world who are hired by the firm at unfair wages). And still other neighbors are simply the down and out of one's city who have no interaction with the employer.

In any of these cases, the point is that the righteous educate themselves about the conditions of the vulnerable. They ask questions about the firm's engagements abroad; they are informed of their local community's news; they make a point of knowing the names of the service workers in their companies. They provide some mental and emotional space for their neighbors' realities. They make room in their hearts for their neighbors' struggles; they allow some of their neighbors' pain to take up residence there.

In a moment, we'll look at what social righteousness is and how we can do justice in and through our work on behalf of those in need. The internal work of cultivating a tender, compassionate heart precedes and makes possible such concrete actions.[11]

OUT

So far we've examined the vertical and internal/personal aspects of righteousness. Also mandatory for the *tsaddiqim* is what we might call social righteousness. Creach describes this social aspect of righteousness eloquently:

> The righteous act in concert with God's will for the shalom of the community. . . . The activity of the righteous shows they align themselves with God's desire to create community well-being, and their activity is part of God's creative, justice-establishing efforts.[12]

Social righteousness is about how we treat our neighbors near and far. It is about how vertical love toward God is expressed in horizontal love toward the world he has made and the people he has created. In short, the righteousness of the *tsaddiqim* involves both personal moral purity and the "attempt to make God's justice a reality where they live."[13]

Both the wisdom literature and the prophetic literature tell us much about the contours of social righteousness. The righteous do not slander or defraud others (Ps 15:3). They do not take advantage of others in tough economic times by lending at interest (Ezek 18:8). Instead they give generously (Ps 112:9). Unlike the wicked, they eschew violence (Ps 11:5). They refuse to accept bribes against the innocent (Ps 15:5). They "do justice" (Mic 6:8) and defend the cause of the widow (Is 1:17). Courageously, they even "snatch" victims of oppression from their oppressor's very jaws (Job 29:17). In contrast to the wicked, they eschew greed and lavish living that is indifferent to the plight of the poor.

As we saw in the previous chapter, the *tsaddiqim* promote justice and shalom. They thread their lives into those painful places where the social fabric is unraveling. As Tim Keller argues,

> What [this] means then is that you must not just be a thread next to the other threads. When you see other people falling out of the [social] fabric, people who don't have the goods, . . . who are being told to fend for themselves and don't have the power to do it, it's your job, it's your responsibility, to get involved with them. And that's what it means to thread yourself. We don't want to be involved—we're so busy. But [we] have to. We have to thread ourselves, our time, our money, our love, our effort, into the lives of people who are weaker than we.[14]

Social righteousness is nurtured when we look "out" at our neighbors near and far and deliberately consider how to advance their good.

Applications to our work lives. Part of looking out involves considering the needs of those among whom we work. First, we simply have to *see* them. We have to make room in our hearts for caring about others. From this heart of compassion springs tangible action. If we have attained a position of authority, we may be able to use our influence to better the working conditions of others. Or we may be in a position to provide job or learning opportunities for people outside our organization. (In chapter nine, we will consider a wide variety of additional ways to seek the common good of coworkers.)

Looking "out" also involves considering the needs of all the stakeholders in our work, such as vendors, customers, partners, investors or neighbors (people living in the communities where our employing organization's facilities are). The call to do justice is applicable in all these relationships. Thus our vocational stewardship may include seizing opportunities to go the extra mile on behalf of customers. Or it may involve using our voice within the organization to mitigate possible harm in the community, such as environmental pollution.

For web designer Justin Kitch, looking out involved creative thinking about how his firm—Homestead, an IT company that helped clients build their own websites and online stores—could promote community well-being. Kitch blessed his Bay Area community by permitting his employees to take two hours per week, or one full day per month, to volunteer in a local nonprofit of their choosing—and paid them for their hours. Since the company had a significant number of employees, this practice provided a few full-time workers annually for free to the nonprofit community.[15] Additionally, the corporate foundation Kitch established when he first launched Homestead has donated tens of thousands of dollars to local charities.

Finally, looking out means taking seriously our potential role in encouraging institutional transformation. This begins within our own workplace. Consider, for example, the ways insurance agent Bruce Copeland sought to live out the call to social righteousness throughout his career.[16] In 1963, Copeland was vice president of a Philadelphia-based insurance company. Concerned by the fact that the company was so male dominated and hierarchical, he used his position and influence to encourage institutional changes within the firm.

Copeland gathered several other managers who shared his views. This team began to promote the rights of women and minorities within the firm. It sponsored a meeting for all of the company's female employees to ask them what needed changing. Fifty women attended the session and came up with five proposals. Copeland was able to adopt three of them immediately and one later. He also brought in trainers who promoted a more participatory, less hierarchical management style. This new approach to management was then implemented in all the divisions under Copeland's charge.

Copeland also sought to influence his firm's decisions regarding where the company invested its money. His role as vice president afforded him a seat at the table with the corporation's senior officers. He advocated vigorously for disinvestment of the firm's stock assets from South Africa, which at that time was still under apartheid. He also tried to get company leaders to earmark a certain percentage of a construction contract for the firm's large new office building to be sourced from minority-owned firms.

Institutional transformation includes actions that can move an entire industry to higher standards of quality or safety or financial transparency or energy efficiency or racial diversity—or other social goods. For an architect, for example, this might involve serving on a commission that reviews the credentialing procedures of architects and encouraging curricular reforms leading to more architecture students being trained in green building practices. For the advertising executive, it could mean establishing internal company guidelines that protect female models from exploitation and then convening a meeting of peers from other firms to seek new industry-wide protocols along the same lines.

For screenwriter Barbara Nicolosi, it has involved starting a nonprofit, Act One, with the mission of creating "a community of Christian professionals for the entertainment industry who are committed to artistry, professionalism, meaning, and prayer so that through their lives and work they may be witnesses of Christ and the Truth to their fellow artists and to the global culture."[17] Act One offers two-week courses and longer training programs that help Christians grow in screenwriting and producing skills. About two hundred students have completed the program and about half are working in the industry. In an interview with *Godspy*, Nicolosi explained her vision for this creative enterprise:

> Our long-term strategy is to emphasize training people rather than producing projects. We're trying to establish an alternative to the top secular film schools. Going to one of those schools is still a tremendous advantage, but their underlying worldview is radically nihilistic. As a Christian, you can learn the craft in those places but everything you believe will be ridiculed by your professors. With Act One, they see that it's possible to live a holy, Christian life and master the craft and create excellent content at the same time. And they've created friendships and Christian community that can sustain them when they enter the industry.[18]

Act One graduates are now better equipped to seed themes of creation, Fall and redemption into the entertainment industry.

Or consider the example of orthopedic surgeon Barry Sorrells from Little Rock, Arkansas. He has used his influence, experience and network to bring about a modest but meaningful change in the preparation medical students receive. "I got to thinking about my profession," Barry explains, "and everybody coming out of medical school says, 'I felt well prepared in medicine, but I didn't really feel prepared for the world.'"[19]

With support from his pastor at Fellowship Bible Church, Barry designed an intensive course that offers brief instruction to medical students on such practical matters as budgeting, first-time home buying and managing credit cards. He brought his idea to the professors at the University of Arkansas medical school, and they embraced it "whole-heartedly."

The highlight of Barry's LifeSkills Institute is a panel discussion called "Wisdom from Medical Practice." He explains that six or seven "gray-haired physicians, well known and well respected in the community" speak with the students for a few hours about life. The goal is to help the future doctors avoid making some of the mistakes they made. The older physicians talk openly about their failings in balancing family and work and about lost marriages due to workaholism or infidelity. From 2001 to 2009, Barry's weeklong LifeSkills Institute was a required part of the curriculum for medical students in their final year at the University of Arkansas.[20]

Two Objections

The Bible's description of righteousness is daunting. I can imagine the material presented thus far provoking at least two reactions. The first is suspicion: that I ought not to be exhorting us to become the *tsaddiqim*, because that is a call to works-righteousness. The second is despair or skepticism arising from the thought *This is an unattainable standard. How can anyone in today's world come close?*

The call to righteousness in this book in no way replaces the doctrine of full reliance on Christ and his righteousness. For one thing, the exhortation here is not to perfection. No matter how much we grow in becoming righteous as depicted in the preceding pages, we still desperately need Jesus and the daily, indwelling power of the Holy Spirit. For another, the call here is not about achieving some level of moral uprightness that puts us in a position of deserving God's favor. God's gift of salvation through Christ's righteousness is free, unearned and utterly gracious.

But this doctrine of God's unmerited favor toward us is not meant to lead us into a passive life, a life unchanged, a life dismissive of the call to grow in holiness. We are saved to be Christ's disciples. And, as Dallas Willard says, "The disciple is the one who, intent on becoming Christ-like and so dwelling in his 'faith and practice,' systematically and progressively rearranges his affairs to that end."[21] Those terms—*systematically* and *progressively*—sound like hard work. They are. And that is perfectly legitimate and orthodox. Why? Because there is a great difference between *earning* and *effort*. There is no place for the former in the Christian life. But it's a different story for the latter. "We must act," Willard says. "Grace is opposed to earning, not to effort."[22]

Regarding the second objection, I'll certainly admit that living as a *tsaddiq* today is very difficult. But it's not a pipedream. I know, because I've met many *tsaddiqim* face-to-face. Let me introduce you to one.

A MODERN-DAY *TSADDIQ*

Perry Bigelow, a Chicago homebuilder, is not perfect. He's humble and knows he needs to rely daily on the mercies of Christ. But I think he is a *tsaddiq* (though he gets embarrassed when I tell him that). He was the kingdom-oriented businessman I was hoping to find in Lindsay's *Faith in the Halls of Power*, but didn't. Perry's pursuit of righteousness in all three of the dimensions we've been discussing—up, in and out—shapes his vocational stewardship.

Perry is the founder of Bigelow Homes, a suburban homebuilding company just outside Chicago. (His son, Jamie, now heads the firm.) Perry's integration of faith and work began from the deep-set conviction that he is the steward, not owner, of his business. The orientation of his whole life, including his professional life, is Godward. Over many years, Perry has prayed, studied Scripture and read thoughtful Christian scholars in order to develop a God-honoring approach to his stewardship of all the gifts and assets he has received.

Based on this foundational desire to please and honor God in and through his work, Perry seeks to obey biblical standards of morality and to imitate Christ's character. This commitment to personal righteousness is expressed concretely in the strict ethics the Bigelow Homes firm expects of itself and its employees. Company policy is straightforward: "We will never knowingly lie to each other, a home purchaser, a supplier or subcontractor, or government official. We place a high premium on personal integrity."[23]

Personal righteousness is also expressed through Perry's desire to imitate the servant-leadership of Jesus. During the years he actively led the firm, that servant heart expressed itself in his management style. Humbly recognizing the limits of his own giftedness and knowledge, he deliberately hired colleagues who possessed strengths that he lacked. Then he placed those people in responsibility over various functional areas of the business. He pursued a consensual management style and emphasized interdependence and collaboration, giving leaders space to exercise their gifts.

In addition to modeling Christ's servanthood, Perry has treated his employees compassionately. The homebuilding industry is notorious for cyclical booms and busts. That means that most construction workers find steady employment a chimera. Bigelow Homes takes seriously a responsibility to keep its labor force on the job. It does so by refusing to overreach in the good times and eschewing the temptations to become big for the sake of bigness. "We aim for careful, sustainable growth," Perry says.[24] This has allowed the firm to go through all but two of Chicago's innumerable housing cycles without laying off anyone—while competitors were shedding as much as 50 percent of their workforce.[25]

Perry and his team have also thought carefully and creatively about the product their business offers. They've advanced two kingdom virtues through the way Bigelow homes are designed. The first is community. Perry is aware of the trend in American culture toward hyper-individualism. His love for the biblical value of *koinonia* (fellowship and co-participation) gets infused in the design of the communities Bigelow Homes builds. These designs aim for "a balance between privacy and neighborliness."[26] For example, Bigelow builds extra-wide sidewalks and multiple "commons" spaces for spontaneous interaction and puts large front porches on each home.

Perry has also advanced the kingdom virtue of sustainability through his work. Through product and design innovations, Bigelow homes are extremely energy efficient. In fact, the company guarantees that homeowners won't have to spend more than four hundred dollars per year on heating bills—in Chicago! "Our innovation in energy efficiency is a direct result of our great respect for God's creation," Perry explains, "and a belief that we should preserve as much of it as we can for our children's children."[27]

Perry and his team have thought wisely not only about their product design, but also about the ways their company's assets—networks, expertise, technical prowess, managerial talent and financial resources—can be deployed to assist inner-city housing ministries. So, for several years, Bigelow Homes has partnered with nonprofits as they work to provide quality, energy-efficient housing for low-income working people in Chicago.[28]

Perry has also sought to design and build neighborhoods that bless the local community in practical, tangible ways. For example, knowing the challenges that vital but modestly remunerated professionals like teachers, police officers and firemen sometime face in finding affordable homes where they serve, Bigelow Homes deliberately builds "workforce housing." These are family-friendly homes with affordable per-square-foot prices.

Bigelow also follows an unconventional model of planning neighborhoods—one marked by deliberate product diversity and what Perry calls "compact development." This approach blesses the school district and the local municipality. Here's how: By offering diverse styles of homes with prices ranging from $150,000 to $350,000, Bigelow subdivisions create demographic diversity. Singles, retirees and families all live in a community. This demographic diversity spins off positive cash flow for the local school district because the total number of students in the subdivision is less than it would be following conventional, suburban-sprawl building practices.[29] Moreover, Bigelow's compact development leads to "high assessed value per acre and less infrastructure." As Perry explains, this is the recipe for municipalities to make a profit from property taxes.[30]

In short, Bigelow Homes' design-building practices challenge the suburban homebuilding industry's conventional wisdom. Perry's company has shown the industry that it is possible to do well by doing good. It has demonstrated that it is possible to build attractive, energy-efficient and yet affordable homes. It has proven that compact development that strengthens a community's tax base can be designed to produce an aesthetically attractive and neighborly subdivision. Through Perry's writings and work with municipal officials, he is bringing this message to the powers that be, advocating reforms in the industry toward the more sustainable approaches Bigelow Homes has pioneered.

Perry Bigelow has stewarded his vocational power to rejoice the city. He has blessed his employees through his compassionate and thoughtful business model. He has brought joy to his customers—many of them first-time homebuyers, many of them working families needing a safe, neighborly, affordable community to live in. He has also blessed the city of Aurora by building a subdivision that contributes to the local tax base, generating revenue for schools and municipal services. And he has blessed future generations by taking the biblical value of sustainability seriously enough to let it shape his product design.

And all the while, Perry has been humble and approachable—a regular guy. He's not a "super saint." His life shows that it is indeed possible to be a *tsaddiq* in modern America.

CONCLUSION: THE *TSADDIQIM* AND THE *ECCLESIA*

In ancient Israel, important public business was conducted by the "assembly at the gate." There, in what we today call "the public square," societal leaders oversaw judicial proceedings. Deuteronomy 21–22 gave instructions to the Israelites about coming to the "elders of the town" to settle family and legal issues. In Ruth 4, we read of Boaz negotiating at the gate to become Ruth's kinsman-redeemer. In 2 Samuel 15 we read of Israelites coming to the gate "for justice."

Ideally, these elders were to be holy, reputable, faithful men. Proverbs

24:7 tells us that there was no place for a fool in the assembly at the gate. The prophet Amos indicated the righteousness of the elders by describing a wicked person as one who hates "him who reproves in the gate" (Amos 5:10 NASB). Job, the Old Testament character whom God himself called upright, was one of these elders at the gate (see Job 29:7). In other words, the assembly at the gate in the Old Testament was an assembly of the *tsaddiqim*. And that matters for us today. Here's why.

When the apostle Paul sought a word to use for "church," he chose the Greek word *ecclesia*. This is a notable selection because other Greek words were available to denote the idea of assemblies or gatherings. *Ecclesia* was the word specifically used in the Septuagint (the Old Testament translated into Greek) to mean the assembly at the public gate—that is, the assembly of the *tsaddiqim*.[31] This means that Paul's word for "church" denotes an assembly of the people who decide matters of common welfare, the people charged to look out for the commonwealth.

For Paul, church was not meant to be a body of people concerned only with their own fellowship. The church was never to extract itself from the cares of the larger community, to form a "holy huddle." No. The church—the *ecclesia*, the assembly at the gate—is to give itself for the life and flourishing of the community. The church, by definition, is missional.

The church is supposed to be a collection of the *tsaddiqim*—people of deep personal piety and intense passion for the kingdom of God. The church is a fellowship of those committed to stewarding their prosperity for the common good, of people who think creatively and strategically about how to deploy their talents to advance foretastes of the kingdom. This is an incredibly exciting and inspirational vision.

Sadly, though, our churches often fall short. In the chapters ahead, we'll try to understand why.

Why We Aren't the *Tsaddiqim*

We get what we preach. . . . How we live reveals the
gospel we responded to and the gospel we believe.

SCOT MCKNIGHT

For over forty years, South African believer Michael Cassidy has faithfully and courageously led evangelicals in a context frequently marked by confusion, violence, injustice and fear. He has thought long and hard about what it means to be a Christ-follower in this broken world. In his book on the fight against apartheid, *This Passing Summer*, Cassidy wrote, "Conversion marks the birth of the movement *out of a merely private existence into a public consciousness.* Conversion is the beginning of active solidarity with the purposes of the kingdom of God in the world."[1]

This arresting view of salvation provides a rich foundation for life as the *tsaddiqim*. Unfortunately, such a definition of what it means to be a Christian is unfamiliar to many American evangelicals. This is because many churches preach an individualistic gospel limited to "having a personal relationship with Jesus." Sometimes even missional church leaders can be weak in this regard. (Even when they are not, they have newcomers to their church who arrive from congregations with an individualistic gospel.)

If we want to make progress in discipling Christ-followers who will live as the *tsaddiqim*, we need to understand the reasons why many do not live that way. The prevalence of an individualistic understanding of the gospel is the number-one reason. In many of our churches, our gospel is too small.[2] While it is rightly centered on the vital atoning work of Jesus on the cross, it fails to grasp the comprehensive significance of his redemptive work. Consequently, it fails to direct Christ-followers into the righteous lifestyle of the *tsaddiqim*, who gladly join Jesus on his grand mission of restoration.

We'll examine this too-narrow gospel in this chapter, observing how it is expressed and reinforced in the popular music and books of current American evangelicalism. Then we'll move on to the second, related reason why most Christians aren't the *tsaddiqim*: our inadequate understanding of heaven and the afterlife. We'll see how failure to grasp correctly our *ultimate* hope as Christians limits our understanding of our proper mission in *this* world. Finally, we'll look at two other reasons that contribute to our failure to live as the *tsaddiqim*: social isolation and lack of accountability. Then, in the next chapter, we'll take up the question of what to do about all this.

THE TOO-NARROW GOSPEL

The most common presentation of the gospel in contemporary American evangelicalism centers on the death and resurrection of Jesus. This gospel begins with humankind's most fundamental and desperate reality: we are sinners separated from God. It then offers the very good news that God, in his mercy, is willing to forgive us. To effect that, he sent his own beloved Son to live the life we should have lived and die the death we deserve to die. Through Jesus' atoning work, we can enter into fellowship with God our Creator and Father. We put our trust in Jesus as Savior, asking God to credit Jesus' righteousness to our account. We admit that we have not lived as we should have (namely, for God's glory), and we "accept Jesus as Lord and Savior." Our profession of faith makes us part of God's family. Because of Jesus' atonement, we are freed from the punishment of sin (eternal death in hell). We receive the gift of eternal life from Jesus. Through faith in him, we can be confident that we will go to heaven when we die.

The Bridge illustration, an old evangelistic tool, portrays the gospel succinctly (see figure 3.1). It emerged in 1981 through the Navigators and has been included in the evangelism training done by such giants as Campus Crusade and the Willow Creek movement, not to mention at hundreds of individual churches. It has been used countless times, and through God's providence it has brought many people to a saving knowledge of Jesus.

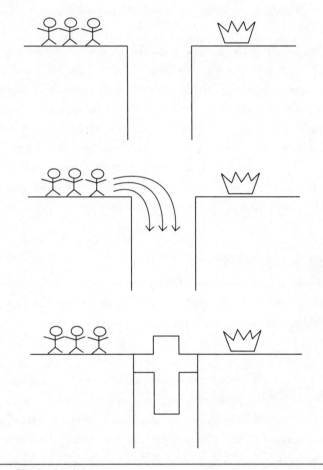

Figure 3.1. The Bridge illustration

The Bridge illustration highlights the atoning work of Jesus Christ on behalf of sinners. It shows a person on one side of a deep canyon. This represents us in our sin. God and heaven are on the opposite side of the canyon. No amount of human effort can get the sinner from one side of the canyon to the other. We can try to jump (that is, earn our way through good works), but we will only plummet to our death. The only way for a sinner to obtain God's eternal life is through the gracious, free gift of the cross. Jesus' cross serves as a bridge that connects the two sides of the canyon. By turning away from our own efforts and relying fully on Jesus' shed blood, we are able to walk across that bridge.

The gospel as depicted in the Bridge illustration is true. It rightly presents humankind's fundamental dilemma (separation from God due to our sinfulness). It rightly gives God glory by showing both his holiness (he will not overlook sin) and his mercy (he offers his Son to pay the penalty our sin deserved). It rightly lifts up the cross of Christ, with its utterly unique power. It puts human beings in their proper place, and God in his.

But this gospel isn't complete.

The glorious truths celebrated in this too-narrow gospel do not, in themselves, capture the full, grand, amazing scope of Jesus' redemptive work. For Jesus came preaching not just this gospel of personal justification but the gospel *of the kingdom.* Jesus' work is not exclusively about our individual salvation, but about the cosmic redemption and renewal of *all* things. It is not just about our reconciliation to a holy God—though that is the beautiful center of it. It is also about our reconciliation with one another and with the creation itself. The atoning work of Jesus is bigger and better than that captured by the Bridge illustration.[3]

PROBLEMATIC WORSHIP MUSIC

One of the ways the too-narrow gospel permeates evangelicalism is through contemporary worship music. The incomplete gospel is not only preached from pulpits but also sung by worship bands. Much of contemporary Christian music cultivates and reinforces a me-and-Jesus mentality. And that matters, because theological shortcomings in the music we hear on Christian radio or sing on Sunday mornings affect our beliefs. As worship leader Keith Getty says, "What we sing becomes the grammar of what we believe."[4]

In 2005, Dick Staub of the Center for Faith and Culture examined the shortcomings of contemporary Christian music (CCM) in a thoughtful essay in *Christianity Today.* He argued that CCM tends to promote "fortification" rather than "real engagement" with the world. Even worse, sometimes CCM fails to communicate the realities we live in, realities that when taken seriously help us understand the need for a profoundly powerful gospel that is able to conquer more than our personal sin. Staub wrote,

> CCM assiduously avoids . . . telling the *full* truth about life, the human condition, our fallen-ness. . . . If we fail to tell the truth about our human condition, which requires nastiness and messiness and is not all that inspirational, we will be unable to explore the riches and depth of the gospel, which is about restoring *all* that unraveled in the Fall.[5]

Brian McLaren, a leader in the emerging church movement, shares Staub's concerns. In his "Open Letter to Worship Songwriters" in *Worship Leader Magazine*, McLaren complained that many lyrics are "embarrassingly personalistic":

> Listen next time you're singing in worship. It's about how Jesus forgives me, embraces me, makes me feel his presence, strengthens me, forgives me, holds me close, touches me, revives me, etc., etc. Now this is all fine. But if an extraterrestrial outsider from Mars were to observe us, I think he would say either a) that these people are all mildly dysfunctional and need a lot of hug therapy . . . or b) that they don't give a rip about the rest of the world, that their religion/spirituality makes them as selfish as any nonChristian, but just in spiritual things rather than material ones.[6]

Intrigued and dismayed by such critiques, my research assistants and I decided to conduct a modest content analysis of the lyrics of today's worship songs. To identify the most popular ones, we relied on two resources. The first was *CCM Magazine*'s 2006 book on "the top 100 Christian worship songs of all time."[7] The second was data collected from Christian Copyright Licensing International (CCLI). From CCLI reports it is possible to identify the worship songs used most frequently in churches.

From these sources, we honed in on 127 highly popular worship songs. Then we rated the lyrics of each of these songs on a 1 to 4 scale, with 1 representing lyrics that reinforced a me-and-Jesus view of salvation and Christian living, and 4 representing a kingdom gospel perspective with a broader understanding of Christ's redemptive work and our call to follow Christ in his mission of shalom. Our average rating for songs was 1.57, skewed toward the too-narrow gospel.[8]

INADEQUATE DISCIPLESHIP

Not only is the me-and-Jesus gospel reinforced in many popular worship songs, it also permeates a good deal of the most popular Christian books. The Christian Booksellers Association and the Evangelical Christian Publishers Association produce lists of top sellers each month. Separate from these lists are lists produced by publishers, book reviewers and evangelical commentators and magazines on the "best books on Christian discipleship." My research assistants and I examined the monthly bestsellers lists for the past several years. We also collected a variety of the "best books on discipleship" lists to identify the discipleship texts mentioned most often. We found thirteen books that commonly made the cut, such as *The Cost of Discipleship* by Dietrich Bonhoeffer and *The Divine Conspiracy* by Dallas Willard.[9]

Notably, the list of top-selling Christian books and the list of best discipleship books did not overlap much. The best *discipleship* books often were marked by a kingdom gospel theology. The most *popular* Christian books typically focused on the individual Christian's relationship to God.[10] To oversimplify, the books strongest on a robust theology that could undergird the life of a *tsaddiq* are generally not the books being chosen by the highest percentages of Christian readers. Just as much worship music does little to move us beyond the individualistic, narrow gospel, many "Christian living" books reinforce that me-and-Jesus mindset.

This is not a new problem. Back in 1983, sociologist James D. Hunter noted the overly individualistic character of evangelicalism. His study of eight prolific Christian presses found that a whopping 87 percent of the books dealt with subjects related to the self.[11] About ten years later, scholar David Wells's *No Place for Truth* lamented that because of the prevalence of the too-narrow gospel, evangelicalism was characterized by a lack of rigorous application of biblical thinking to all aspects of life:

> Being evangelical has come to mean simply that one has had a certain kind of religious experience that gives color to the private aspects of daily life but in which few identifiable theological elements can be discerned or, as it turns out, are necessary. Evangelical faith is pursued as a matter of internal fascination but abandoned as a matter of external and public relevance.[12]

In 2005 Ronald Sider's *The Scandal of the Evangelical Conscience* continued the critique. Sider's book was prompted by various Barna and Gallup survey reports suggesting that evangelicals' practice on a whole host of moral issues (for example, divorce, materialism and racism) is indistinguishable from secular people's behavior. In chapter three, Sider argued that the reason is that evangelicals have exchanged the "whole gospel" for "cheap grace":

> One of the most astonishing ironies of contemporary Evangelicalism is that most evangelicals do not even define the gospel the way Jesus did! . . . Jesus did not define the gospel as the forgiveness of sins, although again and again he offered free, unmerited forgiveness. The vast majority of New Testament scholars today, whether evangelical or liberal, agree that the central aspect of Jesus' teaching was the gospel of the kingdom of God. . . . Forgiveness of sins is at the center of Jesus' proclamation of the gospel of the kingdom. But it is only part of it.[13]

With a reductionist understanding of the good news, Sider wrote, too many believers think they can simply accept the gospel and then "go on living the same adulterous, materialistic, racist life" that they lived before.[14]

Sider's contentions are repeated in the work of another well-informed observer of evangelicalism, Dallas Willard. His 2006 book *The Great Omission* is based on the claim that, because the narrow gospel prevails in evangelicalism, we gain *converts* but not *followers* of Jesus. For the past several decades, Willard says, "The churches of the Western world have not made discipleship a condition of being a Christian."[15] From his years of studying the prevailing preaching and teaching within evangelicalism, he concludes that the gospel is typically presented as all about the forgiveness of sins—period. "In contrast," Willard asserts, "I make bold to say, the gospel of the entire New Testament is that you can have a new life now in the kingdom of God if you will trust Jesus Christ." His conclusion about the tragic results of the dominance of the narrow gospel is essentially the same as Sider's: "If there is anything we should know by now, it is that a gospel of justification alone does not generate disciples."[16]

IMPLICATIONS OF THE TOO-NARROW GOSPEL

A context in which much Christian preaching, music and books emphasize a highly individualistic understanding of the gospel does not provide rich soil for the nurture of believers who will live as the *tsaddiqim*. This too-narrow gospel focuses believers missionally only on the work of "soul winning." It has little to say about Jesus' holistic ministry or the comprehensive nature of his work of restoration. It focuses on the problem of personal sin only, thus intimating that sanctification is a matter only of personal morality (rather than that plus social justice). It focuses believers on getting a ticket to heaven, but doesn't say much about what their life in this world should look like. Put differently, it focuses only on what we've been saved *from*, rather than also telling us what we've been saved *for*.

AN INADEQUATE VIEW OF HEAVEN

If the too-narrow gospel is the first reason we aren't the *tsaddiqim*, the closely related second reason is our inadequate views of heaven. In *Surprised by Hope: Rethinking Heaven, the Resurrection, and the Mission of the Church*, theologian N. T. Wright asserts that most Christians "remain satisfied with what is at best a truncated and distorted version of the great biblical hope."[17] Based on surveys of the British public, Wright says that the prevailing view of the ultimate Christian hope is "going to heaven."[18] This involves a vague sense of our souls being forever with God somewhere "above." This "popular picture" of heaven, Wright laments, is "reinforced again and again in hymns, prayers, monuments, and even quite serious works of theology and history."[19]

Here on the other side of the Atlantic, author Randy Alcorn has noted a similar problem. He says that although the major Christian creeds affirm the resurrection of the body, many U.S. believers "spiritualize" this concept. "They don't reject it as a doctrine, but they deny its essential meaning: a permanent return to a physical existence in a physical universe. Of Americans who believe in a resurrection of the dead, two-thirds believe they will not have bodies after the resurrection."[20]

Against the popular view of heaven as an ethereal existence on clouds, the biblical view is that God will remake both heaven and earth and join them together forever. The picture of the end is "not one of ransomed souls making their way to a disembodied heaven but rather the New Jerusalem coming down from heaven to earth, uniting the two in a lasting embrace."[21] The Bible teaches us that what awaits us in the afterlife is embodied life in a re-created material universe called the new earth. Space, time and matter will all be redeemed.[22]

Distorted understandings of heaven and the afterlife have a corrosive effect on Christians' thinking about how to live *this* life in our routine, workaday world. If we (mistakenly) believe that at the end, the earth will be completely destroyed[23] and that just our souls will live on forever, it's a bit hard to imagine being *tsaddiqim* who are passionate for such things as environmental stewardship or cultural reformation. It's hard to stay committed to such allegedly nonspiritual works if they will all completely disappear in the end. If it's all going to be burned up, isn't our labor here on earth in vain?

To such a query the Bible answers a resounding "No!" In 1 Corinthians 15:58, the apostle Paul exhorts believers to "stand firm" and "give yourself fully to the work of the Lord, because you know that your labor in the Lord is not in vain." Wright explains that this verse comes on the heels of Paul's celebration of the resurrection. The exhortation makes perfect sense when it connects the future resurrection with "getting on with work in the present," says Wright. "The point of the resurrection, as Paul has been arguing throughout the letter, is that *the present bodily life is not valueless just because it will die.* God will raise it to new life. What you do with your body in the present matters because God has a great future in store for it."[24]

This truth has immense significance for our vocational life. What we do in the present—"painting, preaching, singing, sewing, praying, teaching, building hospitals, digging wells, campaigning for justice, writing poems, caring for the needy, loving your neighbor as yourself—*will last into God's future,*" Wright says. Such activities are all a part of "what we may call *building for God's kingdom.*"[25] Our work is not in vain, because we are "accomplishing something that will become in due course part of God's new world."[26]

What all this means when applied to the mission of the church is that we "will work in the present for the advance signs of that eventual state of affairs when God is 'all in all,' when his kingdom has come and his will is done 'on earth as it is in heaven.'"[27]

IT AIN'T THAT EASY TO BE THE *TSADDIQIM*

The inquiry for this chapter is, Why aren't more of us acting as the *tsaddiqim*? What we've seen so far is that with an inadequate theology—a truncated gospel—we don't have a vision for living in alignment with the purposes of God's kingdom. And that's a huge problem, since such alignment is at the heart of true righteousness. Not surprisingly, as evangelicals have preached a gospel that is mainly individual—and this has been reinforced through the songs we sing and the books we read—our conception of righteousness has gotten out of balance. It leans too heavily toward personal piety at the expense of social justice.

Moreover, with a theology that's all about getting a ticket to heaven for when I die, it's not surprising that many Christians don't show much interest in the question of how to live life *now*, in *this* world. When our churches teach a salvation that is only *from* (from sin and death), it's not hard to understand why so many believers don't seem to know what salvation is *for*. And if we preach a gospel that is only, or mainly, about "saving souls," we shouldn't be shocked if we end up with congregations that are not very motivated to care for bodies and material needs.

But these aren't the only reasons we're not the *tsaddiqim*. Another key reason is that the very positions of prosperity and power that make possible righteous stewardship that can advance justice and shalom also serve as sirens calling us away from kingdom sacrifice.

Lack of accountability. Wise sages have taught throughout the ages that power corrupts. Anyone with experience "in the limelight" knows the way such privilege can embolden that fallen inner voice that whispers to us of our self-importance. When the red carpet is rolled out for you, when you're invited into the exclusive gatherings, it becomes ever more difficult to fight an inflated ego. When you are the top dog, it's hard to avoid pride. Add to all this the weight of affluence—the power of riches to turn hearts away from humble dependency on God—and you can understand why many evangelicals who are the prospering would find it tough to be simultaneously the *tsaddiqim*.

The siren songs of prosperity make it imperative that preachers in middle-class and wealthier congregations urge their members to join small accountability groups. There they can ask one another the hard questions about how they are managing the faith-eroding qualities of privilege, wealth and power.[28] In *Faith in the Halls of Power*, Michael Lindsay found that very few of the evangelicals he interviewed were participants in such fellowships. Perhaps this lack of accountability helps explain why he found that so few of his interviewees saw wealth "as a resource to benefit society, not the individual."[29]

The problem of isolation. Finally, beyond this issue of troubling temptations, Lindsay's research identified another problem: the insulation of Christian professionals from people outside their socioeconomic class. Consider this series of Lindsay's observations:

> They tend to interact with the same kind of people, whether they are in Los Angeles, London, or Lima. They may indeed travel more frequently and engage different cultures, but most of the time they remain in a world of social, professional and economic peers. In this way these cosmopolitan evangelicals are sheltered from the world of economic inequality as much as their secular peers are.[30]
>
> [Evangelicals in Hollywood] differ little from others in the entertainment industry. They drive luxury cars, live in exclusive communities, and worry that their fame and talent will evaporate overnight.[31]
>
> Evangelical executives tend to accept the material accoutrements of an affluent lifestyle without question.[32]

Within their homogeneous world of prosperity and privilege, many of the evangelicals Lindsay interviewed never rubbed shoulders with the poor (or even the working class). Their friends were people just like them, from the same elite.

Potentially, the isolation that Lindsay found among the believers he surveyed might have been mitigated somewhat if those individuals were active members in local churches—but many were not. In a thoughtful op-ed in *USA Today* in 2008, Lindsay reported, "I was shocked to find that more than half—60%—had low levels of commitment to their denominations and congregations. Some were members in name only; others had actively disengaged from church life."[33]

This is problematic since personal exposure to needs is often a prerequisite for a lifestyle of deep, sacrificial generosity on behalf of others. Commitments of money, time and personal energy can develop when the prospering truly *see* the suffering of the poor and weak.[34] This exposure can then lead to believers truly growing as the *tsaddiqim*—people who not only *help* the poor but *know* them in real relationships.

CONCLUSION

In the brokenness of South Africa before the fall of apartheid, Michael Cassidy labored relentlessly to nurture white Christians who would live as the *tsaddiqim*. At the heart of his work was solid, biblical preaching about God's grand story of creation, Fall, redemption and consummation. He challenged believers to eschew a private faith that excused them from the hard work of living as Christ's disciples, imitating Jesus' sacrificial, others-centered life. Cassidy worked tirelessly with leaders to help the church get its "act together whereby vertical and horizontal components of the gospel are brought into balance."[35]

Cassidy also labored to show South African believers that Christianity isn't simply about having a ticket to heaven. It is about working for society's renewal *now* in ways that "reflect more truly the lordship of Christ over all spheres of the life of man."[36] He taught that believers were residents of two cities—the heavenly and the earthly—and that they were "not permitted to abandon either." Their charge was to work in this material world as "an outcrop of the kingdom of God on earth." It was to "serve notice" to a watching world that "there is more to reality than meets the eye. . . . Because we love something else more than this world, we love [this] world better than those who know no other."[37] For him, right thinking about our eternal hope shapes right behavior in this life.

Finally, Cassidy knew that as critical as accurate theology is, it was also necessary to help white believers overcome their isolation. Without personal relationships with blacks who were suffering under apartheid, and without personal exposure to blacks' real living conditions, Cassidy knew most white believers wouldn't take the risks required for justice and shalom. Consequently, he organized exchange programs through which white evangelicals would go and live for a week in the homes of fellow Christians in the black townships. Through such programs, Cassidy saw "the penny drop" for his white friends, as they finally came to understand their social reality and the attendant call for courageous engagement on behalf of justice.[38]

Under God's providence, many of the groans of the oppressed in South Africa have been addressed. Happily, that nation shed the vicious policy of apartheid in the early 1990s—and Christians like Cassidy and his followers played an important role in that miracle.

Today, in cities at home and abroad, many of God's children continue to cry out for justice and shalom. Evangelical churches in America have innumerable opportunities to rejoice these communities. This will happen when our churches produce Christ-followers who live as the *tsaddiqim*.

How the Gospel of the Kingdom Nurtures the *Tsaddiqim*

Jesus enticed people into a
kingdom mission from the outset.

JAMES CHOUNG

The too-narrow gospel we studied in the previous chapter doesn't provide an adequate theological foundation for nurturing righteous Christ-followers who practice vocational stewardship. What's needed instead is a strong presentation of Jesus' gospel of the kingdom.

THE GOSPEL OF THE KINGDOM

Jesus' gospel centered on his announcement that the long-awaited kingdom had broken into human history. Understanding what such an announcement meant to its original hearers requires reviewing what some theologians have referred to as the Grand Narrative of redemptive history.

That narrative begins with creation. In the beginning, our loving and lavish God brought into being a wonderful paradise. He set human beings in that paradise, where they enjoyed perfect shalom: peace with God, peace with self, peace with others and peace with the created order.

Tragically, the first humans disobeyed God's one commandment, not to eat of the fruit of the tree of the knowledge of good and evil. Rather than enjoying their place as vice regents under God's gracious sovereignty, they wanted to be in charge. Their sin is known as the Fall, and it changed everything. Their relationship with God was broken, as suspicion and fear misplaced joy and trust. Their psychological well-being was marred as they experienced disorientation and shame. Their relationship with one another became conflictual. They pointed fingers of blame at one another, and they hid from each other. Peace between humans and the created order was also shattered as God banished Adam and Eve from the Garden of Eden and cursed the earth itself. As a result of the sin of the first human beings, suffering, evil, alienation, pain, conflict, toil, futility, scarcity and death entered the world.

Yet even in the midst of this cosmic tragedy, a line of God's amazing grace was visible. In Genesis 3 we see God seeking out his children. He mercifully makes them clothing to cover their nakedness. And, most importantly, he promises them a savior—a redeemer who will crush the head of evil.

From Genesis 3 to the opening of the New Testament, God's grace continues even in the face of his people's chronic sin and rebellion. God often has to bring judgment, but he promises never to abandon his commitment to full restoration. Indeed, he inspires many prophets with visions of that future restoration (including the preview passages we examined in chapter one).

And then, as singer-songwriter Michael Card put it, God spoke his "final word" in the incarnation of Jesus.[1] Jesus is God's "yes" and "amen" to all the promises of restoration and redemption (2 Cor 1:20). Jesus comes announcing that *in him* the promises of the preview passages are fulfilled. His salvation is full-orbed, dealing with every dimension of the Fall. Through his life, death and resurrection, he overcomes *all* the effects of the Fall. He pays the price for our sins and all sin, accepting God's punishment on the cross. His resurrection brings the renewed possibility of shalom between humans and God, within humans themselves, among humans, and between humans and the created order.

Yet while Jesus tells us his kingdom work has begun in the world, he explains that it is not yet complete—nor will it be until he comes again to consummate it. His evangelistic invitation is to come and enter his kingdom now, to embrace him now as the one true King whom the whole cosmos will one day acknowledge. In Jesus' gospel, salvation certainly involves the vital and glorious work of individual redemption. Those who trust Christ for their salvation receive forgiveness of their sin and a restored relationship with God. They enter into the promise of eternal life. However, drawn against the creation/Fall/redemption/consummation story, Jesus' redemptive work is shown to go *beyond* saving individual souls. His redemption has accomplished nothing less than the promise of a restored paradise where shalom in all its dimensions will reign.

In 2008, InterVarsity leader James Choung did the Christian world an invaluable service when he published a new, simple diagram for explaining this gospel of the kingdom.[2] Choung's Four Circles illustration (see figure 4.1) tells the Christian story from this creation/Fall/redemption/consummation paradigm. Unlike the Bridge illustration, Choung's presentation centers the gospel story right away on God and God's mission in the world, rather than on humans and their sinfulness.

Choung's presentation begins by asking nonbelievers their opinion on

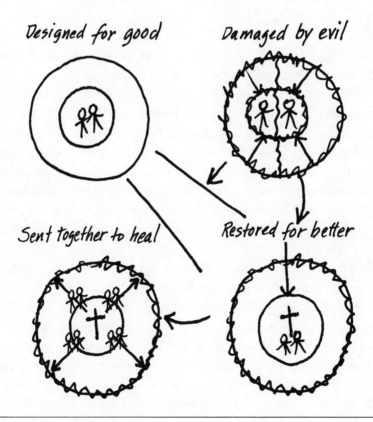

Figure 4.1. Choung's Four Circles

the state of the world—and how they feel about it. Most acknowledge that the world is deeply broken, marked by suffering, injustice and alienation. Most also admit that they feel upset over this, and wish it were different. Choung then draws a first circle representing the damaged world.

Choung then capitalizes on that universal hunger for a better world. Following C. S. Lewis's classic apologetic approach, he argues that just as the universal sense of hunger suggests the reality of food, so the universal longing for a better, more just, peaceful and healthy world suggests that either there once was one or there one day will be one. Then he announces that this is exactly what Christianity teaches.

Now he draws another circle. This one represents the good, created order of Genesis 1. He explains that God originally made a world of shalom, marked by beauty, goodness and harmony. There was peace between humans and God, between people, and between people and the created environment. Then he labels this second circle "Designed for good."

With the stark presence of the first two circles before him, it's easy now for Choung to raise the obvious question: How did we get from the perfect world that originally existed to the messed-up one we now inhabit? At this point, Choung introduces the concepts of evil and sin. Sin is humankind's fundamental turning away from God and his ways, to setting self on the throne. Once people did that, they began to use the natural world and human relationships for selfish gain. This damaged everything—the environment, ourselves, our human relationships and our relationship with God. Thinking that the way of self would lead to life, sinful humans found instead that they were totally alienated. Having departed from God's path of life, they found decay and death. They stood under God's wrath.

Choung then adds more squiggly lines into the first circle to represent all these broken relationships, and he labels it "Damaged by evil." His picture captures the pervasive nature of sin. Unlike the Bridge illustration, which highlights the individual sinner's separation from God, this picture shows how sin affects all four fundamental relationships originally created for shalom. This highlights how everything is tainted by sin; it underscores how only a comprehensive redemption will suffice.

Choung then explains to the listener that God doesn't want to leave us alone in our sin in this damaged world. The good news is that God has mercifully returned to his planet in his Son Jesus to heal it. Jesus enters our broken world, offering the path to reconciliation, the opportunity to return to God through him. Jesus allows himself to be infected by the disease of sin (he bears it on our behalf) and courageously, sacrificially pays the penalty for it himself on the cross.

Now Choung draws a third circle with a big, vertical arrow representing Jesus' entry into our sin-ravaged world. He explains that Jesus came to start a resistance movement against all evil. Through his life-giving ministry, he starts pushing back the curse and offering people foretastes of the new kingdom he is bringing. He dies on the cross, fully paying the penalty of God's wrath against sin. And then he is raised victorious over death, ready to breathe his spirit-life into those who say yes to him.

Those who respond to Jesus' invitation to enter his kingdom receive forgiveness for their sin and healing for their brokenness. He grants them the gift of eternal life and brings them into the family of God. Jesus then shows us a new way to live. He commands us to trust and obey him and places his Spirit within us to empower us to grow to become more like him. As our relationship with him matures, we experience deep inner healing. We gain motivation and power to pursue healed, reconciled, just relationships with others. And the way is opened for us to take up once again our commission as wise stewards of the earth. Now Choung labels this third circle "Restored for better."

Choung then draws a fourth circle. His story of the gospel doesn't end with Christ's sacrifice and our rescue (our "receiving our ticket to heaven"). No, now he draws a horizontal arrow from the "Restored for better" circle to a fourth circle that is labeled "Sent together to heal." Now—appropriately—the conversation about salvation is linked to a conversation about discipleship. Choung explains that Jesus offers us rescue from our sin and the consequences of it (that is, eternal death) *and* that he calls us to join him on his resistance movement against evil. In Choung's depiction of the gospel, we hear Jesus say, "Come, follow me."

The too-narrow gospel presented in the Bridge illustration lacks this discipleship component. It creates the danger of producing Christians who essentially get stuck in the third circle. They remain there with their personal ticket to heaven, in the "holy huddle," enjoying fellowship with God and other believers, but divorced from the mission of God. This is a big part of what motivated Choung to design an alternative way of presenting the gospel. He explains,

> The afterlife takes priority over the mission life in existing gospel explanations. They imply that the gospel is something that happens after death instead of now. Even if they mention a relationship with God in the present, they often emphasize what people can get out of it—joy, peace, healing, prosperity. As a result, we invite people into a relationship with Jesus without mentioning the *missio Dei*, hoping to get to it later. . . . But Jesus enticed people into a kingdom mission from the outset.[3]

IMPLICATIONS OF HOW WE UNDERSTAND THE GOSPEL

The gospel preached in our congregations makes a huge difference in the kind of people our members become. Specifically, congregants' understanding of the gospel affects their views of three arenas crucial to living as the *tsaddiqim*: sanctification, evangelism and mission. This is why it is crucial that missional leaders preach the "big" gospel of the kingdom.

Sanctification. The big gospel helps us understand that sanctification is a matter of conforming not only to the character of Christ, but also to his passions and identity. Missional leaders should of course be quick to affirm that seeking conformity to Jesus' holy character is absolutely essential. Personal morality and growth in the fruit of the Spirit is a critical part of righteousness, but it's also incomplete. Becoming like Jesus also means seeing ourselves as he did, as "sent ones," and being passionate about the things he is passionate about. Let's look briefly at each.

Jesus is passionate for justice and shalom. We see this as he overturns the tables of the greedy moneychangers in the temple (Jn 2:14-16), as he calls the Pharisees to account for their unjust practices (Mk 7:9-13) and as he deliberately reaches out to those society has banished to the margins: the poor, the disabled, the lepers. Jesus is also passionate about reconciliation among diverse people. He reaches across gender, ethnic and religious barriers to minister to the Samaritan woman at the well (Jn 4) and the ten lepers of Luke 17. Unity is also a core value for Jesus; consider, for example, his fervent prayer in John 17. And, like his Father, Jesus is passionate about the poor, the vulnerable, the sick and the stranger. To become like him is to adopt all these passions as our own.

Moreover, genuine sanctification means that we intentionally identify with the *identity* of Jesus. He saw himself as the "sent one," and he calls us sent ones. Listen again to John 20:21: "As the Father has sent me, I am sending you." Sanctification means growing ever deeper into our identity as sent ones—those appointed by God to bear fruit, as Jesus said (Jn 15:16). It's not just the missionaries in our congregations who are the sent ones. We are *all* sent ones.

In teaching this point, missional leaders may want to consider using an attention-getting exercise from missionary Darrow Miller. Miller notes how precious John 3:16 is to many Christians ("For God so loved the world that he gave his one and only Son, that whoever believes in him shall not perish but have eternal life"). In some evangelical churches, Miller reports, to help not-yet-Christians grasp the amazing significance of this great love and to personalize it, evangelists encourage people to insert their own name into the verse, in place of "the world." Thus, John 3:16 comes to say, "For God so loved [Name] that he sent his only Son Jesus that I should not perish but have eternal life."

Acknowledging the validity of this, Miller then suggests that Christ-followers take another liberty with the text that links it to John 20:21. This helps us better grasp our own sentness. He suggests personalizing John 3:16 to read, "For God so loved the world that he sent me into the world."[4]

Now, it should be immediately emphasized, Jesus' sentness is utterly unique. He alone is the Messiah and God's one true redeemer. But, as John 20:21 makes clear, God intends for believers to follow his Son into the world as sacrificial servants. God shows his love for the lost and the least through his Son *and* through all his children who seek, in the power of his Holy Spirit, to be his hands and feet in compassionate service. God and Jesus have sent *us* into the world.[5] Sanctification means following Jesus as he sends us into every place and every societal sphere, giving ourselves to the work of the restoration of all things.

Evangelism. How we understand the gospel also shapes our approach to evangelism. Our presentation will include the vital good news of personal justification by faith in Christ's atoning blood. But we will also talk about the power of Jesus in redeeming *all* our fundamental relationships (with God, self, others and the earth). Moreover, our gospel presentation will rejoice in Jesus' victory over both the penalty of sin *and* the corruption of sin. We will share the good news that through Jesus' redemptive work we can be made clean *and* whole. We will celebrate the good news that he is making us new creatures *and* that he promises the restoration of all things.

The gospel of the kingdom should also reshape the language we use in evangelism. Typically, congregants are trained to encourage seekers to "ask Jesus into their heart." However, this does not mirror the language Jesus himself used. His evangelistic invitation was, "Come, enter my kingdom." Therefore, evangelists of the gospel of the kingdom should encourage seekers to respond to Jesus' invitation to come over and join his heart. Intimate communion with Jesus occurs when we go to him. German theologian Dietrich Bonhoeffer put it this way: "It is not that God is the spectator and sharer of our present life, howsoever important that is, but rather that we are the reverent listeners and participants in God's action in the sacred story, the history of the Christ on the earth. *And only so far as we are there, is God with us today also.*"[6]

The kingdom gospel also leads us to invest more thought and energy in the missional work of *enacting and demonstrating* the heart of God in the world. We acknowledge that our lives as well as our words are messages to the watching world about God. This is what one Californian church learned as it studied and meditated for three years on Luke 10 and Matthew 10, about Jesus sending out his disciples. Pastor Ryan Bell writes,

> We have . . . learned of our need to be continually converted to the gospel. Little by little, the gospel that Jesus gave the disciples to share, recorded in Matthew 10, has been replaced by a disembodied, abstract gospel about going to heaven after you die. But notice in Matthew 10 that Jesus doesn't commission the disciples with anything like a gospel of "going to heaven." He says, "proclaim the good news, 'The kingdom of heaven has come near'" (Matt. 10:7). If anything, this is a gospel about heaven coming to earth, not us going to heaven. It's obvious, too, that this gospel is more about demonstration than presentation. Jesus does tell them to "proclaim" the good news. But how? "Cure the sick, raise the dead, cleanse the lepers, cast out demons" (Matt. 10:8). We have discovered that to be God's witnesses we need to be re-converted to the gospel of the "at-hand" kingdom of God.[7]

Mission. Our understanding of the gospel also influences our view of mission. As we already saw, the gospel of the kingdom highlights the fundamental call for the church to join King Jesus on his mission of offering foretastes of justice and shalom. It shapes our understanding of the church's mission in the world in four additional ways.

First, the gospel of the kingdom illuminates our Lord's top three missional priorities. As articulated in his inaugural address in Luke 4, they are evangelism, compassion and justice.

Second, the gospel of the kingdom draws us to holistic ministry, to addressing people's spiritual and material needs. It does so by pointing our attention not only to Jesus' death, but also to his life. A close study of Jesus' life reveals that he didn't treat people as souls without bodies. His healing ministry mattered. When he sent out the disciples, it was for the task of evangelism *and* the work of healing (Mk 3:14-15; Lk 9:1-2).

Third, the gospel of the kingdom shapes mission by encouraging us to think more "cosmically" about evil than does the too-narrow gospel. The latter focuses on individual sin and personal redemption. The gospel of the kingdom focuses on that *plus* the far-reaching ravages of the cosmic curse. It proclaims not only the redemption of individual sinners but also the destruction of the devil's work and the restoring of all things.[8] Kingdom people thus seek Jesus' power to "tie up the strong man" and "rob his house" (Mk 3:27). They recognize that mission involves pushing back the curse, fighting evil and injustice.[9]

Finally, the gospel of the kingdom shapes the direction of our mission. With our focus on Jesus' life and ministry as our model, we come to see that while he loved everyone, his steps tended to lead him toward the poor. In this Jesus is simply following in his Father's footsteps. The Bible teaches that God "shows no partiality" (Deut 10:17). But it also paints a very consistent picture of God acting vigorously on behalf of the poor, the orphan, the widow and the stranger. He regularly exhibits a special concern for them. Our mission work should too.

THE *MISSIO DEI*: WE HAVE A ROLE

The big gospel presented through tools like James Choung's Four Circles puts the mission of God, the *missio Dei*, front and center. We see that God is on the move, doing his work of restoring all things. Such a vision should provoke our awed worship: How amazing a savior is our God, who is conquering all evil and is about the work of re-creating paradise! But it should provoke another response as well. Namely, it should move us to a startled, humbled-yet-confident embrace of our own personal role in building for the kingdom.

Australian missionaries Michael Frost and Alan Hirsch make this point so powerfully in their book *The Shaping of Things to Come* that it is worth quoting them at length:

> We Protestants have generally struggled to affirm our place in God's plan of redemption for fear of developing a salvation by works. In our efforts to ensure that God's sovereignty remains unsullied, we have tended to downplay the vital part that God has set for humanity in the redemption of the world. We have tended to make a formula of "all of God" and "we are nothing." Not only is this highly questionable theologically, loaded as it is with dualistic self-hatred, but it has not necessarily brought God any glory. In actual fact it might actually have served to diminish the sheer value of the investment he has made in human freedom and the preciousness of his image that he has placed in the human being. . . .
>
> We partner with God in the redemption of the world. *This is not just an issue of theology or spirituality; it is an issue of a thoroughly reorienting missiology. It will provide God's people with a new sense of purpose, a divine connection to daily actions. We need to grasp the fact that in God's economy our actions do have an eternal impact. We do extend the kingdom of God in daily affairs and activities and actions done in the name of Jesus.* We live in an unredeemed world. But out of each human life that is given over to God and committed to his creation, a seed of redemption falls into the world, and the harvest is God's![10]

As N. T. Wright said, "[Christians] are not just to be a sign and foretaste of [the] ultimate salvation: *they are to be part of the means by which God makes this happen in both the present and the future.*"[11]

God's plan is to bring shalom to this broken world, but he wants to do that in partnership with us. This can sound absolutely astonishing to those of us deeply schooled in the realities of our own sin. I attend a church where we confess our sin every Sunday. This is appropriate, but it can risk communicating to believers that the Christian story began in Genesis 3 instead of Genesis 1. We were made with original glory; all human beings bear the dignity of being made in God's own image. Sin has greatly marred that image but has not extinguished it.

Moreover, believers redeemed by Jesus are called saints throughout the New Testament. A proper understanding of our (new creation) selves is that we are saints who sin. As one of my former pastors liked to say, we are crooked sticks, but God can strike straight blows through us. If we think of ourselves only as hopeless worms who sin constantly and have nothing to offer, we won't believe ourselves capable of fulfilling our calling as God's coworkers who have been designed by him for good works (Eph 2:10).

Now, God doesn't *need* us—let's be clear on that. He is omnipotent. It is not from some lack that he looks to us as partners. No, we are his partners because he has chosen to act with us. We are his partners because of his invitation. It's simply the way that the all-wise Creator of the universe has determined it to be.[12]

Meanwhile, though we have this calling to join him in his kingdom work, we are utterly unable to do so apart from our total reliance on him. So God still gets all the glory. The laborers labor in vain if he doesn't build the house. We only do the "greater things" Jesus predicted in John 14 if we abide in the vine. "Apart from me," he warns us, "you can do nothing" (Jn 15:5). Affirming the strange and wonderful partnership that God has designed between himself and us frail humans to get his work done in the world does not diminish his glory. It accentuates it—for how loving it is of our Father to invite us into such colaboring.

The story told of the Christian's life in the too-narrow gospel does not capture this awesome reality and privilege that we—saved sinners—are part of God's plan to heal the world. The too-narrow gospel tells us what we've been saved *from*: sin, hell and death. And that is very good news indeed. But the gospel of the kingdom tells us not only what we're saved from, but also what we're saved *for*. We have a purpose, we have a sacred calling, we have a God-given vocation: to partner with God in his work of restoring all things.

What could be more exhilarating than that?

PART 2

Discipling for Vocational Stewardship

Integrating Faith and Work

THE STATUS QUO IS INADEQUATE

*In nothing has the church so lost Her hold on reality as
in Her failure to understand and respect the secular vocation.*

DOROTHY SAYERS

In future chapters, we will meet Christian architects, engineers, business owners, historians, entertainers, photographers, chemists, dancers, sales reps, lawyers and real estate appraisers. Their stories of vocational stewardship are exciting and illuminating. Often, though, they began on a sad note. Many of these Christ-followers received almost no teaching from their churches on how to integrate their faith and work. As a result, many of them wondered early in their Christian lives whether their commitment to Jesus meant that they should leave their "secular" profession to go into "full-time Christian ministry."

Their stories—and the three years of research undergirding this book—have convinced me that today thousands of Christian professionals sit in the pews, wondering, *Can I participate in Jesus' mission—and do so using the gifts and skills God has given me?* The answer is a resounding *yes*—but such a word is tragically uncommon in many Christian congregations.[1]

Princeton University's David Miller, who directs the Faith and Work Initiative there, has conducted years of research on this subject. He reports,

> The Church generally shies from the topic [of work], and our divinity
> schools and seminaries are no better. *Fewer than 10 percent of regular church-*

goers, surveys say, can remember the last time their pastor preached on the topic of work. When he or she did preach on work, inevitably the tone was critical—if not hostile—and painted all businesspeople as greedy and uncaring. Seldom do pastors honor the work world as a place for parishioners to live out their high calling. Whether you're a secretary or a CEO, people in the pews seldom hear from the pulpit that God has a plan that includes your work, and that your faith can help inform how you approach your work.[2]

Moreover, key periodicals addressed largely to clergy and church leaders do not often cover issues of faith and work integration. My research assistant and I culled through many years of back issues of *Leadership Journal*, *The Christian Century* and *Discipleship Journal*, looking for such pieces. Online keyword searches revealed 152 matches on the word *vocation* at *Leadership Journal*—but over 95 percent were on the vocation of the pastorate. We turned up only nine results searching on *vocation* in *The Christian Century*, and three of those were on the pastoral calling. *Discipleship Journal* gave us forty-one matches, but only one was about faith-and-work integration by laity.

While many Christians are not receiving guidance from their churches, they may be hearing about faith/work integration from parachurch sources. Hundreds of books have been written on this topic.[3] There are also many marketplace ministries available for Christian businesspeople to join. According to Steven Rundell and C. Neal Johnson of Calvin College, "By one estimate there are now at least 1,200 organizations that promote, in various ways, the integration of faith and work, not to mention dozens of events held annually around the world that encourage businesspeople to 'bring their faith to work.'"[4]

And still other believers participate in a Christian professional society. Roughly forty of these associations are in existence.[5] They range from the Affiliation of Christian Geologists to the Christian Veterinary Society. Christian artists, actors, chefs, doctors, dentists, economists, foresters, journalists, librarians, nurses, pharmacists, political scientists, sociologists—and more—all have professional fellowships available to them.

In short, although Christians aren't hearing much about how to integrate faith and work in the pews, there's a significant quantity of resources and organizations in the broader Christian community they can turn to.

To disciple their people well for vocational stewardship, congregational leaders need to understand what their members may have learned from these sources about faith/work integration.

CHRISTIAN THOUGHT ON THE INTEGRATION OF FAITH AND WORK

Scholar David Miller's book on the history of the Faith at Work movement begins by noting, "This modern quest for integration has ancient theological roots."[6] Throughout Christian history, Miller explains, the faithful have mused on the question of how to express their faith in and through their labor. Theologians of the Reformation, for example, were deeply interested in "vocation in daily life and work."[7]

Focusing on more recent history, Miller examines three waves of the Faith at Work (FAW) movement: the social gospel era (c. 1890s–1945), the era of lay ministry (c. 1946–1980) and the modern FAW era (1980 to the present). He discusses the players, organizations, events and ideas of each wave. Toward the close of his book, Miller describes the major themes in the movement as falling into four main categories or quadrants: ethics, evangelism, enrichment and experience. Each of these ways of expressing faith through work is discussed below.

Quadrant one: Ethics. Individuals and organizations in the ethics quadrant have primarily integrated faith at work "through attention to personal virtue, business ethics, and to broader questions of social and economic justice," Miller explains.[8] Activities in this quadrant include everything from ethics seminars to Christian business fellowships that provide members with the opportunity to discuss moral dilemmas and hold each other accountable. Christians in this quadrant are concerned about appropriately balancing the demands of work and family. They desire to grow in wisdom in handling the temptations of secular success as well as the immoral social activities permitted or even encouraged within the organizations that employ them. Issues tackled here might include cheating on expense reports, putting corporate interests over human relationships, or navigating the toll taken on marriage by long periods of business travel.

Generally, discussions of ethics are limited to personal morality. A few members in this quadrant, however, do go beyond this to issues related to "social righteousness." As Miller explains,

Other FAW participants in the [ethics] type, while not indifferent to personal ethics, focus more on business ethics and topics affecting the broader *mezzo* level of the corporation. The FAW participants with this accent address issues such as product selection, quality, safety, whistle blowing, loyalty, and advertising. Others focus on *macro* ethical questions involving corporate responsibility to society at large and economic justice as it pertains to all stakeholders and beyond. Typical business issues addressed by groups with macro ethical orientation include environmental analyses of manufacturing and product decisions, offshore working conditions and wages, and executive compensation.[9]

Quadrant two: Evangelism. As the label suggests, people of faith in this quadrant are primarily interested in integrating their faith and their work through evangelistic efforts. This includes cultivating friendships with coworkers from other (or no) faiths; sponsoring Bible studies at work; hosting events or conferences that offer platforms for believers to share their testimonies with nonbelievers within their organizations; or providing spiritual counselors or chaplains in the firm. The Full Gospel Businessmen's Fellowship International and the Fellowship of Companies for Christ International are two of the leading groups in the evangelism quadrant. Miller also puts the Center for FaithWalk Leadership as well as Priority Associates (a division of Campus Crusade) in this category.[10]

Efforts and activities by the groups within this quadrant have borne much fruit. According to Os Hillman, director of the Atlanta-based nonprofit Marketplace Leaders, "America is now home to 10,000 workplace Bible-study and prayer groups, with new initiatives starting at companies such as Sears, Coca-Cola and American Airlines."[11]

Quadrant three: Enrichment. The third theme in the FAW movement is personal transformation and spiritual nurture. The organizations here (which Miller notes are often religious hybrids like "Christian Buddhists" or New Age) want individuals' experience of work to be a means of self-actualization and transformation. They are interested in healing, prayer, meditation—therapeutic and contemplative practices to aid workers. Such practices can help discouraged or downsized workers, or they may bring a new level of peace to over-stressed corporate executives. Maximizing one's potential is also a major focus in this quadrant.

Quadrant four: Experience. This quadrant is composed of those FAW groups that examine questions of "vocation, calling, meaning, and purpose in and through their marketplace professions." Importantly, for this group, work "has both intrinsic and extrinsic meaning and purpose. That is, the particular work someone does, in and of its own right, is of theological value," Miller says.[12] Christians in this quadrant lament the common view that somehow secular work is "second class" or that only through a "ministry career" (such as pastoring or being a missionary) can a person truly live out her or his faith. These organizations provide counsel, books and conferences to help individuals discover their calling and align their natural and spiritual gifts with careers in which those talents can be well deployed.

THE EVERYWHERE INTEGRATOR TYPE

Miller rightly affirms the strengths of each quadrant while simultaneously asserting that the healthiest approach is one that combines all these themes. He found a few examples of FAW groups that embodied this "Everywhere Integrator" type, including the Laity Lodge Leadership Forum and Campus Crusade's CEO Forum.[13] These rare groups take seriously *all* the issues raised in the four quadrants.

Miller's Everywhere Integrator type gets closest to the concept of vocational stewardship for the common good. It takes seriously the three dimensions of righteousness (vertical, internal and social). Evangelicalism could produce more believers who act like the *tsaddiqim* in and through their professions if its marketplace ministries, professional societies and books on faith/work integration helped move people as much as possible toward the Everywhere Integrator type Miller describes. How well are we doing in that?

MARKETPLACE MINISTRIES

To answer that, my research assistants and I examined the vision and activities of fifteen evangelical "marketplace ministries."[14] We concluded that most of them fall into Miller's quadrant one (ethics) or two (evangelism). Twelve of the fifteen groups were principally focused on winning people to Christ at work through Bible studies, evangelism and prayer and/or encouraging their members to be good witnesses. These ministries tend to offer small groups, conferences, events and meetings in which testimonies are shared and prayer and counsel are offered. They promote personal discipleship and evangelism.

The mission of Fellowship of Companies for Christ International (FCCI), for example, reads, "In pursuit of Christ's eternal objectives, we equip and encourage business leaders to operate their businesses and conduct their personal lives in accordance with biblical principles."[15] The main objectives of FCCI are to facilitate fellowship among Christian businesspeople and to "better prepare them to handle daily business situations in a manner glorifying Christ in spirit and truth."[16]

In addition to emphases on personal morality, fellowship/encouragement and evangelism, some of the organizations we examined showed elements of quadrant three (enrichment). These groups encourage workers to rely practically and daily on the indwelling Holy Spirit to empower their labor. They offer Bible-study curriculum and devotional guides and encourage Christians in business to form prayer groups. Henry Blackaby's monthly "God in the Workplace" Bible study, for example, "focuses on helping people know how to practically walk in a real and personal relationship with God in their work place."[17] This ministry also offers online courses that help people to grow spiritually and to recognize the presence of God in their daily life.

None of the marketplace ministries we examined fit into quadrant four (experience), where the work *itself* is valued and deeply contemplated. And none reflected the Everywhere Integrator type.

This imbalance probably helps explain why Michael Lindsay, upon interviewing more than one hundred evangelical business leaders for his book *Faith in the Halls of Power*, discovered few with an *advanced* vision and practice of faith/work integration.[18] Such businesspeople are not getting adequate discipleship from their churches, and many who participate in marketplace ministries are not being pushed very far creatively there either.

Let me be quick to say that marketplace ministries have played an important and valuable role in the kingdom. They have strengthened the discipleship of believers in the midst of the jungle of the modern workplace. They have helped earnest executives to stay the course in the face of very difficult personal and corporate temptations. They have contributed to marital stability and helped Christian executives avoid making their careers idols. And they have introduced non-Christians in the marketplace to Jesus in winsome, friendly and relevant ways. All this is very good and laudable. It's just that there is room for deeper, richer, more creative faith/work integration.[19]

CHRISTIAN PROFESSIONAL SOCIETIES

What about evangelical workers outside the business community? How robustly and creatively are they integrating faith and work? To begin to get a handle on this question, my staff and I analyzed the vision, mission and programs of twenty-three Christian professional societies.[20] We found that the majority of associations were more internally than externally focused. That is, their principal aims had to do with member support, fellowship and peer-to-peer learning.

About half of the professional societies had a significant focus on evangelism. Not many had an explicit focus on ethics. It didn't appear that members faced ethical dilemmas as much as they did intellectual challenges to their faith. In several of the groups, much discussion focused on understanding the professional discipline from a biblical worldview. The principal aim of the Association for Christians in Mathematical Sciences (ACMS), for example, is to help members "explore the relationship of their faith to their discipline."[21] This is accomplished through conferences and a journal.

ACMS and other academic groups primarily seek to be support and networking associations with particular emphasis on peer-to-peer learning and discussion of discipline-related issues. The Christian Neuroscience Society, for example, describes itself as "a group of Christians who are interested in furthering the dialogue between neuroscience and the truth of the Christian faith."[22]

A smaller number of the associations were involved in externally focused activities. Groups like the Association of Christian Librarians and the Christian Legal Society, for example, engaged members in practical missions work using their professional skills. The librarians support peers overseas, helping schools establish libraries. The lawyers donate their time to serve the poor through legal aid clinics.

The Christian Engineering Society (CES) is an interesting blend of internal and external focus. Members gather annually for very robust conferences, with presenters tackling a wide variety of issues. These events foster fellowship, networking, prayer and peer-to-peer learning. At the same time, paper topics are heavily weighted toward practical action in the world. As one presenter said,

> Engineers fulfill a special place within God's Creation Mandate. There are few professions whose purpose is more directly involved in subduing creation for the benefit of mankind than engineering. The engineering profession is everywhere concerned with making the world a little better for mankind while extracting and making use of its resources to produce great benefits for people everywhere.[23]

CES promotes member involvement in hands-on opportunities for vocational stewardship through such nonprofits as Engineers Without Borders, Engineering Ministries International, Water Missions International and TechServe International.

Just about a third of the professional associations, particularly those related to art (Christians in Theatre Arts, Christians in the Visual Arts, Christian Dance Fellowship), focus largely on promoting excellence in their craft. In March 2010 the website for Christians in the Visual Arts, for example, described its purpose as "encourag[ing] Christians in the visual arts to develop their particular callings to the highest professional level possible."[24] In academic associations such as Christians in Political Science, Christian Association for Psychological Studies and the Christian Sociological Society, members are encouraged toward excellence in teaching, research and publishing.

A few of the organizations, most notably the Christian Medical and Dental Society (CMDA), fit Miller's category of the Everywhere Integrator type:

> CMDA promotes positions and addresses policies on healthcare issues; conducts overseas medical evangelism projects through its mission arm, Global Health Outreach; coordinates a network of Christian doctors for fellowship and professional growth; sponsors student ministries in medical and dental schools; distributes educational and inspirational resources; hosts marriage and family conferences; provides Third World missionary doctors with continuing education resources; and conducts academic exchange programs overseas.[25]

CMDA is involved in evangelism on several fronts (on medical school campuses in the United States and through medical missions abroad). It wrestles with complicated questions of bioethics. It seeks to help its members find meaning in their work as well as balance in the demands of that work against competing claims on members' time. And it facilitates numerous opportunities for members to practice their professional skills on behalf of vulnerable populations.

(LARGELY) MISSING: A VISION
OF INSTITUTIONAL TRANSFORMATION

A vital part of vocational stewardship for the common good is a focus by believers on transforming the institutions in which they work. As James Hunter argues in *To Change the World*,

> The church, as it exists within the wide range of individual vocations in every sphere of social life (commerce, philanthropy, education, etc.), must be present in the world in ways that work toward the *constructive* subversion of all frameworks of social life that are incompatible with the shalom for which we were made and to which we are called. As a natural expression of its passion to honor God in all things and to love our neighbor as ourselves, the church and its people will challenge all structures that dishonor God, dehumanize people, and neglect or do harm to the creation.[26]

My (admittedly imprecise) examination of marketplace ministries found no evidence that these business fellowships are discussing how Christian executives can reform practices within their particular industries that might be problematic from the perspectives of justice and shalom. Some of the Christian professional societies have taken some steps in this direction. For example, some are trying to expand the topics given consideration by members of their guild by publishing their own journals. Others encourage their members to participate in key conversations happening within their field, such as when the CMDA encourages members to publish in leading journals in the guild on questions of bioethics. And the already-noted emphasis on excellence within artistic societies could eventually influence their field. If Christian artists create works of exquisite quality, their artwork may have a better chance of being noticed by elite cultural institutions (for example, being put on display in the most influential galleries or being reviewed in the arts pages of the *New York Times*).

On the whole, though, our cursory examination of Christian professional societies did not indicate that discussions of reforming their discipline were a common, central, animating feature of these associations.

CONCLUSION

The average Christian professional sitting in the pew hears little from the pulpit or in Sunday school about how her life with God relates to her life at work. She may receive general guidance about being salt and light in all the spheres of her life, including her workplace. Overall, though, her church offers little specific guidance about why her work matters, how God can and does use it, or how her vocational power can be stewarded to advance his kingdom.

Lacking this guidance, some Christians simply "turn off" their faith at work; they function as "practical atheists" on the job.[27] They have no vision for what it means to partner with God at work, to bring meaning to their work or to accomplish kingdom purposes in and through their work. Others look outside their local congregation for guidance, joining a marketplace ministry or a Christian professional society. These individuals receive some good counsel and personal support, and, depending on which fellowship they belong to, may also hear a fairly robust vision of vocational stewardship.

More often, though, they are simply instructed to be people of strong integrity and to seek to win coworkers for Christ. These emphases on ethics and evangelism are needed and valuable, but they are insufficient for equipping Christians to steward their vocational power to advance foretastes of the kingdom. We need to get beyond the status quo.

Inspiration

Vocation is integral, not incidental, to the
mission of God in the world.

STEVE GARBER

Doug Spada, the leader of WorkLife, Inc., offers pastors a vivid metaphor about a church's proper identity:

> From this day forward, I would like you to think of your local church as an aircraft carrier. Unless our churches assume the rightful and biblical positions in the battles we face in the workplace, we cannot fully advance. It's only as the carrier arms, equips, briefs on the battle plan, fuels the jet and then launches the pilots out on their mission that they assume their maximum dominion. . . . Unfortunately, many of our churches operate like a cruise ship. Think about it, what do you do on a cruise ship? You go to be entertained, you eat a lot, there's very little accountability. And think about a cruise ship: it goes out, hits a couple points and comes back to the very same place—rarely advancing forward into new territory. If the enemy of our souls can disarm the carrier, confuse the pilots, break the catapult system, then we essentially continue to function as a cruise ship. . . . God may very well be asking you to be a catalyst for work life reformation in your church. The church is not a cruise ship but an aircraft carrier.[1]

Churches whose self-identity is as aircraft carriers place a high value on affirming and equipping laypeople for their ministries out in the workaday world. They teach people just how much their daily work matters. Like Pastor Tom Nelson of Christ Community Church in Leawood, Kansas, they inspire their members by reminding them that their work is "central to [God's] redemptive story and his redemptive aim in the world—not only now but also in the new heavens and new earth."[2]

Missional church leaders know that the church is formed of both the "gathered" and the "scattered." They affirm that ministry is not solely about what happens inside the four walls of the church; in fact, it's usually much more about what happens outside them. They don't make the mistake of defining ministry as "church work." Therefore, they affirm laypeople in the ministries that they have in and through their "secular" jobs.

It is from this high view of members' daily work that pastors are positioned to offer inspiration to their flock. Carrying out this task of inspiration involves teaching a biblical theology of work and providing practical advice to members regarding the "vocational sweet spot."

THE BASICS OF A BIBLICAL THEOLOGY OF WORK

To inspire their flock about their daily work, congregational leaders need to start with the vital truth that work preceded the Fall. This truth is foundational for faithful vocational stewardship. Work is not a result of humankind's fall into sin. Work is central in Genesis 1 and 2. There it is—right in the midst of paradise, right in the picture of God's intentions for how things ought to be. Work is a gift from God. *Work is something we were built for, something our loving Creator intends for our good.* Work is not evil, nor is it a side effect of sin. This truth can be hard for congregants to trust when they are frustrated in their jobs or unfulfilled in their careers. It's certainly true that the curse of Genesis 3 brought toil and futility into work. Ever since, our experience of work involves pain as well as pleasure. But work itself is good. It has intrinsic value.

Labor's intrinsic value: How we participate in God's own work. Human beings are made in the image of God, and God is a worker. Human labor has intrinsic value because in it we "image," or reflect, our Creator. In *Faith Goes to Work,* author Robert Banks discusses God as our "vocational model," describing the various sorts of work he does and how myriad human vocations give expression to these aspects of God's work.[3] Banks's model is very helpful for teaching congregants the intrinsic value of work. Pastors can explain the various ways in which God is a worker, and then encourage their congregants to identify where their own labors fit. God's labors include the following:

- *Redemptive work* (God's saving and reconciling actions). Humans participate in this kind of work, for example, as evangelists, pastors, counselors and peacemakers. So do writers, artists, producers, songwriters, poets and actors who incorporate redemptive elements in their stories, novels, songs, films, performances and other works.

- *Creative work* (God's fashioning of the physical and human world). God gives humans creativity. People in the arts (sculptors, actors, painters, musicians, poets and so on) display this, as do a wide range of craftspeople such as potters, weavers and seamstresses, as well as interior designers, metalworkers, carpenters, builders, fashion designers, architects, novelists and urban planners (and more).

- *Providential work* (God's provision for and sustaining of humans and the creation). "The work of divine providence includes all that God does to maintain the universe and human life in an orderly and beneficial fashion," Banks writes. "This includes conserving, sustaining, and replenishing, in addition to creating and redeeming the world."[4] Thus, innumerable individuals—bureaucrats, public utility workers, public policymakers, shopkeepers, career counselors, shipbuilders, farmers, firemen, repairmen, printers, transport workers, IT specialists, entrepreneurs, bankers and brokers, meteorologists, research technicians, civil servants, business school professors, mechanics, engineers, building inspectors, machinists, statisticians, plumbers, welders, janitors— and all who help keep the economic and political order working smoothly—reflect this aspect of God's labor.

- *Justice work* (God's maintenance of justice). Judges, lawyers, paralegals, government regulators, legal secretaries, city managers, prison wardens and guards, policy researchers and advocates, law professors, diplomats, supervisors, administrators and law enforcement personnel participate in God's work of maintaining justice.

- *Compassionate work* (God's involvement in comforting, healing, guiding and shepherding). Doctors, nurses, paramedics, psychologists, therapists, social workers, pharmacists, community workers, nonprofit directors, emergency medical technicians, counselors and welfare agents all reflect this aspect of God's labor.

- *Revelatory work* (God's work to enlighten with truth). Preachers, scientists, educators, journalists, scholars and writers are all involved in this sort of work.

In all these various ways, God the Father continues his creative, sustaining and redeeming work through our human labor. This gives our work great dignity and purpose. Vocational stewardship starts with *celebrating* the work itself and recognizing that God cares about it and is accomplishing his purposes through it.

It is worth lingering on this point because much teaching on the integration of faith and work neglects the inherent value of work. Church leaders should indeed teach and preach on becoming certain types of workers—honest workers, ethical workers, caring workers, faithful workers and salt-and-light workers. But such teaching is insufficiently biblical if there's never any mention of the inherent value of the work itself. As my brilliant friend Ken Myers likes to say, we should seek to be more than "adverbial Christians."

Our work lasts. We saw earlier that a further reason why our work truly matters is because it *lasts*. Work—pleasurable, fruitful, meaningful work—will be an eternal reality. Preview passages about life in the consummated kingdom, such as Isaiah 60, depict humans bringing all manner of culture-making, craftsmanship and economic production into the new age. Revelation 21:24 describes how "the kings of the earth will bring their splendor" into the New Jerusalem. It is good for pastors to remind their congregants of this grand truth, because believers sometimes get discouraged by the seeming futility of their labors. Consider Lesslie Newbigin's profound insight:

> Every faithful act of service, every honest labor to make the world a better place, which seemed to have been forever lost and forgotten in the rubble of history, will be seen on that day [at the final resurrection] to have contributed to the perfect fellowship of God's kingdom. . . . All who committed their work in faithfulness to God will be by Him raised up to share in the new age, and will find that their labor was not lost, but that it has found its place in the completed kingdom.[5]

COUNTERING FALSE IDEAS ABOUT WORK

Pastors need also to be aware that sin and our fallen culture have twisted many Christians' views on work. As church leaders teach the goodness of work, they also need to unmask and reject our secular culture's false understandings of work.

Because we are fallen, we sometimes act as though success at work equates to a successful life. It doesn't. Sometimes we make an idol of our careers. We need to repent. Sometimes we make decisions about jobs as though the ultimate purpose of work were self-fulfillment. It's not. Sometimes we judge people's worth based on their career position or status. We should seek God's forgiveness. Sometimes we allow work—which is just one dimension of our lives—to crowd out family or worship or relationships or play or Sabbath. We must resist.

False ideas about work emerge not just from the secular culture but also from poor theology. Therefore, church leaders must guard zealously against sacred/secular dualism that can produce an exaltation of the soul over the body (and thus of the so-called spiritual over the material) and/or a hierarchy favoring the work of clergy over that of the laity. Pastor Tom Nelson from Christ Community Church—who has been teaching his members about the redemptive value of work for ten years—takes this very seriously. "We're language police around here," he says. "We try very hard as a team to help each other avoid that dichotomist thinking and language."

Church leaders also need to address the fuzzy thinking some of their parishioners may have regarding work satisfaction. We've seen that for Christ-followers, the primary motivation for work is *not* self-fulfillment, self-enrichment or self-promotion. That cuts directly across our secular culture's claims. Christianity insists that our lives—including our work—are all about God and his work, his mission. This should be inspirational, because it provides profound meaning to our labor.

Pastors who begin teaching more on work may find that their congregants have some misplaced fears: Does the fact that their work is not "all about them" mean that God intends for labor to be only drudgery? Is he indifferent to our joy? Does he call us to work that we loathe? Are we only in the center of his vocational call if our work is miserable, painful and unfulfilling? No, no, no and no again!

Church leaders must help their people recognize that Satan delights in distorting our understanding of the Father and his loving purposes. Even believers who have walked for years with God can get tangled up by the enemy of our souls, feeling guilty when they engage in work they love—as though that is a sign that the work must be selfish. It's not.

Dying to self in the context of our work does not mean that we must search for and take on the job we think we'd most dislike. God creates us each with passions and talents. He then endows his followers with spiritual gifts. He sovereignly arranges our circumstances and experiences. He forms us with unique personalities and designs. He puts in us the capacity to find deep joy and purpose by serving him through work that draws on our unique, God-given combination of natural and spiritual gifts. We serve him as we serve others through our work, because he has called us to be his hands and feet in the midst of our beautiful but broken planet. That work is often difficult and may be draining, but it also can bring rich satisfaction and reward. As author Frederick Buechner says in his pithy definition of vocation, "the place God calls you to is the place where your deep gladness and the world's deep hunger meet."[6]

Encouraging Movement Toward the Vocational Sweet Spot

Buechner's definition provides some helpful guidance that is needed when the shackles of a dualistic view of work are discarded. Pastors should celebrate when their members break free of the muddled idea that some jobs are sacred while others are secular. But to say that there's no sacred/secular divide is not the same thing as saying that all secular pursuits are equally worthy.

Some jobs, we know, are morally out-of-bounds. No preacher worth his salt is going to encourage his congregants to start a brothel, take a job at an "adult" bookstore or enroll as a mercenary soldier. Hopefully, few Christians need specific instructions to avoid such career paths, but some may need to be challenged about degrees of good—to be encouraged to ask whether the way they are investing their work time (typically forty hours or more a week) reflects what really *matters* in light of God's priorities and the world's needs.[7]

Church leaders should inspire their congregants to choose jobs that, to the greatest extent possible, offer them the best opportunities for directing their creative talents toward the end of advancing shalom for the common good. Some secular organizations and companies are engaged in putting creativity to work in directions that are substantive for human flourishing; for example, in innovations that advance health or environmental steward-ship. However, other secular companies invest their creative energies in ways that simply produce more needless things and new consumer waste. Again, in some companies, creative talent is directed toward the end of finding answers to critical problems in our broken world. In others, cre-ative talent is directed toward providing answers to "problems" that are not really problems (consider the efforts that go into cosmetic changes in pack-aging or to the creation of new colors of lipstick).

Working for a company that directs the bulk of its creative energy in those kinds of directions isn't morally wrong. But pastors should ask their parishion-ers, "Why, as a follower of Christ, would you choose to give your creative talents to these sorts of exercises, when you could employ them instead in businesses or organizations that are meeting genuine needs?" In a world as broken and needy as ours—and with all the talent, privileges and opportuni-ties that God has granted us in middle- and upper-class America—church leaders should question the validity of believers giving fifty years of their working life toward creating new flavors of dog food or 1,500-dollar sterling silver canisters for tennis balls or gold-plated staples. It's time to admit that some things are just trivial, and if we can avoid them, we should.

Unlike the bottom billion of the world's poor, who do the jobs their ancestors before them did in order simply to survive, many believers in middle- and upper-class America have been given the precious gift of vo-cational choices. They need to be encouraged to choose wisely when they have more than one option. Some believers in today's downturned econ-omy may not have as many occupational choices as they might have in more prosperous times. Other believers continue to be privileged with multiple job options. The latter do well to remember that "to whom much has been given, of him much will be required" (Lk 14:28 ESV).

The diagram below paints a picture of what I call "the vocational sweet spot." The sweet spot is that place where our gifts and passions intersect with God's priorities and the world's needs. To the greatest extent possible, Christians should seek to work there.

FINDING THE SWEET SPOT

Church leaders need to communicate that finding the sweet spot is usually a journey. It takes time, and the process looks different for different people. Consider the journeys taken by Jill and Cynthia.

For twenty-nine-year-old Jill Sorenson, the process began with a deep inner desire to be an architect:

> I still remember the moment when I was twelve that I decided to become an architect. My dad [a contractor] had taken me to his office. I sat in the lounge and looked at magazines. One was a self-plan book with many designs for different house plans. I remember asking if I could take it home. That night I pulled out my mom's gridded cross-stitching paper, took one of the [house] designs and totally redid it. I changed walls around, and decided this was going to be my dream home someday. And if I wanted to build it, I knew I needed to be an architect.[8]

Unlike most college students, Jill never changed her major. "The more I got into the profession, the more I fell in love with the merging of an analytical side of me—the thinking side of me—and [the] creative, artistic side," she says. "I feel like architecture is at its best when you find where those two things collide."

But as a growing Christian, Jill wrestled with the validity of her profession. The Baptist Student Union she belonged to didn't seem to have a category for thinking of architecture as ministry. "I was really struggling

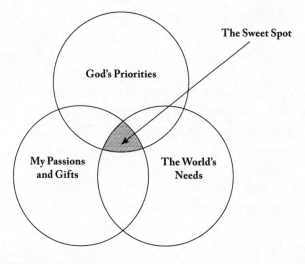

Figure 6.1. The vocational sweet spot

with how my faith and design passion merged," she recalls. "I knew [architecture] was something God was calling me to, and I knew that it couldn't be at odds with my faith. I knew there had to be an answer, there had to be some way for these things to fit together."

She ended up talking with her dad about how his faith shaped his work as a contractor. "He told me, 'You know, I thought about going into the ministry, but I knew that I could reach and affect more people through my work on the job site than from behind the pulpit.'" The affirmation rang true to Jill. "I just really appreciated his missional mindset. There wasn't a separation for him of the 'sacred' and the 'secular.'"

After a special summer ministering at a camp where the staff sought to love youth from many different faith backgrounds in ways that met spiritual, physical, intellectual and emotional needs, Jill returned to college with fresh enthusiasm for reaching out to her fellow students in the architecture school at Kansas State. She felt that developing solid relationships with nonbelievers in her field was an expression of faith/work integration.

In her final years at university, her understanding of how faith affects work deepened further. "I was starting to want to narrow in on what I was going to focus on as an architect," she says.

> I decided I wanted to use my profession in a way that helped people or was [environmentally] responsible. I was looking at either healthcare or sustainability, because I had worked on too many high-end condo projects that I didn't feel had any impact on the way people lived or added value to their life, at least value in the way I measured it. . . . I wanted to design buildings to create healing spaces. Or I could promote sustainability. I just wanted to be a better steward of buildings' purposes, resources and materials.

To prepare herself further, Jill became the first architecture student at Kansas State to achieve the Leadership in Energy and Environmental Design (LEED) certification.

Today Jill runs a small consulting business in the Bay Area, offering help to clients desiring to build more sustainably. She has also volunteered her architecture skills in economic development projects abroad with Engineering Ministries International and is the president of the board for Rebuild Sudan, which designs and builds "green" schools in Sudan.

For Jill, despite her love for her field, figuring out what her vocational sweet spot looked like was an unfolding process. For interior designer

Cynthia Leibrock, sixty-one, the journey to the vocational sweet spot began with dissatisfaction.

Leibrock went into design because she wanted to make things beautiful. She gained success, but it felt hollow. "I'd achieve my goal. I would . . . finish a project and have it completed, and I wouldn't feel satisfied with it. I'd look at it and I'd say, 'Well, what's the point?' I mean, it all seemed so empty to me."[9]

Then Cynthia got a design job for a doctor's office. It went "exceptionally well" and led to the client asking her to consider a part-time position overseeing a project to build a home for the developmentally disabled. She says,

> I didn't really have any experience working with disabled people, and I didn't know anything about developing housing . . . for disabled people. But they offered me this job. . . . I wasn't that satisfied in interior design, as I mentioned before, and suddenly here was this new avenue that I could pursue. I prayed about it and I really felt that the Lord wanted me to be in this. And so I accepted it [and] worked for two years to develop a 15-bed home for developmentally disabled people.

The project marked a major turning point for her career as she realized that design could contribute to independence. As she told a *New York Times* reporter in 2009, "I want people to know [that] no matter whether they have mental or physical disabilities . . . they are only disabled if they can't do what they want to do. Architecture can eliminate disability by design. . . . If you are in a house where you can do what you want to do, you're not disabled anymore."[10]

Cynthia has earned national recognition in the field of universal design, has been invited to teach courses at Harvard and is a champion of the "aging in place" movement. She is contributing to the transformation of the design industry.

She and her husband—aided by numerous corporate contributions—built their Colorado home, Green Mountain Ranch, as a "showcase, laboratory and training center for those interested in universal design." The home includes numerous aging-in-place design elements, like a hidden bathtub lift and kitchen cabinets with a ten-inch drawer in the kick space that can be removed to lower the counters to wheelchair levels if needed.[11]

In recent years, Cynthia launched Rehabitat, an initiative to help congregations come alongside disabled or elderly parishioners looking for ways to remain in their homes for as long as possible. Often minor adjustments—such as the installation of grab bars, ramps or handrails—can permit a person to stay in his or her home. Rehabitat gathers volunteers from churches that can donate labor to remodel homes. Its mission is "to show God's love in action as we help families to provide modifications that enhance independence and prevent disabling accidents."[12]

Jill and Cynthia each found their vocational sweet spot, and they are integrating their faith and work in deeply thoughtful ways.[13] Along the way, their sense of the meaning of their work deepened, their understanding of vocational stewardship matured and their joy increased. As Jill writes in her blog, "I see the world through the eyes of a designer, as one responsible for the built environment and the effect space has on life. I'll never be the same; I'll never shake this passion." She continues:

> With each step I take, it becomes more clear to me that these two paths, as an architect and as a disciple, are not meant to be walked separately and independently of the other. The longer they overlap and intersect, the further they intertwine and correspond, the more alive I become and the greater glory He is given.[14]

UNDERSTAND THE SEASONS

I'm encouraging church leaders to invite people to find and live in their vocational sweet spot because of the joy it brings to the worker, the hope it brings to those served and the glory it brings to God. Simultaneously, in their encouragement, leaders should employ "caveat" language—suggesting that people *to the greatest extent possible* seek that sweet spot. Such language is imperative because not every congregant can in fact work in their vocational sweet spot, and some who are able to do so may be able only for limited seasons of life.

Right now, for example, it's not hard to imagine that some Christian dad is working in the dog food industry because the salary and benefits are excellent. He needs that job to care well for his family, since it includes a severely disabled daughter. The dog food company is in the same town as his in-laws, who provide his wife with much-needed respite care. The family relies on his salary alone because Mom has her hands full car-

ing for their daughter—as well as their three healthy boys. This couple
has no idea what they would have done without the dog food company's
good health insurance policy, which has paid the bulk of expenses for
their daughter's thirteen surgeries. Dad may wish he could find work in
his vocational sweet spot, but that's just not realistic now, given his other
commitments.

Or consider Sally, another fictional character. She has her eyes reso-
lutely set on her vocational sweet spot: being a family court judge. It's a
terrific career goal from a kingdom perspective. Such judges have enormous opportunity to do good. They have significant influence on the lives
of abused children, kids in foster care and the like. Sally's aspirations are
laudable—but she will not spend her entire career as a family court judge.
It's going to take some time to get there. She'll likely spend a season as a
law student, then as a law clerk and then perhaps as an attorney in a practice related to family law. She might not reach her vocational sweet spot
until she's forty-five or fifty years old, if then.

It's important to remember that we live our lives in seasons, and that
our lives are about more than just work. Right now, some people in your
congregation may not be working in jobs or careers that, in an ideal world,
make the *best* use of their God-given talents. Perhaps, for example, the
job works for the individual in terms of balancing family and career. Or
perhaps the job is located where the individual needs to be so he can take
care of his elderly parents. Perhaps the individual's physical or emotional
health has been compromised for a season, and this job is a good fit. Or
perhaps he just can't find the job he really wants in today's downturned
economy.

In situations like these—and others we could imagine—working within
the vocational sweet spot is not a given. So pastors must be careful not to
make parishioners feel guilty when, for any number of legitimate reasons,
they are not able to be in that sweet spot.

BE READY TO EXHORT

Some congregants, though, may need to hear a word of challenge to get
them questioning whether they really are in the best place they could be
for stewarding well the vocational gifts God has given them. It's just a fact
that we sometimes drift in this life, rather than living *intentionally*. Drift-

ing in terms of our jobs may happen even more often than other kinds of drifting, because of how little explicit teaching about work Christians hear from the pulpit.

So, to inspire people with a robust understanding of work, church leaders may need to exhort congregants to examine whether they're in the right place vocationally. Some believers may need to reassess *why* they are in their jobs. What are the reasons—and are they good reasons, kingdom reasons, God-honoring reasons? How much of a role do comfort, convenience, pride, fear or materialism play in explaining why we're staying in our current jobs? Is the congregant staying in the job out of wrong motivations like "a slavish need to please one's parents," "lust for prestige and status" or a "desire to justify oneself by achieving significance in the larger scheme of things?"[15] Admittedly, these are uncomfortable issues to raise. But to help congregants follow Jesus faithfully, pastors must be willing to ask these kinds of penetrating questions.

SHOWCASE MODELS OF VOCATIONAL STEWARDSHIP

A final aspect of inspiring the congregation involves searching for people in the church who are modeling vocational stewardship and telling their stories. A pastor can preach all day about the call to integrate faith and work, and to see our work in a God-centered, service-centered way. But without living, breathing examples of this, church members may have difficulty putting that teaching into practice.

Part three of this book is peppered with stories of Christians living out vocational stewardship in a variety of ways. Many more real-life examples like them exist in every church. Staff need to find those individuals, learn their stories and invite them to testify about their journey of vocational stewardship. Their stories can help their peers in the congregation gain vision for what's possible and plausible. They may aid parishioners in envisioning new, creative ways they could deploy their own vocational gifts and assets for kingdom purposes.

CONCLUSION: A MODEL SERMON

A sermon given by Pastor Adam Hamilton from Church of the Resurrection (COR) in Leawood, Kansas, is an excellent model of inspirational leadership in vocation.[16] Seated on the stage in the worship auditorium

behind a stereotypical office desk bedecked with a phone, stapler and coffee mug, Hamilton began by noting that committed believers from the
ages of twenty-five to sixty-five who regularly attended Sunday services at
COR would log about 2,266 hours in the pew. By contrast, he estimated
that they would spend roughly 96,000 hours at work during those forty
years. "The workplace," Hamilton concluded, "is the primary place where
we live out our faith."

He went on to debunk the sacred-secular divide: "Your five-day-a-week
job has sacredness; it has value to God," he stated. "It is innately good."
Exegeting the morning's reading from the early chapters of Genesis, Hamilton underscored fundamental biblical principles: that God is a worker;
that, made in his image, we are his coworkers; and that work is good. He
offered practical advice on being the kind of worker who recognizes that
God truly is the boss, whose character is impeccable and who serves humbly and loves coworkers well.

Hamilton then went beyond the familiar themes of "vertical" righteousness and "personal" righteousness to the topic of how congregants can advance justice through their work. Looking out at the thousands gathered,
many of whom had significant influence in their workplaces, he challenged his hearers to ask themselves, "How can what we do as a company
be done in such a way that it brings good to others?" He didn't proceed to
bash the congregation's businesspeople. Instead, he held up real-life examples of vocational stewardship among members.

Hamilton told of executives from the Kansas City–based GEAR for
Sports who have worked diligently to ensure fair and just working conditions in their textile factories in Latin America. As Sam Brown, executive
director of the Fair Labor Association, said in a 2000 press conference,
"GEAR for Sports has taken a leadership role in the issue of human rights
for many years. GEAR is an important ally in our mission of improving
workers' rights."[17]

Then Hamilton talked about a contractor from COR whose commitment to racial reconciliation motivated him to practice special procure-
ment policies. This business owner guaranteed that "with every contract
he led, he was going to hire proportionally the same number of ethnic
minority subcontractors" as there were those ethnic groups in Kansas
City's population, according to Hamilton. If the city's population was 18

percent African American, this contractor followed hiring policies that ensured that 18 percent of his subcontracts went to black-owned businesses.

Hamilton also told of a conversation he enjoyed with another church member, Irv Hockaday, the former CEO of Hallmark Cards. Irv, he explained, let his faith shape decisions about the product offerings at the company. He reported that Irv said,

> We decided we would make greeting cards for people who had loved ones who were dying. These were for people who were in hospice. We realized there was no profit to be made on this. We couldn't sell enough of these cards to make a profit. But we felt like it was the right thing to do to help people be able to care for their loved ones during times like this.

Then Hamilton offered some practical examples for congregants in other vocations. He praised teachers from COR who had left comfortable jobs in the suburbs to teach in Kansas City's distressed public schools. He thanked a meteorologist from the congregation who had been public about his faith on television. He commended a boss who made it his habit to visit any employee who was in hospital.

Drawing to a close, Hamilton then challenged every listener at COR to grasp that they were "missionaries," regardless of what field or industry they worked. He concluded, "If 12,000 of us realize that we're missionaries first and we go out into our workaday world everyday on a mission to bless, to love, to heal, to bring justice, to serve God in the workplace— then when we finally begin to do that, I tell you, the world is going to be different."

Amen, pastor.

Discovery

I am more than my spiritual gifts. I am my story,
I am my wounds, I am my successes.
Discovery has to be holistic.

SUE MALLORY

God calls church leaders to the work of equipping the saints for ministry (Eph 4). I've never met a clergy person who disagreed with that. I've also never been in a church that didn't affirm the importance of helping people to steward their "time, talent and treasure" for God. Such talk, however, is not always joined to intentional action.

Beyond casting an inspirational vision to congregants to steward their vocation for God's glory and the good of their neighbors, church leaders need to provide a *system* that helps their people to examine their gifts, passions and "holy discontents," and the dimensions of their vocational power. We can't expect congregants to steward well that which they don't recognize they possess. As congregants take time to explore their unique, God-given design, they begin to discover their particular niches for serving in his kingdom.

Pleasant Valley Baptist Church in the Kansas City metro area is a national leader in walking members through this process of discovery and equipping for service. Willow Creek's Bill Hybels has lauded its work, and veteran church consultant Don Simmons compliments it as "the best equipping church in the country." Every year congregational leaders line up to participate in Pleasant Valley's E² mentoring program to learn how they can create a vibrant culture of engaged laity serving inside and outside the church.

In the first half of this chapter, we'll look at Pleasant Valley's approach. In the latter half, we'll see how members of my own congregation have brainstormed on the specific dimensions of vocational power. Finally, we'll look at how a sermon series from The Well Community Church in Fresno, California, helped listeners identify their holy discontents.

A SYSTEMATIC APPROACH TO DISCOVERY AND EQUIPPING

Pastor Vernon Armitage has led Pleasant Valley for more than forty years and reports that he's been talking about Ephesians 4 since day one.[1] He admits, though, that the church made little concrete progress in seeing laypeople flourish in their gifts until it deliberately systematized its efforts. This involved putting both new staff and new structures in place.

One of those staff people was his wife, Charlene, a full-time director of equipping. Not all congregations need to hire a paid staff person. But any church serious about vocational stewardship needs to designate a specific individual or team, paid or unpaid, that devotes time and energy to the work of equipping the laity.

Pleasant Valley's equipping system is composed of staff training, a thoughtful adult education curriculum, one-on-one coaching and a database tool called Church Community Builder (CCB).[2]

Charlene mentors staff members both in the theology of Ephesians 4 and in practical how-tos. "We went from talking about Ephesians 4 to walking out Ephesians 4," she says.[3] Intentional training is necessary, she explains, because staff typically find that it is easier to do things themselves than to work at equipping lay members. They may understand that as leaders their call is to equip others for the work of ministry, but functionally, they don't operate in this manner. Lay mobilization expert Sue Mallory agrees: "Pastors are not taught to think this way in seminary."[4]

Church staff, Charlene reports, need to understand the biblical imperative of equipping as well as the long-term benefits of this approach to ministry. She describes her training efforts as moving staff from being "DOTs to DOPs: from doers of tasks to developers of people."

In addition to getting staff onboard with the philosophy of lay mobilization and equipping, congregational leaders need to establish deliberate pathways for helping members to discover and apply their talents. At Pleasant Valley, the first steps on that pathway unfold through its four-week "Discover Your Design" course. This course relies heavily on Saddleback Church's SHAPE assessment as well as assessment and spiritual formation tools that Pleasant Valley has crafted. Congregants learn through the class to identify their spiritual gifts, passions, skills, abilities and personality traits, and the key life experiences that have shaped them.

At the final class, the next step on the pathway is introduced. Trained volunteer coaches meet with preassigned class participants to get acquainted. These pairs then plan a one-on-one meeting for the upcoming week to debrief using the participant's SHAPE profile. That meeting is aimed at reviewing the self-assessment process the church member has just gone through over the previous four weeks. The goal of this debriefing and coaching is to clarify and confirm the member's sense of gifts and calling and to help her or him begin thinking through how and where those gifts could be strategically deployed.

Pleasant Valley typically offers its "Discover Your Design" class seven times per year. This affords their large congregation multiple opportunities to participate at a convenient time. The course is especially marketed to newcomers, because church leaders want newcomers to understand that equipping is an essential part of Pleasant Valley's "DNA." They want those in the pews to understand that staff see members not as spectators but as the implementers of the church's mission in the world.

This high view of laity is emphasized in Vernon's preaching from the pulpit. That preaching is then reinforced by the strong emphasis leaders put on having all congregants take the "Discover Your Design" course. Charlene estimates that 60 percent or more of newcomers to the church do complete the course. She reports that they have seen significant increases in the numbers of congregants engaged in serving both inside and outside the church since they launched this system.

SPIRITUAL GIFTS ASSESSMENTS:
IMPORTANT, BUT INSUFFICIENT

Charlene and other equipping veterans emphasize that the task of discovery includes, *but must go beyond,* the traditional emphasis on spiritual gifts assessments. Texts such as Romans 12 and 1 Corinthians 12 teach that God endows all Christ-followers with spiritual gifts. Consequently, many churches offer adult education classes that focus on helping members to identify their spiritual gifts. This emphasis on discovering spiritual gifts is necessary and valuable. However, many church leaders wrongly equate equipping with implementing a spiritual gifts assessment. This is problematic for at least three reasons.

First, for congregants to find their best niche for serving, an assessment that goes *beyond* spiritual gifts is critical. As Simmons explains:

> There's a whole lot more to me (or any person) than my spiritual gifts. If a church helps me discover my spiritual gifts, they have only found one part of me. They are going to miss a whole lot of experience that God's given me; they're going to miss events and activities, and my geography, and my spiritual journey.[5]

Unfortunately, very few discovery tools for sale in the Christian marketplace today seek to get beyond spiritual gifts.[6] Pleasant Valley uses SHAPE because they have found that congregants serve longer and more joyfully in roles that match their passions, not just their spiritual gifts. "We spend quite a bit of time assuring people that we want to know what their passions are," Charlene says.

A second problem with equating equipping with simply conducting spiritual gifts assessments is that when those assessments include recommendations for how people can actually employ their specific gifts—not all assessments even get to this—their recommendations typically focus only on service *within the church*. "The only 'now what?' in their verbiage is serving the church," Mallory laments.[7] In other words, the vast majority of these assessments don't help congregants to see how they can apply their spiritual gifts in the context of their daily work or in volunteer service outside the four walls of the church.

What's needed instead, say Charlene and other equippers, are tools that guide congregants to think more holistically about the deployment of their gifts. Members who discover they have gifts of leadership or administration, for example, could be encouraged to consider service as a church elder *or* service on the city school board.

Moreover, members need to consider what their gifts discovery process means for their daily labors. Those with the gift of teaching could be encouraged to look for ways to utilize this skill more fully in their current job, such as by offering to lead training sessions. The debriefing conversation following the discovery class should involve reflection on the ways congregants are already serving God's kingdom purposes through their daily vocation—and what more they might do there. It should not be focused exclusively on how members can use their talents in volunteer roles. "Your *greatest* place of service might be your workplace," Charlene says. "We hold that up as extremely important."

Third, the use of any spiritual gifts assessment or the more broadly focused tools like SHAPE must be wedded to an intentional process of teaching and debriefing. As Simmons says, "Anybody can do an assessment. It's what happens afterward that matters." He encourages churches to be sure that congregants have opportunities to discuss their assessment results. Like Charlene, he believes that congregants need thoughtful dialogue about how the assessment provides insight into how to better integrate their faith and work in their day job, as well as how they might use their gifts for volunteer service.

Simmons's home congregation, The Well, does its debriefing via a small-team model. He explains: "We think the best place to do discovery is in a small group, in community—definitely not on your own. The gifts are given for use *in* community. And your talents are given to be *for* community. So why would you find out [about your talents] in isolation and not have any community to verify it?"

DIMENSIONS OF VOCATIONAL POWER

Pleasant Valley has matured the discovery and equipping process more than most congregations. However, when discussing vocational stewardship with Charlene, we agreed that the church needed to go deeper. Specifically, to encourage vocational stewardship, church leaders need to include in the discovery process more deliberate attention to the various dimensions of congregants' vocational power. The SHAPE assessment begins this process by honing in on people's abilities and skills—many of which are vocational skills. But vocational power is broader than just skills.

As I've brainstormed with groups of Christians about the dimensions of vocational power, seven categories almost always come to the fore (see figure 7.1). Church leaders should facilitate opportunities for their members to walk through the process of identifying these various elements of their vocational power. This could happen in a classroom setting, a small group or through one-on-one coaching. This intentional "dissection" process can illuminate for congregants elements of vocational power they had not recognized or thought about.

At my own church, I've witnessed how this process excites congregants as they gain new appreciation of their potential to serve God's kingdom in and through their work. I've also facilitated a few discussion sessions on this topic while teaching an adult Sunday school course on "rejoicing the city." It's not been unusual for participants to walk away from this process saying, "Wow, I have more vocational power than I realized."

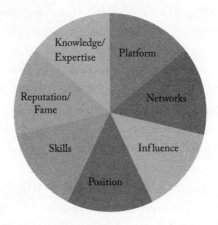

Figure 7.1. Dimensions of vocational power

The seven dimensions of vocational power my fellow church members and I have identified are knowledge/expertise, platform, networks, influence, position, skills and reputation/fame.

1. Knowledge/expertise. Workers accumulate specific knowledge for the industries or fields they are in. This results from educational and vocational preparation as well as on-the-job experience. The first way a Christian faithfully stewards this expertise is by applying it to achieve the highest degree of excellence in his or her work. As Dorothy Sayers once wrote, since the work itself intrinsically matters, the worker has a duty to "serve the work."[8] One implication of this is that Christian workers should seek where possible to pursue professional development opportunities that increase their knowledge so they might make even greater contributions in their daily job. Additionally, Christian professionals may discover that some of their knowledge and expertise is transferable to new contexts. Discerning where that is the case can facilitate additional expressions of wise vocational stewardship.

After graduating from culinary school, chef Tim Hammack apprenticed at a restaurant in Berkeley, California, which he calls the "epicenter of the American gourmet food revolution."[9] Then he landed a job as assistant chef at the prestigious Bouchon, a gourmet French restaurant in Napa Valley, California. There he learned about artful creations, ingredient combinations and precision teamwork in the kitchen.

One day Hammack's old school friend Dave Perez asked to meet with him for coffee. Perez had a vision to share about a culinary arts training program—for homeless men. He told Hammack, "I want you to run the kitchen and teach these guys. You'd be perfect. You've definitely got the cooking skills."[10] So today Hammack draws on that expertise as chief chef at the Bay Area Rescue Mission in Richmond, California.

There, in addition to running the training program, he coordinates the feeding of about 1,200 homeless people per day—on an annual food budget of about ten thousand dollars. Most of the ingredients are donated. "We never really know from day to day what we're going to get," Hammack says. "So it's kind of like triage at a hospital—we separate the good, the bad, the ugly and make do with what we got."[11] He remembers that his Grandma Nola, who grew up during the Depression, had this expertise. She'd always make a feast out of whatever happened to be ripe in her garden. Hammack says, "Just like Grandma Nola, I've gotten pretty good at conjuring delicious food from what looks like scraps."[12]

2. Platform. Some professions provide workers a voice, an opportunity to get a message out or to shine the spotlight on an issue, cause, person, place or organization. Consider, for example, the role journalists, photographers, videographers, newspaper columnists, documentary filmmakers and talk-show hosts play in society. As the Pulitzer Prize–winning photographer Stan Grossfeld said, "It's an honor to be a journalist. If I care about something, I can make a half a million people care about it."[13]

Possession of a platform is a heady responsibility. Stewarding it wisely involves a relentless commitment to truth and accuracy. It also requires great sensitivity to human dignity. For example, it can be helpful for Christians to use their platform to draw attention to stories of human suffering. But they have to strive to present those plights without sensationalism, invasions of privacy or dehumanizing photography.

Christians in these fields can also use their platform to shine the spotlight on stories that typically go unnoticed. Journalist Russ Pulliam, for example, a columnist at *The Indianapolis Star*, sometimes draws attention to the good work done by faith-based nonprofits in the city. He has taken opportunities to tell positive stories about neighborhoods that typically receive negative media coverage. He has given attention to small, grassroots groups working quietly but faithfully to bring new life and hope in some of the city's most troubled communities.

3. Networks. To take stock of vocational networks, congregants can begin by listing current and former coworkers. Then they can identify friends and colleagues from their time of vocational preparation (college, graduate school, training programs); colleagues they have met at professional conferences; and customers, vendors, partners, mentors and public officials they have interacted with on the job. Most people are surprised to see just how wide their network is. Next comes the task of thoughtfully and carefully considering how to steward that network for the purposes of shalom.

Radiologist Simon Chiu from Christ Church of Oak Brook (Illinois) has plumbed his network to recruit many doctors and other health care professionals for volunteer service at the Lawndale Christian Health Clinic in inner-city Chicago. Chiu himself is an enthusiastic participant.[14] Likewise, real estate developer John Phillips from Willow Creek North Shore Community Church in Northfield, Illinois, has drawn on his network in finding affordable space to rent for the inner-city youth ministry he's been helping.[15]

Christians with strong networks within their professional guild can convene peers for discussions of issues affecting the guild and industry— or jump-start new initiatives that address problems guild members are concerned about. In other words, one of the means of promoting institutional transformation within a field is using one's network to organize interest groups, coalitions, issue task forces and the like.

Andy Macfarlan, the family practice doctor we met in chapter one, brought his concerns about the medically uninsured in his city to his colleagues at the Albemarle County Medical Society. He cast vision there for a coordinated system of pro bono care for working adults who lacked health insurance. Fellow doctors committed to the vision, and together Andy and these partners drew on their networks to recruit primary care physicians, specialists, pharmacies and medical laboratories into the new Physicians Partnership Network program.

4. Influence. In 2003, a book called *The Influentials* by Ed Keller and Jon Berry made the case that the kind of power known as influence—the capacity to cause an effect in indirect or intangible ways—is not synonymous with position. That is, people can have substantial influence without holding high positions. All Christians, regardless of their position within an organization, should consider what degree of influence they possess in their work setting—and how that influence can be used creatively for good.

Helen Bach is not the CEO or president of the organization she works for, nor does she have high seniority. But she found a way to use her influence to advance kingdom foretastes of wholeness at her workplace—and beyond.

Helen has served for six years as an administrative supervisor at Olive Crest, in Santa Ana, California, an alternative school for youth with emotional disturbances. However, for more than two decades, she has raised and trained dogs, winning American Kennel Club titles in the highest levels of obedience competition.

Several years ago, Helen learned about the use of dogs in therapeutic settings. She got her own pet, Luther, certified as a therapy dog and then went on to receive certification herself as an evaluator of potential therapy dogs. It didn't take her long to recognize that Luther could probably do a lot of good on the Olive Crest campus.

Helen spoke with her supervisors about bringing Luther in to work. "Initially, they didn't know what to do with [this idea]," Helen says.[16] But they permitted her to try it out. So each morning, Helen positioned herself and Luther—who was always dressed up in some kind of silly hat or sunglasses—right at the spot where the teens went through a security check. Helen noticed right away that Luther could bring a smile to the faces of these hardened teens. "They'd come over and pet him. You could see how they could give and receive affection from him in a way that they couldn't with adults. Before long, teachers at Olive Crest started using "time with Luther" as a reward for good behavior. The dog's positive influence was so noticeable that administrators visiting from group homes for troubled students began asking Helen to bring him to their facilities. She has since lined up therapy dog visits with other certified dogs for many of the group homes in the area.

5. *Position.* Some congregants have attained powerful positions within their organizations or professional fields. *Position* is a dimension of vocational power that involves the degree of authority one has within an organization based on seniority or title or reputation. It also denotes the standing or credibility a person has that comes from the positional power of her or his organizational affiliation (for example, an academician has more "position power" if she teaches at Harvard than if she teaches at a community college).

Truett Cathy, founder and chairman of Chick-fil-A, used his position as the company's head to make a countercultural decision: to close all his restaurants on Sundays to honor the Sabbath. Baroness Caroline Cox has stewarded positional power as a member of Britain's House of Lords to draw attention to the plight of Christians around the world who are persecuted for their faith. David Aikman, a former senior correspondent with *Time* magazine, has leveraged his position to highlight the history-changing role that key Christian leaders in the twentieth century have played and has shined the spotlight on the potential implications of massive Christian revival in China.

6. *Skills.* Sometimes people are so used to simply performing their jobs that they don't often stop to take stock of the many different skills they are using in the process. Individuals in various vocations possess an almost endless array of skills. In their helpful collection of assessment tools, *Live Your Calling*, authors Kevin and Kay Marie Brennfleck include an assessment listing sixty-two specific skills.[17]

Vocational stewardship involves making an inventory of one's skills and then asking, "*For whom* could I deploy these?" Thinking creatively—and prayerfully—about the answer to that question can open up new avenues of service.

Nashville-based professional singer/songwriter Craig Pitman, for example, decided some years ago to use his skills not just for his own career advancement in the Christian music industry; he also offers his musical talents freely to his local community. Craig leads monthly hymn sings at his church; the price of admission is a bag of nonperishable food for the church's food pantry. Additionally, after being inspired by the Bible story of David playing his harp for a tormented Saul, Craig decided to find church members who were "going through trials" with the aim of offering such sufferers his musical skills. Craig wrote about ministering to a family that had suffered a tragedy:

> I have played concerts all over the southeast for over twenty years, and have recorded my songs and have had them recorded by others. I have led worship services when I thought the glory cloud would fill the sanctuary by the way the congregation sang; but that night, in the living room of that dear family, God gave me the privilege of seeing real music ministry, when in the privacy of the home, tears of sorrow turned to tears of hope and hearts were poured out over the psalms, hymns, and spiritual songs that rose in that room. I got to see God use my handiwork to strengthen and comfort my brothers and sisters in a way I never before had experienced. There is not a recording contract in the world nor a concert stage I would trade for that night.[18]

7. Reputation/fame. Some professionals achieve a high level of name recognition within—and sometimes beyond—their vocational field. This can afford them entrée to powerbrokers, capacities for mobilizing a large following or strategic opportunities to direct wide-scale attention to a particular issue or cause.

International rock star Bono is perhaps a premier example of stewarding fame. He has leveraged his global reputation to draw attention to the AIDS pandemic and world poverty. Likewise, successful Christian comedian Carlos Oscar has leveraged his fame to raise money and awareness through benefit shows for the fight against child sex slavery. And world-famous pediatric neurosurgeon Ben Carson capitalizes on his reputation to encourage investments in the Carson Scholars Fund, which has provided academic scholarships to more than 4,300 disadvantaged youth.[19]

HOLY DISCONTENT

Finally, beyond identifying spiritual gifts and dimensions of vocational power, the task of discovery involves encouraging congregants to discern their holy discontent. This is not an area Pleasant Valley has focused much on, but The Well Community Church has.

A holy discontent is that passion that "wrecks" a person—that issue that "keeps you up at night; something in the world you want to fix," says The Well's pastor Brad Bell.[20] In September 2009, he preached a sermon series on the topic, using the book of Nehemiah as his text. His words proved to be life changing for at least one listener, thirty-three-year-old Tim Schulz.

Tim had been working in construction with a Fresno residential developer for several years. He had a long-standing interest in several key areas: homelessness, creation care, unemployment and design. Prior to listening to Bell's sermons, Tim had been wrestling with how to integrate these interests into a new social enterprise that could capitalize on his vocational skills, experience and network. The Nehemiah sermons, he says, "really pulled the trigger" for his ideas.[21]

When Bell first used the phrase "holy discontent," something clicked for Tim. "It really gave a name to what I was experiencing," he says. "I was finally able to say, 'That's it! That's what I'm going through.'" Tim was grieved over unemployment and homelessness and was passionate that better ways be found in the construction industry to reduce waste that ends up in landfills. Following Nehemiah's example, Tim took his holy discontent to God in prayer. Slowly, the diverse concerns he'd been grappling with took on a coherent shape.

In July 2010, Tim incorporated ReVive Industries with a multifaceted vision. ReVive will contract with builders to engage in deconstruction services. The firm will salvage usable items and leftover building materials, then use those to make custom-designed furniture. Tim plans to partner with the Fresno Rescue Mission by employing homeless men in its recovery program. He will train the men in furniture making and employ them in deconstruction projects. The idea is to salvage lives, not just scrap materials.

ReVive gives Tim a vehicle for deploying his unique design and vocational power. It capitalizes on all that he is—a designer who's been drawing and doodling since he was tiny; a builder with a solid network of connections in the construction industry; an environmentalist who is teased by his family for being "obsessive" about recycling; and a Christ-follower whose heart has been broken by the plight of the unemployed homeless. Tim admits to being somewhat nervous in stepping out in this new venture. But Bell's sermons on holy discontent have taught him that "if it is God leading, then [you] just obey and walk."

Formation

*Jesus is actually looking for people
He can trust with His power.*

DALLAS WILLARD

Faithful vocational stewardship is not only about *doing*, it's also about *being*. To deploy their vocational power for the common good, believers must possess a character that handles this power humbly and eschews its misuse. This is why discipling for vocational stewardship involves not only the work of inspiration and discovery but also an emphasis on formation. This aspect of preparing parishioners for vocational stewardship is less about how-to mechanics and more about the heart. Equipping is not complete until church leaders provide the teaching, exhortation and nurture needed to shape their members' character appropriately.

A close reader of the last few chapters might conclude—correctly—that it's imperative that people avoid underestimating the talents and vocational power they possess. Now I want to balance that by underscoring how vital it is to avoid *over*estimating them. The danger here lies in people acknowledging the position, knowledge or skills they possess—but then over-esteeming them.

Many congregants in middle- and upper-middle-class churches are successful and gifted. They possess significant vocational power. Many are leaders; many are high-capacity, type-A individuals with significant abilities and competence. Sometimes such believers need to hear again Jesus' warnings that some very gifted people will end up surprised on the last day. They will say to him, "Lord, did we not . . . cast out demons in your name?" And he will reply, "I never knew you" (Mt 7:22-23). Jesus is speaking here of people with remarkable talents. Such talents *may* be evidence of God's anointing, but apparently they can exist also in people who do not even know God.[1] Clearly, it is very important not to equate such gifting with spiritual maturity.

In this chapter, we'll look at the two components of the work of formation: cultivating proper character and imitating God's way of stewarding power. Congregational leaders who invest in this work help ensure that as they launch their members off the "aircraft carrier," which is the church, they do good rather than harm.

CULTIVATING THE CHARACTER REQUIRED FOR VOCATIONAL STEWARDSHIP

Preparing believers for wise vocational stewardship begins with cultivating at least four key character traits: servanthood, responsibility, courage and humility.

Servanthood. Congregants who steward power well see their primary identity as servants. To nurture this attitude among their flock, church leaders can begin by teaching the Hebrew word *avodah*. This term is used to express three notions: worship, work and service. It is difficult to think of a more beautiful and fitting term to describe vocational stewardship. When we labor using our God-given talents to participate with King Jesus in his mission of bringing foretastes of the consummated kingdom to our neighbors, we are living out the idea of *avodah*. We awaken to the truth that our work can be a means of worship of God and service to neighbor.

Avodah also includes God-dependent prayer as we undertake our work, God-focused attention as we do the work with him as our audience and God-guided love for others as we consider the kinds of work we should do. Commenting on *avodah*, Rabbi Michael Strassfeld says, "Work . . . is a form of service to the world, to the rest of humanity, and to God. . . . It has the potential to accomplish *tikkun olam*, 'repair of the world.'"[2]

Another ancient word can also help church leaders seeking to shape their people for vocational stewardship. This one is *vocare*, a Latin term meaning "to call." It is the root of our English word *vocation*. The Christian's fundamental call comes from Jesus' invitation "Come, follow me."

The call is to be like Jesus, which means at least two things: to be sent and to be servants. Indeed, our fundamental vocation (calling) is that of a servant. This is why the apostle Paul starts so many of his epistles with a statement of his identity: "I, Paul, a servant of Jesus Christ."

Our work as servants varies as it takes expression in scores of different occupations. Service is our common vocation; the specific ways we serve depend on our individual gifts, passions and opportunities. The point is this: our work is fundamentally about serving others. Congregants who deeply grasp this are more prepared for vocational stewardship than those who don't.

Mariners Church, a megachurch in Orange County, California, is largely populated by affluent, successful, highly competent and powerful people. Kenton and Laurie Beshore have served the church for nearly three decades. Knowing the composition of their flock and knowing God's Word has motivated them to highlight serving as a "pillar" of the church. "Self-centeredness and individualism are the ways of life these days," Kenton Beshore says. "Jesus came and turned everything upside down and showed everyone a countercultural way to live. . . . He came from a position of power, yet served humbly."[3]

As part of its efforts to unleash its congregants' time, talent and treasure into the local community and the world, Mariners encourages every member to participate in a foundational ten-week course called "Rooted." The course is conducted in a small-group format and emphasizes that Christianity is about being like Christ—and Christ was a servant. "How are we supposed to live the new life of faith?" Beshore asks. "We live as Jesus did. We need to have the heart of Jesus. 'For even the Son of Man came not to be served but to serve others and give his life as a ransom for many.'"[4] Two of the study weeks focus on the servanthood of Jesus. The key memory verse is from Paul's words in Philippians about imitating Christ's nature: "Don't be selfish; don't try to impress others. Be humble, thinking of others as better than yourself. Don't think only about your own affairs, but be interested in others, too, and what they are doing. Your attitude should be the same that Christ Jesus had" (Phil 2:3-5 NLT).

Responsibility. In chapter two, we saw that Jesus felt kicked-in-the-guts compassion for those who were suffering, and this deep mercy led him to sacrificial action. The *tsaddiqim* exhibit similar compassion. They develop it by intentionally growing as people who see. They strive to pay attention in this broken world, so that they can hear others' groans. And then they allow themselves to be implicated by what they see. They willingly accept responsibility.

In his book *The Dangerous Act of Loving Your Neighbor*, Mark Labberton argues that lack of action by Christians in the face of tragic injustice and need in our world stems from our failure to see what's going on and take responsibility to act. We do not hold injustice "clearly, unmistakably, and urgently in our field of vision," he says.[5] This results from the great distance between our privileged world and that other world "over there," where tragedy, disease, destitution and oppression simply *are*. We misperceive this suffering as *their* problem, not ours, Labberton says. We live "with a clear conscience, believing that we are not the perpetrators of injustice while also believing that injustice is beyond our power to change. We think this is just the way things are." But, he reminds us, "the consistent witness of Scripture is that each of us is, in all times and places, implicated, deeply implicated, in the problem of injustice."[6]

The *tsaddiqim* practice seeing and perceiving rightly. Labberton, a former pastor, says that congregational leaders can help their members do this by implementing practical corporate exercises. For example, while leading First Presbyterian in Berkeley, California, Labberton invited a Ugandan bishop to visit and tell the congregation about children vulnerable to capture by rebels in the Lord's Resistance Army (LRA). This led to practical actions—but only because step one was reframing how church members saw these kids. "You won't know what to do," Bishop Zac explained, "until they are first *your* children."[7]

To cultivate that mindset, members posted photographs of the Ugandan children around the sanctuary. Corporate worship regularly involved prayer for them. Following Labbberton's personal example, some parishioners began subscribing to online Ugandan newspapers to stay informed and wrote letters to politicians to express their concerns.[8] One member's heart was pierced by the tragedy of girls captured and sexually brutalized by the LRA. She led an initiative to craft handmade quilts to send to them at a rehabilitation hospital in Goma, Uganda, that the church supports. Prior to shipping them, the quilts were draped over the pews in the sanctuary. Members were invited to "wrap themselves in these expressions of

God's beauty and love," and in silence to imagine the recipients wrapped in a dignifying, loving embrace.

Courage. To accept responsibility for acting in a world of injustice and brokenness takes courage. And courage is not something our culture regularly calls us to. Our culture idolizes comfort, happiness and safety. In response, as Rev. Tim Keller from Redeemer Presbyterian Church has put it, Christians must be "a counterculture for the common good."[9] This involves making choices to be brave rather than safe.

Importantly, this does *not* involve abandoning the things we do well, the strengths we possess or the vocational expertise we've accumulated. It *does* mean employing those God-given gifts on what author Gary Haugen calls "more demanding climbs."[10] In other words, this bravery is about devoting our gifts and talents to the purposes of God's kingdom, not our own little kingdoms. It means seeking to do God-sized things with our talents, tasks we cannot accomplish alone, outside of his help. We bring all our powers to God and admit they are not enough for accomplishing the work of bringing foretastes of the kingdom. We look, as children, in desperate dependence to our heavenly Father. Haugen writes,

> This is not a resignation of [our] gifts or passions or training, *but a deployment of those endowments to a place beyond safety*, beyond [our] ability to control the outcome and beyond [our] own power to succeed. It's a place where God is desperately needed and a work in which he delights to engage—for it is his own work.[11]

The pathway to this kind of courage is through the struggle for justice in this world.[12] Church leaders encourage the development of godly courage in their members when they call those members to participate in doing the work that truly matters to God. That work is his mission of pushing back the kingdom of darkness with fresh expressions of the kingdom of light. It is the work of bringing foretastes of justice and shalom to broken people and broken places. Calling congregants to this work requires bravery on the part of church leaders. It takes courage to point out that some things to which we Christians devote our attention are simply trivial and others are expressions of a lack of trust in Jehovah Jireh.

Joining Jesus on his mission of restoring all things reorders our priorities. It forces us to stop spending all our time building the kingdom of self. It takes us away from time invested in accumulating more worldly wealth or acquiring greater worldly status. It requires that we actually start trusting God to take care of us rather than trying to ensure that care by constructing myriad safety nets for ourselves and our loved ones. It demands that we start to function as though we really do believe that if we seek first the kingdom of God and his righteousness, he will make good on his promise to give us everything we need (Mt 6:33). The courage we need, in short, is both the fortitude to go with King Jesus to the places of suffering and the bravery to take God at his word.

Outreach Pastor Brad Pellish of Bethany Bible Church in Phoenix has called his flock to greater bravery in the face of a particular injustice in his city. It has taken some guts on his part, too. Two years ago, Brad raised some eyebrows at the church when he invited former strip-club dancer Harmony Dust to address the congregation. Brad had been learning some harsh truths about the commercial sex industry in Phoenix. He thought his flock should know about the despair the women behind the NUDE GIRLS signs felt. He suspected they'd be horrified to learn that many prostitutes in Phoenix are just thirteen years old—and that brutal pimps forcibly keep many girls in this lifestyle. Brad wanted his church to join him on a new mission into some dark and scary places.[13]

By God's grace and empowerment, they did.

Bethany Bible decided to begin by supporting local vice squad officers. First, church members purchased three thousand dollars in gift cards to twenty-four-hour fast-food restaurants to give to the officers. That's because, when officers arrested underage streetwalkers, they often spent their own money to get them some food. (Though the girls were hungry and might have cash on hand, they didn't dare risk their pimp's wrath by spending their earnings on food.) Vice Officer Chris Bray, a veteran of the Phoenix Police Department, was shocked; no church group had ever done anything like that before. Bethany also launched a prayer initiative called Vice Undercover to "keep the vice squad under the cover of prayer."

Several women from Bethany traveled to Harmony Dust's Treasures ministry in Los Angeles to receive training on effective ways to communicate Christ's love to strippers. Through the new program, church volunteers deliver cards and gift bags on weekend nights to the dancers. They seek to jump-start conversations and new friendships that could help these women find a way out of the commercial sex industry.

Humility. Many church leaders are in congregations filled with individuals with significant vocational power. Stewarding that power well requires deep humility—a character trait with which highly successful, competent people sometimes struggle.

Congregational leaders can help their members avoid the mistake of over-esteeming their talents by reminding them that love, not gifts, is the preeminent evidence of God's work in our lives. Just before the great "love chapter" of the Bible, 1 Corinthians 13, the apostle Paul encourages his readers to desire spiritual gifts eagerly but then says he will show them "the most excellent way" of love (1 Cor 12:31). Gifts are good, the apostle teaches, but they can't hold a candle to love. We could say the same thing about our natural abilities or vocational expertise.

To steward their power, abilities and gifts well, believers must pursue growth in love, reflected in kindness, faithfulness, patience, humility and self-control. The one who has learned to love well is the one who employs his or her talents well. Jesus has promised to supply his followers with Holy Spirit power for our lives and work. But, as Dallas Willard put it, the Messiah is looking for those he can trust with his power: "Only constant students of Jesus will be given adequate power to fulfill their calling to be God's person for their time and their place in this world. They are the only ones who develop the character which makes it safe to have such power."[14]

Willow Creek North Shore outside of Chicago is a congregation with numerous highly talented, successful people. Pastor Steve Gillen is candid about what he and his staff must do to shepherd this flock well. When a congregant approaches the staff with ideas on how to use his or her vocational power for service, Loretta Jacobs, a staff member, interviews him or her. The purpose of that initial meeting is twofold: to learn about the congregant's skills and dreams *and* to screen for inappropriate attitudes or motivations. Gillen explains:

> If your church is empowering [vocational stewardship by high-capacity parishioners] . . . you have to be careful of who you invite into it. That is part of why Loretta sits right across from every one of these people. We want to make sure they have got the character in place before we unleash them. . . . There is just no room for [power issues]. What we talk about is when you put that serving towel over your arm in these initiatives, you serve others,

and if there is any question on motive, then we are going to have a conversation and our support for them is going to wane if [they] don't show the right attitude.[15]

SHARING POWER: RECOGNIZING THE GIFTS OF OTHERS

The first part of the work of formation involves church leaders seeking to develop within their members the character of compassionate, engaged, humble servants. The second part of this work involves educating congregants in the right manner of deploying power—namely, doing so in a way that accords with how God manages his power. Put simply, God manages his power by sharing it, and we must imitate that modus operandi.

GOD'S MODUS OPERANDI

Consider the creation story. In Genesis 1 and 2, we get a picture of God's normative intentions for the world. In this ideal world, we see God sharing power with the weak—because he shares it with humans. (Compared to God, we are weak.) God shares his power with Adam and Eve and makes them his vice regents. He places human beings in charge of his created order. Remember Genesis 1:28, in which God told Adam and Eve, "Be fruitful and increase in number; fill the earth and subdue it. Rule over the fish of the sea and the birds of the air and over every living creature that moves on the ground." A chapter later, this cultural mandate is repeated: "The LORD God took the man and put him in the Garden of Eden to work it and take care of it" (Gen 2:15).[16]

This story's familiarity is a bit dangerous, because it can cause us to overlook something critical. We need to see that God did not have to share his power this way with the first human beings. He could have put humans in the Garden and said, "This is paradise. Don't mess with it!"[17] But he didn't. God had such a great time being Creator that he wanted us, his children made in his image, to enjoy the lifework of creating. Made in God's image, we have talents from him and *authority* to use them. We have vocational power. And it is God's gift.

Remarkably, this power sharing continues even after the Fall (Gen 3). Having thoroughly messed up our commission from God to work and tend the Garden, we'd expect God to decide that this power-sharing plan wasn't such a great idea. However, against that reasonable expectation, God surprises us. God does indeed cast Adam and Eve out of paradise, but he does not strip power from them and does not retract their cultural mandate.

We can be certain about this for two reasons. First, Jesus as God's Son continues to operate according to the Father's modus operandi of power sharing. When we observe Jesus with his disciples, we see power sharing. The royal King shares his power with commoners, disciples who, like us, are so often marked by folly, pride, weakness and cowardice. Jesus gave the twelve power to cast out demons and heal the sick—and then sent them out to do it. Later he did the same thing with the group of seventy-two. They went out two by two and found great joy as they ministered and blessed people, healing them in Jesus' name, using their power to bring foretastes of shalom to their neighbors. Then, near the end of his life, Jesus promised even more power through the Holy Spirit to his future disciples and predicted that they would do "even greater things" (Jn 14:12).

Second, consider the picture of the consummated kingdom of God presented in the book of Revelation. In the restored, reconstructed paradise in the new earth and the new heavens, what do we see? We see power sharing as we humans continue to be God's vice regents, sitting on thrones with Jesus and ruling in the new earth (Rev 3:21; 5:10).

God's modus operandi is sharing power with humans, who are weak, frail and often sinful. He gave us creativity, talent, potential and resources, and he wants us to deploy all that. God simultaneously recognizes our frailties *and* his divine stamp on us, and he gives us potential.

Here is the application of all this for today. In this world, there are power disparities. Some people possess more power than others. That is just a fact. Another fact is that middle- and upper-class American Christians are among the world's powerful. From our position of relative power, we are called to avoid despising those who, in the eyes of the world, are not powerful. We are called to see the poor and the dispossessed as *more* than just poor and dispossessed. We are called to see their potential, their dignity, their latent capacities. We're called to labor *with* them. We do not impose our vocational power *on* them or even use it *for* them. We are called to bring it *alongside* them.

What Andy Crouch says about the stewardship of cultural power in his

insightful book *Culture Making* should be applied to the stewardship of
our vocational power:

> When God works in history, he does so through partnership between pow-
> erful and powerless alike. *The basic thing we are invited to do with our cultural*
> *power is to spend it alongside those less powerful than ourselves.* The more cus-
> tomary phrase would be spend it on behalf of the powerless, but that is not
> the way power works in God's economy. The way to spend cultural power
> is to open up for others the opportunity to create new cultural goods, add-
> ing our resources to theirs to increase their chance of moving the horizons
> of possibility for some community. . . . We do not approach the relatively
> powerless as recipients of our charity but as sources of a power that we who
> are relatively powerful may not even know. When we put our power at their
> service, we unlock their creative capacity without in any way diminishing
> our own.[18]

MAKING IT THREE-DIMENSIONAL

Antiques dealer Martha Rollins from Richmond, Virginia, offers an in-
structive example of just this sort of humble stewardship of vocational
power. For years, her shop was repeatedly voted Richmond's Best Antiques Store. Her work was trumpeted in industry magazines. She possessed a wide professional and social network and enjoyed a healthy income from her business. In short, Martha was prospering in the way
Proverbs 11:10 describes.

Martha says she started to get serious about her faith when she hit
middle age. Although she briefly flirted with the idea of heading to seminary in order to "serve God," her pastor wisely counseled her to find ways
to deploy her business knowledge, skills, experience, wealth and social
network—that is, her vocational power—for the kingdom of God. So she
began praying and seeking input from friends about how she might use her
marketplace talents to fight poverty in Richmond.

Soon she got the germ of an idea. What about starting a used-goods
store somewhere in the inner city that needed a retail business investment?
Such a store could provide employment, sell gently used goods at reasonable prices that could help stretch tight household budgets and perhaps
breathe some new life into an economically depressed neighborhood. The
notion made sense, but she did not know which community in Richmond

would be a good choice for the investment. Since she'd always been someone with an activist personality, Martha decided just to hop in her vehicle and start looking. Soon her white van became a common sight traveling slowly through the east side's tougher neighborhoods.

As she drove and observed, she also prayed persistently, asking for God's guidance. In 2001 God crossed her path with Rosa Jiggets. Rosa is a middle-aged African American woman from Richmond's Highland Park neighborhood, an economically challenged community. She grew up in an entrepreneurial family—her father had operated a "mobile mini-mart" for years.

Rosa's and Martha's shared business interests and common faith helped the two women to hit it off. Their partnership brought together different types of power. Martha had certain kinds of power that Rosa did not; she had wealth and access to credit and a very large social and business network. Rosa had power that Martha lacked: local knowledge, cultural capital and a good reputation in the neighborhood. Both had the power of business acumen. By combining their talents, they implemented a ministry that is bringing transformation to several city blocks in Highland Park.

Since 2002, these two women have grown their ministry, called Boaz & Ruth, into a multifaceted social enterprise that is imparting life. As Martha came to understand more about the community from Rosa and other neighbors, she learned that Highland Park receives a disproportionate number of men and women coming out of Virginia prisons. She discovered that recidivism rates are about 66 percent and that very often this is because former inmates can't find work.

Rosa began introducing Martha to some of these men and women, and Martha had eyes to see them as more than only ex-cons. In the next five years, she used her political connections, money, business network and marketing prowess to launch seven more local businesses in Highland Park, each of which employs ex-offenders. These men and women join Boaz & Ruth's apprenticeship program and work for a year or more at the Second Harvest store or in the moving business, the furniture restoration business, the eBay business, the restaurant or another of B&R's enterprises. By sharing her power with Rosa and the other members of the community, Martha has contributed to some glad rejoicing in the city blocks of Highland Park.

Martha loves to say of everyone involved at B&R, from staff to volunteers to program participants, "We believe everyone is a 'Ruth' with needs and also a 'Boaz' with gifts."[19]

CONCLUSION

As church leaders look out at their flocks, they see many individuals blessed with education, privilege, opportunities and influence. These congregants have much to offer. Some need to be challenged to direct their considerable talents toward the common good, overcoming inclinations toward comfort and affluence. Others are eager to help others but may need to grow in sensitivity in managing their power in the midst of people with less power.

Hopefully, as a result of being inspired and going through intentional discovery processes that have enabled them to clarify the unique talents God has given them to share, many congregants will be itching to get out there and do something. Before unleashing this energy, however, church leaders should work hard to strengthen their members' "inner self" so that their service in the world truly brings God glory and genuinely helps their neighbors.

PART 3

Pathways of Vocational Stewardship

Deploying Vocational Power

FOUR PATHWAYS

At most you will spend about
5 percent of your waking hours in [church].
Ninety-five percent of your life you spend in the world. . . .
The scorecard is about the 95 percent [lived] out in the world.

PASTOR VICTOR PENTZ

Church leaders may believe that if they preach the right message (inspiration), provide the tools and forums that help their people identify their gifts, passions and dimensions of vocational power (discovery), and help their members develop mature character for handling their power in a biblical manner (formation), then their members will simply begin stewarding their vocational power effectively. While it's possible that a few smart self-starters may be able to do just that, many parishioners need further practical help. Having seen *why* they should steward their vocational power and *what* that power is, they now need help in discerning *where* to invest their efforts. This is the work of deployment.

In part three, we will closely examine how congregational leaders can equip their members for vocational stewardship along four possible pathways. I introduce them here and offer some comments on the temptations of each pathway that congregational leaders will want to be aware of. Table 9.1 summarizes key ideas about each pathway.

Table 9.1. Overview of the Four Pathways

Pathway	Key Word	Description	Church type	Temptations
1	Bloom	Promoting the kingdom in and through your daily work	All: any size, any outreach strategy	Pietism, triumphalism
2	Donate	Volunteering vocational talent outside your day job	Small to midsize; those with an outreach strategy emphasizing partnerships	Impatience; arrogance toward volunteer or nonprofit organizations and staff
3	Invent	Launching a social enterprise	Midsize to large; those with a high percentage of leaders and "halftimers"	Reinventing wheels; failure to partner; vainglory
4	Invest	Participating in the church's targeted initiative	Midsize to large; those with a narrow and deep outreach focus	Failure to do "ministry *with*"; failure to recognize mutuality of ministry

INTRODUCING THE FOUR PATHWAYS
OF VOCATIONAL STEWARDSHIP

Pathway 1: Blooming where you're planted. The primary and most important avenue for deploying vocational power is in and through one's present work. The first place believers should look to conduct their foretaste-bringing mission is right at the current job they hold. I call this "blooming where you're planted."

Blooming involves reflecting and promoting God's glory in our current vocation. The *tsaddiqim* do this by seeking to live out, in the power of the Holy Spirit, the vertical, personal and social dimensions of righteousness in the context of their vocation. We got a good glimpse of what that looks like when we considered the example of homebuilder Perry Bigelow in chapter two. We bloom when we acknowledge God as our director and audience, and conduct our work in functional, daily reliance on the Spirit. We bloom when we honor God through our ethical practice and when we intentionally and creatively seek to advance shalom for *all* our organization's stakeholders. And we bloom when we act as "intrapreneurs"—people who innovate needed reform within their company or industry sector.[1]

Every congregation, regardless of size, can and should place primary emphasis on equipping their members for this expression of vocational stewardship. Some may also have the capacity to equip members for one of the other pathways, and megachurches may have the ability to support all four pathways. Unlike pathway one, though, the other pathways are optional.

Temptations of pathway 1. The temptations in this pathway are two (at least). One might be called pietism; the other, triumphalism.

The pietistic temptation emerges when congregants mistakenly define the mission of faith/work integration too narrowly. That is, they seek to be people of integrity on the job and perhaps attempt to evangelize coworkers, but they do not muse deeply over the work itself. They don't invest time considering how their work images God in his ongoing providence in creation or how their work participates in God's redemptive purposes. They fail to discern how people can bear witness to the *missio Dei* through work in ways other than placing Christian plaques on the wall or leading Bible studies.

Steve Garber, president of the Washington Institute, tells of bringing some Christians onsite to visit a hamburger restaurant owned by a friend of his. This friend has thought very deeply about how to serve God through his business, and he has chosen to adopt some specific policies. Seeking to promote the kingdom virtue of wholeness, this businessman avoids commercial grain-fed beef that contains antibiotics that may have negative health effects. Seeking to promote the kingdom virtue of creation care, he purchases all his produce locally. The visiting Christians that Steve brought to the restaurant were unable to see the kingdom value of this. They could not discern what was "Christian" about this hamburger joint, since the owner wasn't talking about converting his employees and he didn't have any Christian literature prominently displayed.[2]

A second temptation in pathway one is triumphalism. This can occur when Christians in their secular workplaces forget the doctrine of common grace—the notion that God has granted degrees of wisdom and insight to nonbelievers and that he can advance his purposes through non-Christian institutions. Triumphalism rears its head when Christians assert that only *they* can perceive the true, the good and the beautiful. It surfaces when Christians carelessly use language about "taking" their institution or

vocational sector "for Christ." Such language can cause great consterna-
tion among secular colleagues. Triumphalism is revealed when believers
fail to be good listeners to people of good will who do not share their
Christian faith, when believers are inhospitable toward others' views.

Academician Kim Phipps, now president of Messiah College, offers
practical advice to Christians in her profession on how to avoid triumphalism. She urges scholars to practice "intellectual hospitality." This
involves

> care and concern for the person, and it also necessitates inviting others into
> conversation, listening without prejudging, and affirming the value of oth-
> ers and their perspectives even when legitimate disagreement exists. Most
> important, intellectual hospitality involves the virtue of epistemological
> humility, which roots our openness to the views of others in the recognition
> that our own mental powers are limited and that the cognitive, experien-
> tial, and affective insights of others, especially when they are different from
> our own, can truly deepen and extend our understanding of others and the
> world that surrounds us.[3]

This hospitality is not mere relativism, and it does not require accepting
every scholarly opinion. In fact, Phipps notes, intellectual hospitality requires acknowledgment of legitimate conflict. Christians can and should
make rigorous arguments based on a biblical worldview. The point is to
avoid labeling opponents unfairly, breeching civility, refusing to see the
image of God in the people who disagree, and lacking the humility to realize that we can learn from others whose views are different. Phipps's
advice for Christian scholars in the often unfriendly environment of secular academia is applicable to Christians in any secular workplace.

Church leaders equip their flock to resist the temptations of pietism
and triumphalism when they teach a robust view of faith/work integration and remind their members of God's common grace. As they celebrate
members who are living out vocational stewardship along pathway one,
they need to affirm a wide range of examples. They need to showcase
those who start Bible studies at work *and* those who achieve workplace
reforms that advance justice, those who promote employee care and those
who convince their firms to be more green. As they exhort congregants to
influence their fields positively, they should employ the language of servanthood, not conquest. The idea is to encourage congregants to be salt,

to be seed sowers, to be secret givers, to be reweavers of social fabrics that are torn—to be a "faithful presence," in sociologist James Davison Hunter's words. "If, indeed, there is a hope or an imaginable prospect for human flourishing in the contemporary world, it begins when the Word of shalom becomes flesh in us and is enacted through us toward those with whom we live, in the tasks we are given, and in the spheres of influence in which we operate."[4]

Pathway 2: Donating. The second pathway of vocational stewardship involves donating our skills to organizations other than our regular employer. This includes volunteer service at churches, nonprofit ministries or private or public agencies that can make good use of our particular vocational knowledge and experience in their labors here at home or abroad. This pathway is unique in its concern that volunteer service intentionally capitalizes on vocational power. It's about getting bankers to serve as bankers, carpenters to serve as carpenters and architects to serve as architects. Such an approach is obviously commonsensical; but in most congregations, there is little or no effort to mobilize members for service according to their vocational talents.

Many congregations may have capacity to equip their congregants for vocational stewardship along this pathway in addition to pathway one. If the church's outreach strategy focuses on partnering with local agencies (rather than launching new church-sponsored initiatives) pathway two will be a natural fit.

Temptations of pathway 2. The main temptations of this pathway involve impatience, arrogance and failure to appreciate work styles or work environments/cultures different from those with which one is most familiar and comfortable. High-capacity marketplace professionals are likely to find the nonprofit world a different animal than the corporate world. Some of those differences point to weaknesses in nonprofit culture, but others may reveal its strengths.

Pro bono volunteers need eyes to see both, rather than just getting irritated by inefficiencies or the lack of shipshape policies and procedures. They also need to cultivate an appreciation for the talents and skills of nonprofit staff. These individuals may not demonstrate the same kind of "smarts" that the professional volunteers have. They may lack the same level of formal education or training. Consequently, church leaders should be intentional about reminding their well-educated members that there are many different types of smarts in the world and that a "street education" can count in nonprofit work as much as or more than a college education.[5]

Leaders can also foster an attitude of respect for the community organizations with which they are partnering by modeling that respect. All communications about the congregation's work alongside these partnering organizations should emphasize the mutuality of the relationship. Leaders should do nothing that communicates, "Well, those nonprofit partners of ours are certainly lucky to have the support of our flock, given how talented and well educated and competent we are." Avoiding such obviously patronizing language is fairly simple, but leaders need to watch their words diligently when they are praising their members for their service. Affirming should always be done in ways that acknowledge the dedication and talents of the partners as well as the achievements of the congregants.

Pathway 3: Inventing. Vocational stewardship along the third pathway is a form of what author Andy Crouch calls "culture making." In his book by that name, Crouch argues that "the only way to change culture is to create more of it."[6] Pathway three involves drawing on our vocational power to launch a new social enterprise that seeks to advance the kingdom in a fresh way. It is about creating new or alternative institutions (big or small) that implement innovative ways of addressing social problems. Vocational stewardship along this pathway brings foretastes of shalom first to the direct beneficiaries of the services provided by these new organizations. In some cases, it can also bring about significant, far-reaching cultural or social change. Social enterprises like the Grameen Bank, for example, which birthed the modern microfinance industry, have revolutionized life for millions of people worldwide.

Churches with significant numbers of high-capacity congregants or "halftimers" (professionals at a point in their career where they are seeking greater significance in their marketplace work) may want to build structures for supporting pathway three.

Temptations of pathway 3. The principal temptation of pathway three involves failure to listen or to partner. Excited about her new idea, a high-capacity Christian may fail to realize that others have been working on the problem long before she came along. In this circumstance, church leaders may need to ask the entrepreneur gently whether she's done thorough homework and familiarized herself with what others have tried. If others are already laboring in the same vineyard, church leaders should urge their entrepreneurs to consider how they might partner with existing programs rather than reinvent the wheel.

In the same way, professionals who have proven themselves excellent problem solvers in the business realm may fail to see where there are limits on the transferability of those skills. In this circumstance, church leaders should remind the entrepreneur that an idea or approach that worked marvelously in the corporate or technical sector may not succeed in the social sector.

Church leaders need also to be "as wise as serpents" about the sad reality that some of the social entrepreneurs in their flock may be motivated by vainglory and disinterested in partnering with others because they want to "do their own thing." The ego is a persistent little devil. Church leaders need to discern whether a potential entrepreneur's proclaimed desire to serve others through his or her venture is actually masking a hunger for personal recognition.

Pathway 4: Investing. Finally, pathway four involves participating in a targeted, intensive initiative by a congregation to serve a particular people group, neighborhood or cause in a way that strategically employs our vocational power. Some congregations have chosen a narrow but deep strategy for affecting community renewal. They've honed in on a particular neighborhood or a particular problem, such as failing schools or the troubled foster care system or international sex trafficking. The aims of such initiatives are bold—and to accomplish their goals, these congregations need to garner the vocational power of all their members. They seek to create on-ramps for service by members of all different professional skill sets. Pathway four funnels all the diverse talents of congregants toward the same target.

Obviously, if the church's outreach strategy is built on this narrow-but-deep approach, supporting members in vocational stewardship along this pathway makes sense.

Temptations of pathway 4. The principal temptation to fight on this pathway is the failure to undertake the work in a "ministry with" paradigm as opposed to a "ministry to" paradigm. For example, if a church has targeted an economically distressed community, it must guard against its talented, fast-paced, powerful members running roughshod over community residents in so-called helping initiatives. As Steve Corbett and Brian Fik-kert explain so well in their recent book, sometimes such "helping" actu-ally hurts.[7] The biblical approach is one of shared power, mutual respect and equal dignity.

As in pathway two, believers with significant vocational power to draw on must do so without an inflated sense of their importance and with genuine regard for the different skill sets that those they are serving bring to the table. Leaders of a targeted neighborhood initiative must engage the residents of that neighborhood, learning what *their* desires and dreams for the community are. Community residents must be involved in the design, implementation and evaluation of the initiative. Church leaders mobilize parishioners to come alongside local residents to assist them in advancing their dreams by drawing on their own particular vocational assets, knowl-edge and networks. Similarly, when the focus is on an issue rather than a place, Christians stewarding their vocational power should partner with the people most affected by that issue and seek *their* input into diagnosis, prescription, implementation and evaluation.

Finally, church leaders on pathway four can also help congregants to avoid the temptations of paternalism or superiority by taking care to point out the *mutually* beneficial character of ministry. They should emphasize that both sides can learn much from one another and that God's desire is to see both transformed.

Pathway 1

BLOOM WHERE YOU'RE PLANTED

The church exists for the mission, for the sake of the world.
Yet it is organized to build itself up as an institution.
It blesses the work its members do within the
institution but pays no attention to the
work they do "outside" the church.

REV. DAVIDA CRABTREE

In 1985, Tom Hill's company, Kimray, was experiencing hard times. The Oklahoma City firm, which produces sophisticated control gauges and thermostats for oil and gas companies, was in a bust cycle. This was not unusual in that industry. In fact, several years earlier, Kimray had gone through an even worse time. Hill remembered that recession all too well. Back then, he had allowed the firm to grow too large during a boom cycle, not placing funds in reserve. When the market tanked, the subsequent layoffs he was forced to make were gut wrenching.

This was an experience Hill never wanted to repeat. He vowed then and there to God that he would operate Kimray debt-free in the future. "We put back reserves in good times to carry us over during the lean times," Hill says. "That commitment alone enables us to operate successfully under varied economic climates."[1] When the bust of 1985 arrived, Hill found himself with a financial reserve but more employees than he had work for. His response was that of a *tsaddiq*.

Out of his strong commitment to his city and his employees, Hill contacted Oklahoma City Mayor Ron Norrick to ask if Kimray could put its employees to work for Oklahoma City. Hill recalls,

> It took us about two and a half months to make that arrangement, but [we] did, and we also put employees to work in other companies. We had employees who worked for Macklanberg-Duncan and for several non-profits, some where [sic] they could be paid, some at minimum wage, some in jobs with no pay, and we would make up the difference in their wages. It resulted in 92 employees working for somebody else for a period of 18 months, and we paid the difference in their salary or paid all of their salary.

By 1987, Kimray's business had picked back up, and Hill brought all ninety-two employees back to work at the plant.

Kimray's unusual response to the 1985 recession has not been forgotten. In an interview years later, Hill said, "Many of the employees we have now were here then. They remember that [time], and they appreciate it." For his part, Hill says he's just thankful that Kimray was able to demonstrate "our commitment to our employees and our community. . . . Our goal is not just to sell products. Our goal is to provide jobs to the community, to be part of the community, and to have an impact on the community."

Christian marketplace professionals like Hill are not born; they are made. The Word and the Spirit of God form them into people who look out for the common good, rather than focus exclusively on themselves. The nurture of believers like Hill, whose faith shapes their daily work in profound and creative ways, is a primary task of the church.

In this chapter we'll examine what church leaders around the country are doing to disciple these kinds of workers. Without a vision, the Scriptures tell us, the people perish. The stories here about church leaders and church members can help fuel a vision for raising up *tsaddiqim* who advance the kingdom in and through their daily work.

NURTURING *TSADDIQIM* WHO BLOOM

Three key commitments mark congregational leaders who are effective in encouraging their members to steward their vocations for the common good: affirmation, education and support (see table 10.1). A variety of churches around the country offer insights for engaging in these three activities.

Table 10.1. How to Nurture Congregants Who Bloom

Affirmation	Education	Support
• Preach the missional value of daily work	• Offer work-related short courses	• Sponsor career counseling
• Use workplace illustrations in sermons	• Hold gifts discovery retreats	• Partner with WorkLife, Inc.
• Visit members at their workplace	• Host book groups	• Organize vocational groups
• Use "vocational" prayers	• Host special faith/work conferences	• Provide tools
• Commission laypeople for work in society		

Affirmation. Nurturing the *tsaddiqim* to bloom at their job begins with solid preaching based on the theological convictions examined in previous chapters. At The Falls Church, a large Anglican congregation just outside the Washington, D.C., Beltway, Rector John Yates recognizes the vital importance of affirming parishioners in their daily ministry on the job. Yates believes that the church in America today resides in Babylon and that the prophetic word to "seek the peace and prosperity of the city to which I have carried you into exile" (Jer 29:7) is the relevant paradigm for ministry. In such a context, affirming and encouraging the marketplace vocations of the laity is more important than ever. As Yates advised a group of seminary graduates in a commencement address in 2008,

> God has called us to Babylon. This is our home for now, and this is where we are called to build disciples and build churches. God will give you people to shepherd and serve, and they may actually be more effective for Christ's kingdom, and influential in our culture as laymen, than you or I. Encourage them, believe in them, pray for them. Be patient with them. Don't attempt to insulate them from Babylon, but tell them they are Christ's seeds, sent out to produce fruit, and they will.[2]

Congregational leaders at churches from a variety of denominations share this perspective and this commitment to pulpit leadership that affirms members' work in the world. At San Diego's Harbor Presbyterian Church, leaders say simply, "We believe people can—and must—live out the Gospel in and through their work."[3] At Grace DC, a Presbyterian Church in Washington, D.C., former associate pastor Duke

Kwon, who oversaw the congregation's vocational stewardship initiative, explains that,

> theologically, we've always maintained what some refer to as a Kuyperian worldview, teaching the Lordship of Christ in all spheres of life, rejecting the secular/sacred divide. . . . That commitment in terms of ministry philosophy was in place from the beginning, and it [is] communicated through our classroom and pulpit ministries.[4]

In addition to preaching, other activities during the Sunday worship service also help affirm congregants in their daily labor. At The Falls Church, for example, in the congregational prayer every Sunday, four or five church members are specifically prayed for by name and vocation. At Colchester United Church of Christ in Colchester, Connecticut, Rev. Davida Crabtree took this notion of vocational prayers one step further. With help from selected parishioners, she composed a special prayer for each Sunday that focused on a different occupation. She placed a symbolic object from that career on the altar (such as a hair dryer for beauticians or various tools of the trade for carpenters or plumbers) and then offered a prayer for church members from that occupational field.[5]

Church leaders can also affirm their marketplace professionals by formally commissioning them during worship services. Many churches currently commission missionaries or laypeople who teach Sunday school. That's not a bad thing, but in the absence of similar kinds of commissioning of laity in the marketplace, it reinforces the message that only "spiritual" or "church" work is truly missional. So, at The Falls Church, Rev. Yates commissions various laypeople in all their diverse callings in the marketplace.[6] Meanwhile, inside the D.C. Beltway, Church of the Savior has developed special liturgies for ordaining church members for their work in society.[7]

Pastor Tom Nelson from Christ Community Church in Leawood, Kansas, has been preaching on faith/work integration for a decade. To affirm his congregants, he deliberately uses workplace illustrations in sermons and invites testimonies from marketplace members. He and his staff also visit church members at their work sites. "We want to understand their world," he explains.[8]

Nelson's intentional affirmation and frequent preaching on vocational themes has helped businessman Dave Kiersznowski and his wife, Demi,

think more creatively and intentionally about how they can advance foretastes of the kingdom through their business, DEMDACO. Dave reports
that Nelson challenged them to think about what their business would
look like if they were "viewing all of life through a biblical lens."[9]

So, when the Kiersznowskis were planning the design of their new
company headquarters, they began to think deeply about that physical
space where their employees spent so much time. They determined that
the new office should be "a place that's beautiful, creative, pleasing, and
full of light."[10] They also wanted a family-friendly workspace. So the new
DEMDACO headquarters included a room dedicated to nursing moms
and a room filled with games, videos and arts-and-crafts supplies. The
latter is intended to encourage parents who work for the company to have
their kids visit them at lunchtime.

Nelson's strong preaching on vocational stewardship also led Dave
Kiersznowski to reexamine his company's health insurance policy. He realized that it was "generous to those who wanted to start a family through
natural birth," but didn't have benefits for those who wanted to adopt. So
DEMDACO "instituted an adoption aid program as a way of meeting the
needs of widows and orphans."[11]

Education. In addition to affirming their members' daily work, church
leaders can promote "blooming" by offering adult education opportunities
devoted to faith/work integration topics. Harbor Presbyterian, Grace DC
and Christ Community Church have all hosted special weekend conferences and retreats, and two have sponsored multiweek adult education
classes on the topic. These have ranged from the general, such as teaching
on the biblical theology of work, to the specific, such as Harbor Church's
mid-week course "StrengthsFinder for Job Seekers."

Under Crabtree's leadership, Colchester UCC sponsored gifts-discovery
retreats, using formal assessment tools to help people better think about
matching their personality and passions with job choices. The congregation
also hosted a weekend conference titled Beyond Sunday Christianity, fea-
turing well-known faith/work integration guru William Diehl.

At Grace DC, Pastor Kwon brought in Steve Garber, author of *The
Fabric of Faithfulness,* to teach on vocation at a retreat. Afterward, Garber
returned to the church to lead a five-session adult-education class for
young professionals on Sunday mornings. As a follow-up, Kwon recruited

a lay member to host a discussion group on the book *Engaging God's World* by Cornelius Plantinga. "It is a wonderful book on the issue of vocation," Kwon explains, "and it's also just a wonderful review of the gospel story."

In Atlanta, Peachtree Presbyterian Church organizes its educational efforts to promote vocational stewardship under its WorkLife ministry. The church's website describes the philosophy animating the WorkLife initiative in this way:

> For followers of Jesus, who we are is a person created in the image of God. Your work—whether you are in banking, or a homemaker, or a teacher, or in medicine, or retired, or whatever you do, is important to God. Your work, your life, is vitally important to God, and He invites you to partner with Him in that, just as he invites you to worship Him.[12]

In 2007, the WorkLife ministry launched its My95 initiative. "No matter if you sign up for everything that moves here at Peachtree," Senior Pastor Victor Pentz explained to congregants, "at most you will spend about 5 percent of your waking hours here on these premises. Ninety-five percent of your life you spend in the world. Now this 5 percent is critical in giving us a navigation system to help orient us in the Christian life. But the scorecard is about the 95 percent we live out there in the world."[13]

The My95 initiative has included direct teaching through sermons on the missional life and faith/work integration. My95 small-group gatherings on Sunday nights with facilitated discussion segments allow congregants to analyze their spiritual gifts, discern their calling and identify the purposes for which God has gifted them. Additionally, video testimonies of individual congregants talking about how they serve God through their work help cast vision and build excitement.

Peachtree members like Bonnie Wurzbacher, senior vice president for Global Customer and Channel Leadership at The Coca-Cola Company, deeply appreciate Peachtree's My95 program and the deliberate efforts that Pentz has taken to help marketplace leaders think theologically about their daily work. Raised in a Christian family—a preacher's kid and a granddaughter of overseas missionaries—Bonnie explains that she "grew up thinking that the way to best serve God is in 'full time Christian service' or by supporting your church."[14] It took her years to overcome this sacred/secular dichotomy in her thinking.

Today Bonnie has a deep theology of how to serve God through business, honed over years of personal study and rich conversations at Peachtree. "God has an important purpose for every institution," she says. "His purpose for business is to advance the economic well-being of communities throughout the world. And as the sole source of wealth creation, business enables every other institution to exist—schools, colleges, missions, churches, government, everything." This means that when a business fails, everything is impacted. Business "is very important, noble work throughout the world," she says.

Bonnie has been at Coke for twenty-six years now. This mega-corporation is active in two hundred countries, and the majority of the firm's profits remain in the local economies, through its franchised business model. Bonnie reports that economic impact studies show that "on average, for every one job we create directly, another twelve are created indirectly." She says enthusiastically, "I believe that I am helping to bring God's kingdom here on earth when I participate in a successful, ethical, effective business that helps communities improve their economic well-being and enables everyone associated with it to contribute to the larger good in the world."

Support. Some churches have found that gathering members into vocationally based small groups is a good strategy for helping believers deepen their understanding of and commitment to faith/work integration. Redeemer Presbyterian Church, a megachurch of more than four thousand attendees in New York City, leads the oldest initiative of this sort that I found in my research. Its Center for Faith and Work, launched in January 2003, seeks to "equip, connect, and mobilize our church community in their professional and industry spheres toward gospel-centered transformation for the common good."[15] Founder Katherine Leary Alsdorf says the center's work is based on the "practical theory of cultural renewal [that] most [believers] will have our biggest impact through our work." Having a clear vision for that, as well as the perseverance required for being salt and light in secular work environments, requires support. "We wanted to create community," Katherine says. "People need to build relationships and help challenge one another."[16]

Today the center boasts fifteen vocationally based fellowships in which everyone from advertising executives to fashion designers to engineers to dancers can gather with peers for prayer, discussion and mutual support.

The newest group is for professionals working in international diplomacy.

The groups bring in older Christians with many years of experience wedding their faith to their work. They host dialogues, book studies, prayer groups and social events. Some seek to serve nonprofits through their specific vocational skills. All the groups aim at encouraging kingdom-oriented vocational stewardship for the common good. As the website for the Fashion Industry Group proclaims,

> As Christians involved in the fashion industry, we hope to discover the bursts and inflections of God's restoring work through our creative and vocational endeavors. As we are being restored to His image by the Holy Spirit, both individually and in community, so He also desires to break forth His glory in new creative concepts, designs, partnerships and business models which will produce a foretaste of the coming Renewal of all things.[17]

It has been important to Katherine since the beginning that the groups not only talk about issues, but actually "do something." The most mature expression of that is seen in one of the oldest vocation groups, the Entrepreneurship Initiative, which sponsors an annual business-plan competition. Through it, entrepreneurs present their vision and implementation strategy for a venture, for-profit or non-profit, that has a high potential for "gospel-centered social impact" and growth and sustainability.[18] Since the first competition in 2007, Redeemer has awarded twelve winners grants from five thousand to twenty-five thousand dollars.[19]

Churches much smaller than Redeemer have also implemented vocationally based groups. At Church of the Good Shepherd in Durham, North Carolina, Associate Pastor Sean Radke taught an adult education class on rejoicing the city over several weeks. Out of this grew interest in establishing vocational groups. Today church members in the legal field gather in the Justice Matters fellowship. Already this group has launched a free legal clinic in the city. A group for medical professionals and one for businesspeople are in formation.

In Washington, D.C., at Grace DC, vocational fellowships began organically when Kwon simply sent out a church-wide email asking if members had interest in meeting with peers in a similar vocational field. He says church leaders expected that perhaps they'd be able to launch two or three small groups as a pilot program. "But," he reports, "120 people ended up signing up for it!"[20]

Churches can also support their marketplace professionals by partnering with parachurch organizations that focus on faith/work issues. In Atlanta, Peachtree Presbyterian pays for membership in the Crossroads Career Network. This allows parishioners who are seeking new jobs or desiring to explore alternative careers free access to Crossroads's training seminars, workbooks, and online resources and tools. Peachtree also partners with WorkLife, Inc., which offers an online coaching tool called Maestro WorkLife. Maestro provides marketplace professionals biblically based resources that address a variety of topics related to daily life on the job.

Wendy Clark from Durham has developed her understanding of business as mission by reading all the books she can get her hands on, attending weekend retreats and conferences, and dialoging with other marketplace Christians and thoughtful preachers like Sean Radke.

In 1994, at age twenty, Wendy launched a business called Carpe Diem Cleaning. Initially, she says, her sense of what it meant to be a Christian businessperson was that her firm could generate profits—and then she could give generously to missions. Only years later were her eyes opened to see that her business *itself* was a means of ministry.[21]

Today Wendy advances the kingdom value of compassion at Carpe Diem through her attentive care for her employees, mostly Latina moms. She has changed Carpe Diem's hours to accommodate their schedules "so that they aren't stressed out trying to get their kids to school, running late to work and getting home on time." Additionally, instead of holding training sessions in Durham, she takes the women—and their kids—to a family camp in the country. That way, the families get a vacation they probably wouldn't have had otherwise. Wendy says business "is not just about profits. It's about investing in the people who are working with us."

BLOOMING AND THE GREAT COMMISSION

Every church leader is familiar with the Great Commission of Matthew 28. Pastors typically preach this as the missionary call to go "to the ends of the earth" to spread the gospel. In his book *To Change the World*, James Davison Hunter offers a different spin on the Great Commission. He argues that it can also "be interpreted in terms of social structure." In other words, the call to go is not only geographical but also sociological. He writes,

> The church is to go into all realms of social life: in volunteer and paid labor—skilled and unskilled labor, the crafts, engineering, commerce, art, law, architecture, teaching, health, and service. Indeed, the church should be *sending people out* in these realms—not only discipling those in these fields by providing the theological resources to form them well, but in fact mentoring and providing financial support for young adults who are gifted and called into these vocations. When the church does not send people to these realms and when it does not provide the theologies that make sense of work and engagement in these realms, the church fails to fulfill the charge to "go into all the world."[22]

For church leaders who want their members to bloom, this is a vital perspective. It properly expands our understanding of the mission in the world that we are calling members to. That call is to go into every sector of society and there bring shalom.

To help their people catch and live that vision, congregational leaders should tell stories—lots of them. It's imperative to make the call three-dimensional. I was once teaching third-graders about missions, and asked them if they knew what a missionary was. Their responses showed how their imaginations had been captured by missionary biographies, missions conference slide shows and the film *The End of the Spear.* "A missionary," one little girl told me soberly, "is like a superhero." We need to get to the point in our churches where even children can describe what "vocational stewardship" is. They will be able to do so if we regularly tell the stories of what it looks like in every sector of society.

Toward that end, below are some short stories to start with.

ACADEMIA: A HISTORIAN PROMOTES
RACIAL RECONCILIATION

Historian Anne C. Bailey from SUNY-Binghamton focuses her research on what Christians in earlier ages did to combat the injustices and prejudices of their day, in the hope of learning lessons for today. Her research into European missionaries who sought freedom for individual slaves uncovered the uncomfortable truth that these Christians did not always leverage their power and privilege to the extent they could have to oppose the slave trade. Bailey says, "It made me think in which ways I had other opportunities, other things that I can do, right here in the place that I stand, in order to effect change for the places that I care about."[23]

One thing Bailey cares a great deal about is racial reconciliation. "Coming to the Lord helped me to look at racial reconciliation issues in a different and [deeper] light," she told an interviewer in 2008. "And frankly with much more hope."[24] That hope has been bolstered further as she has learned of the tenacious and often generous faith of slaves. A believer in the concept of "living history"—that events of the past are connected to contemporary issues—Bailey chose as her research specialty African American history and African Diaspora studies.

In studies that led to her book *African Voices of the Atlantic Slave Trade: Beyond the Silence and Shame* (Beacon Press, 2005), Bailey found that "a number of the slaves were deeply committed Christians." Among some, love for Christ led them to a remarkable place: intercession for their masters. "So you have many ex-slaves talking about their masters, worrying about their nominal Christianity and wishing that they had a heart for a relationship with Jesus," she reports. "They would pray for themselves, and they would also pray for their masters."[25] Telling of their exemplary faith through her writings affords Bailey the opportunity to promote racial reconciliation among Christians today.

ART: A DANCER PROMOTES SOCIAL JUSTICE

Jeannine Lacquement has been dancing all her life. She did ballet as a little girl and jazz and modern dance in high school.[26] She then majored in dance at Goucher College in Maryland. For her, dance has always been about serving others. When working in a nursing home, Jeannine launched a therapeutic dance class. Later, as the live-in director of a residential facility for the handicapped, she involved several disabled kids in a dance troupe she formed.

Today, as head of the nonprofit youth development organization Children of the Light Dancers, Jeannine takes her troupe of teen dancers out to perform at nursing homes and inner-city Vacation Bible School programs. In 2007 and 2008, the troupe composed and danced a special "Seek Justice" performance to highlight the tragedy of international human trafficking and raise funds for International Justice Mission, a leading Christian human-rights organization. Two teens from the troupe, Megan Parker and Alys McAlpine, have also choreographed dances to dramatize the plight of terrorized children in Northern Uganda, who nightly flee to hide from forced recruitment into the Lord's Resistance Army.

BUSINESS: AN ENTREPRENEUR CREATES ECONOMIC OPPORTUNITY

Milt Kuyers from Milwaukee has stewarded his vocational power to create economic opportunity for African Americans from a distressed inner-city neighborhood. Years ago he became president of Star Sprinkler, a struggling manufacturer of fire protection equipment. Milt already had more than two decades of business experience and was ready for the new challenge of turning a company around. Shortly after, a friend invited him to a conference on microenterprise. There, with several other Christian businesspeople, Milt dialogued late into the night about how God could use them to fight poverty at home and abroad. The conference put a fire in his heart. "For the first time he recognized that his position and skills as a businessperson were gifts from God, entrusted to him for a significant function in God's kingdom."[27]

Milt decided to find an urban ministry partner with whom he could work to provide job opportunities for the unemployed. Several ministries turned him down, suspecting this white "do-gooder." Milt persevered. He met one day with Pastor James Carrington of Light House Gospel Chapel, a small congregation in one of the more dangerous neighborhoods of Milwaukee. He told Carrington of his dream to provide jobs to unemployed church members, who would then be supported and kept accountable by the rest of the congregation. After turning Milt down twice, Carrington finally said yes.

Carrington invited his parishioners to hear Milt out; nineteen showed up for the meeting, wanting jobs. It was "overwhelming," Milt remembers, but he dutifully took down everyone's name. And then God performed a miracle: he sent a huge surge in orders to Star Sprinkler. Milt was able to hire every person on his list. Light House Church rallied behind the newly employed, providing transportation and, later, childcare services. Over time, Carrington and Milt became friends, with the pastor contacting Milt whenever one of the church-member employees was having unusual difficulties. Eventually, more than one hundred members of the church benefited from this unique partnership.[28] They weren't the only beneficiaries, Milt reports. "I've had more joy in that part of my life than any other time in my work life."[29]

ENTERTAINMENT: A COMEDIAN PROMOTES TRUTH

Professional comedian Carlos Oscar is a salty presence in the entertainment industry. He integrates his faith into his work first by being a clean comic. He doesn't use profanity, and his humor isn't prurient and sexualized. "I think it makes me a more creative person because I don't have to go that route," he says.[30]

Carlos's dream is to land a contract with a television studio for the production of a sitcom starring an Hispanic family, a sort of Latino version of the *The Cosby Show*. He wants to be able to portray family life in a healthy way, where the dad is "silly but not stupid" and where the kids are respectful. "Today," Carlos says, "television tends to show that the kids are in charge, to show the dumb father. . . . Kids look at these shows and they see grownups as just 'in the way' instead of being there to help them get to the next level in life." He wants to push against that trend by offering a truer, more godly version of parent-child relationships. "I believe God wants all of us to go into different areas of the world and to hopefully show some of the values, the Christian values, that we hold dear, because the entertainment industry is a very influential industry."

GOVERNMENT: A SENATOR ADVOCATES FOR THE VULNERABLE

Pia Cayetano, the youngest member of the Philippines Senate and one of only three women in that body, expresses her faith by being an advocate for the vulnerable.[31] Trained as a lawyer, Cayetano first ran for political office in 2004. While in the senate, she has been a consistent voice for the underdog, particularly women, children and senior citizens. She has worked to pass legislation facilitating access by the poor to cheaper prescription medicines, to establish a Food and Drug Administration to promote food safety, and to bar the detention of indigent patients on account of unsettled medical bills.

Cayetano has been a vocal advocate for the protection of women and children in war-torn areas, particularly against the problem of sexual abuse by peacekeeping forces. As she said in a 2005 interview with the Inter-Parliamentary Union, "There are specific sex crimes that happen to women and children which a lot of people either do not recognize, or just turn a blind eye to. In a lot of areas the situation arises where such crimes are almost tolerated, because men are occupying the field and men have needs. It has to be made known that it is absolutely not acceptable."[32]

FASHION: A DESIGNER PROMOTES CREATION CARE

Fashion designer Bora Aksu, a Briton from a Turkish background, made headlines when graduating in 2002 from the prestigious Central Saint Martins College of Art and Design. At its annual fashion show highlighting the work of its MA graduates, Aksu's designs garnered the loudest acclaim. This led to contracts with high-fashion companies like Dolce & Gabbana.[33]

Today the successful designer promotes the kingdom value of creation care through his work. In 2007, Aksu joined People Tree, a leading voice internationally for eco-friendly fashion, as one of their signature designers.[34] From the beginning of his design career, he has made a point of using only natural fabrics—100-percent wool or silk—in his designs. Work with People Tree has enabled Aksu to branch into some new materials. "I was really excited about using People's Tree's handwoven and hand dyed fabrics," he says.[35] Now he will also be designing creations using recycled materials.

AGRICULTURE: A FARMER PROMOTES
SAFETY IN HIS INDUSTRY

Chicken hatchery owner Jacob A. Schenk, a Pennsylvania Mennonite, launched his business at age thirty-two.[36] In multiple ways he worked for institutional transformation in his field. His business practices with vendors and suppliers, for example, were remarkable. Schenk paid above-market prices for the eggs and chickens he bought in order to get the highest-quality products and to ensure good relationships with his suppliers. He even had a policy of profit sharing with his suppliers, giving them bonuses according to how profitable his hatchery had been that year.

Schenk's unconventional practices gained him significant financial success and great respect from those in his field. He then leveraged his platform to lead his industry in consumer and product safety. Well aware of the devastation that could be caused to farmers by contagious diseases among the livestock, he instituted annual flock-owners meetings, which drew chicken farmers from a wide region. Schenk would bring in special speakers to talk about innovations in ways of preventing disease and controlling its spread when chickens get sick.

BEYOND WEARING A WWJD BRACELET

The professionals profiled throughout this chapter demonstrate that it is possible for Christians in the marketplace to go far beyond the traditional ways of connecting faith and work (that is, practicing personal morality and studying the Bible with others in the workplace). Their stories point to several additional arenas where kingdom values can be advanced, such as how employees are selected, treated and managed; how a firm's profits are used; how an organization practices environmental stewardship; how its products are designed; how it relates to others in its industry; and how it contributes to its community. As church leaders encourage their members to wed their faith and work, they should challenge them to ponder this question: "In my current job, am I doing all I can to deploy my vocational power to promote kingdom foretastes? Am I truly blooming where I'm planted?"

BUT I'M NOT THE CEO

As church leaders share stories like those in this chapter, they may hear a question from some members: "Those people were high up in their companies. How can I, not being the CEO, really make any difference at my work?"

Fear that one lacks any authority to influence positive change in the workplace is a legitimate concern. The good news that pastors can share, though, is this: even believers with limited authority at their workplaces can be creative about stewarding the level of influence they *do* possess. Specifically, church leaders can respond with the following.

First, they can encourage church members to educate themselves about the working conditions of everyone *below* them in their organization. Believers can strive to develop friendly, respectful relationships with those workers, learning their names, inquiring about their families. This little step may have more punch than expected. Too often, the lowliest workers in a company can be virtually invisible to those above them. Others fail to acknowledge them, fail to see them. And that's problematic, since Christ-followers should never treat people like furniture.

Church leaders can encourage their parishioners to take time at work to notice the janitor, the woman who empties the trash, the groundskeepers and the folks down in the basement mailroom. They should observe the conditions these employees labor under. They might discover, for instance, that the janitorial staff doesn't have as nice a lounge as do the white-collar workers, or that lower-level employees face overly restrictive rules concerning phone use or break times.

Second, aware of such things, believers in the firm—including those not high up themselves—may be encouraged by church leaders to improve the quality of life for the lowest-level workers in some simple, practical ways. What if, for example, a mid-level Christian employee at a hotel took up a collection from her peers to buy a nice coffee maker, some comfortable chairs and some green plants to fix up the housekeeping staff's break room? That would be a practical way to introduce a little bit of the kingdom foretaste of beauty.

Moreover, regardless of what position a believer holds at the firm, he could start a quiet, intercessory prayer ministry. Step one might be to get a few other believers at the company on board. Step two could be requesting permission to place a prayer box in some common space in the office (a locked box with a slot where index cards—provided next to the box—can be inserted). Employees can be informed that a prayer group has started and that anyone with a prayer request could jot it down on an index card—anonymously if they desire—and put it in the box. Then the intercessory group would open the box once or twice a week and pray for those matters. This would be a tangible demonstration of love for fellow workers.

Third, church leaders should remind their congregants that, in many firms, even employees in the lower echelons can offer suggestions about ways the organization could be more engaged in the community. It could not hurt for a believer to ask for a meeting with the head of the firm's human resources or marketing departments, for example, and propose that the company start a corporate volunteering program.

There is also nothing to stop a small group of believers at an organization from forming their own emergency benevolence fund. They could seed the fund with their own contributions and then invite other employees to contribute. They could also invite participation in a benevolence committee that would be in charge of distributing the funds. To keep things as simple as possible, the committee could outline a limited eligibility—for example, the fund would only help employees in cases of serious medical illness in their immediate family.

Additionally, even employees with modest positions or low seniority can suggest small, doable reforms in terms of the organization's energy and resource use, to inch the firm in a "greener" direction. Such suggestions could include using energy-efficient light bulbs, launching a campaign to help remind all employees to turn off their computers over the weekend, recycling used paper, or encouraging a serious reduction in the use of plastic and paper cups.

Another strategy involves tweaking initiatives that already exist at the company in order to promote the values of equality or opportunity. For example, suppose an organization already has a job-shadowing program or a summer internship program for young people. A Christian employee at the firm could learn who tends to benefit from these initiatives. If the programs largely cater to white, middle-class (or wealthier) kids, the believer could suggest an alternative approach to the program's director. The program could be expanded or redirected in ways that could spread its benefits to young people with greater needs. If the director is open to the suggestion, the Christian employee might volunteer to do some of the legwork in identifying new partners—such as a Christian school in the inner city that is eager to expose its youth to professional careers.

The point is this: congregants need to understand that wherever they are, regardless of their status, they can probably do at least one thing that advances kingdom values like justice or beauty or compassion or economic opportunity or creation care.

What About the Traditional Church Teaching on Work?

Many of the stories in this chapter have something of a "sexy vibe" to them, as my twenty-something friends say. How astonishing it is that Tom

Hill paid his employees to work for Oklahoma City for a year and half; how impressive it is that young Wendy Clark has created not just jobs but a deeply supportive work environment for low-income Latinas who would more typically face grueling labor conditions. As the twenty-somethings would say of these actions: "How cool is *that*!" And these actions are indeed impressive.

In addition to telling these kinds of inspirational success stories, though, there remains a role for church leaders to continue to teach on some less "sexy" familiar topics as they disciple their people for blooming. One is *ethics*. Since the workplace is fallen, there will always be a place for strong teaching from the pulpit on personal holiness on the job. The second is *evangelism*. Church leaders should regularly remind their flocks that the amazingly good news of the good news needs to be shared with our non-believing coworkers. Finally, church leaders should continue emphasizing one other E-word: *excellence*.

Recently I learned that a friend has a malignant brain tumor. Right now, more than anything else, I want her doctor to be *really good* at brain surgery. Right now, I care more about that than I do about whether he offers his services pro bono at the free clinic or if his management style is hierarchical. Similarly, when I'm driving over a long bridge, I trust that the bridge inspector is someone who takes her job very seriously, who is highly competent and vigilant. I want the chemists and engineers at our region's nuclear power plant to be diligent, careful experts in the safe operations of the facility. I want my veterinarian to be on top of the latest research that can help my sick pet. The quiet, faithful, diligent pursuit of excellence in a vocation can be absolutely vital.

Telling stories of excellence may feel less exciting than showcasing the sorts of stories we've looked at here. But every vocational stewardship initiative should be careful to include teaching on this virtue. Indeed, in some cases, given the weight of their individual responsibilities, some believers may need to view excellence as the highest among the kingdom values they are seeking to live by as they bloom for Jesus in their profession.

Pathway 2

DONATE YOUR SKILLS

I want [congregants] to have moments with God
that take their breath away because of the activation and
deployment of a gift that He gave them that makes them feel
like difference-makers in a broken world. And we as
church leaders have that gift to give every volunteer.

BILL HYBELS, FOUNDING PASTOR,
WILLOW CREEK CHURCH

Paper chemist Dan Blevins doesn't see himself as an extraordinary guy. He grew up in a small town in Michigan, went off to college and got a job after graduation. He found a wife, started a family. They joined a church. At Mt. Pisgah United Methodist Church in Atlanta, Dan sang in the choir and volunteered with the recreational ministry as a soccer referee.[1]

In April 2003, Dan turned fifty. He'd worked for Dow Chemical Company for nearly a quarter-century. He heard about a missions conference coming to downtown Atlanta in June and decided to attend. Given his recent milestone birthday, he chose to follow the track at the conference organized by the Finishers Project. (Finishers Project's mission is to connect midlife adults with "global impact opportunities for God.")[2] On the last day, Dan attended a workshop titled "Finding Your Place in Ministry: Your Skills are Needed."

"The instructor began his presentation stating that regardless of what your skills were, there was a ministry somewhere that could use you," Dan says.[3] Then the presenter said he'd ask each person in the room a little about her or his job, and then make a recommendation of a ministry that could make use of those skills. "He started around the room to my left," Dan says, "and the examples began to flow. Teacher, electrician, nurse— and with each person [he'd] reel off ministries and places in the world where they could be involved." When the presenter got to Dan, though, he was stumped. He wasn't sure how God would use a paper chemist.

"Suddenly, from the back of the room a voice called out," Dan recalls. Someone announced that they'd met a ministry leader in the exhibitors hall that needed a paper chemist. Dan rushed to that ministry's booth after the session.

There he learned that Village Handcrafters, a livelihood ministry among squatters outside Manila, had engaged about forty people in making handmade paper products from hemp. The enterprise provided jobs and generated revenue to support three Filipino church plants. When Dan contacted the ministry's founder, Ed Landry, and explained his professional background, Ed didn't hesitate to say, "We are self-taught amateurs. We really need you to come to the Philippines and help us."

Dan says, "That was enough for me. It was clear that God had hooked me up with a ministry that needed my special knowledge. Wow!"

During Dan's first ten-day visit to Manila, he was able to help Village Handcrafters cut their processing time for a batch of hemp pulp from nine hours to three and to reduce their chemical costs per batch by nearly 90 percent. "It was really in the sweet spot of what I like to do: technical problem solving," he reports. During subsequent trips, Dan taught his Filipino friends new wastewater treatment processes, another one of his areas of expertise. His most recent involvements have been in leading teams from Mt. Pisgah to Kenya to install water purification systems that utilize a technology he learned from his work at Dow Chemical.

Serving abroad by using his unique vocational skills has brought Dan profound joy and has deepened his Christian faith. While he had fun serving in Mt. Pisgah's music and recreational ministries, they did not enrich his spiritual life the way this vocational stewardship has. Because God led him to serving opportunities so customized to his skills, Dan's faith in God's personal care for him deepened.

When you see something that calls you so specifically to an area that you're prepared for and you really love to do, that's when it feels really, really personal. That's when you say, "Yeah, I know God knows me, knows my name, and he cares for me." When he really grabs you by the shirt and says, "Come here, do this thing over here," it's just really tremendous reinforcement of these things that we often talk about and believe. I deeply believe it's true based on what has happened to me.

While Dan doesn't see himself as extraordinary, his story has become catalytic at Mt. Pisgah. On the church's website, on the Volunteering page under "Global Mission," the text reads, "If God can use the skills of a paper chemist for the cause of world evangelism (just ask Dan Blevins his story!), then God can use whatever skills, talents, and willingness to serve that He's given you!"[4]

Dan's experience led church staff to focus more intentionally on helping members find ways to deploy their specific skills in ministry. And his wife leads an adult education class called "Finding Your PLACE in Ministry,"[5] which combines spiritual gifts assessment with personality, interests, work style and background assessments. "The idea is that you can serve in lots of ways but you're not really going to be happy unless you find something that's your sweet spot," Dan explains.

He continues, "We've got a number of businesspeople [in the congregation]. They're marketers or management people or business executives, and they've said, 'Okay, where do I fit into this?'" Several of these congregants are serving through a ministry Mt. Pisgah partners with called International Leadership Institute. "It's largely a ministry that goes and holds leadership conferences lots of places around the world," Dan says. "And [for] a lot of businesspeople, that's how they see themselves: 'Gee, I'm an organizational leader, and this is how I can influence [others].'" Teaching abroad has been very rewarding for these business executives, Dan says. "They really find it exciting because they use [these skills] in their corporate business setting, and it resonates with what they like to do and what they know how to do."

• • • • • •

In the previous chapter we saw that the primary expression of vocational stewardship that church leaders should encourage is "blooming where you're planted." But sometimes employees have additional energy to give outside their daily job and are eager to deploy their vocational skill on behalf of a ministry. In other instances, believers face obstacles to blooming. Some church members are young workers new in their jobs. They may feel that their inexperience, lack of seniority or lowly position significantly limits their scope for advancing kingdom foretastes. Other congregants may be working in jobs that don't match their vocational gifts, such as the aspiring artist who is currently waiting tables. And even older congregants with seniority at their workplaces may face institutional constraints to blooming, such as a hostile boss or a powerful bureaucracy that limits his or her voice.

Such workers may need to be challenged to think harder and more creatively about how they could bloom.[6] But in some cases, these individuals may have more capacity for deploying their vocational talents *outside* their regular job. Pathway two of vocational stewardship is about donating vocational skills to nonprofits and ministries—within the church, in the local community or abroad—that can use them to advance God's kingdom. Churches with the ability to promote not only blooming but also this pathway may discover that many congregants respond enthusiastically to meaningful opportunities to use their job skills on their off time.

A COMMON-SENSE—YET DISCOURAGINGLY RARE—APPROACH

Encouraging congregants to serve using their unique vocational skills by volunteering in a ministry or nonprofit that is advancing the kingdom is not a particularly innovative idea. It makes much common sense. After all, it holds obvious promise for the servants. If they already enjoy their profession, it's not surprising they'd find pleasure in donating those skills to ministries—just like Dan Blevins has. It is also a good idea in terms of needs commonly cited by nonprofit organizations. In April 2009, the Deloitte consulting firm released a study reporting that 95 percent of nonprofit leaders say their organizations desire more pro bono services by professionals. While they appreciate volunteers who can help them provide direct services (tutoring kids, cleaning up polluted rivers, serving meals), their greater need is for skilled professionals who can assist them in strengthening their organizational structures so that they can be effective and sustainable.[7]

Findings from a 2004 study by the Urban Institute were similar. It reported that nonprofit organizations are seeking greater numbers of volunteers with specialized skills.[8] Yet despite the fact that this kind of service would be of obvious benefit to both the server and the served, most congregations have no specific, intentional focus or programs to identify their congregants' occupational skills and match those to serving opportunities.

The reasons why vary. Understanding them helps position church leaders to overcome barriers to implementing pathway two. The reasons boil down to two basic types: administrative and attitudinal.

With regard to administration, some churches do not use any sort of database to gather information on their parishioners. Consequently, they do not collect vocational information that could be useful in matching members to relevant volunteer opportunities. In churches that do use database programs, it is rare that occupational or skills data is collected. Moreover, even churches with ministries focused on equipping the laity sometimes fail to utilize assessment tools that specifically identify members' vocational skills and expertise. In all these cases, church staff don't know much about the wealth of professional skills resident in their congregation.

The second reason many churches do not support vocational stewardship along pathway two is fear. Some clergy are not enthusiastic about helping their members to plug in to service opportunities best suited for their skills when those opportunities are *outside* the church's own programs. As veteran church consultant Sue Mallory laments, "The average church in America has the mindset of scarcity, not the mindset of abundance." Church leaders, she reports, often feel they do not have enough support for getting the church's work done and so there is reluctance to "send people out."[9]

Gordon Murphy from the Barnabas Group, a parachurch ministry that seeks to connect Christian marketplace professionals with Chicago's inner-city nonprofits, agrees. He reports that some clergy are fearful about losing resources:

> I've tried to meet with dozens of pastors, and they just don't seem interested. . . . They're afraid if they start referring their sheep out, even though [nonprofits] might use their skill set better, they have this sense: "Well, then I'm going to lose the sheep. Even though I'm not using the sheep

well, they'll like [the outside nonprofit] more than they'll like me and they'll give their time, talent and money to them and they won't give it to our church."[10]

For nearly forty years, author and church consultant William Diehl has been a voice crying in the wilderness about these problems. With their internal focus on building the institution of the church, clergy are reluctant to scatter the flock out into serving opportunities in the community, he says. Some years ago he was invited to teach a course at Princeton Theological Seminary on the ministry of the laity. Initially excited, he ended up disappointed. He recalls, "As we progressed, it was very clear to me that what the students were looking for in taking the course was a better understanding of the laity so that they could better use them in serving the church institution. And that was all they got out of it. I might as well have taught a course on how to use audiovisual equipment."[11]

OVERCOMING THE OBSTACLES TO PATHWAY 2 INITIATIVES

Overcoming administrative obstacles. Congregational leaders have pioneered four strategies for overcoming administrative obstacles: implementing new technology; rethinking traditional approaches to engaging volunteers; partnering with a local "volunteer clearinghouse"; and providing formal coaching.

First, at Grace Community Church in Noblesville, Indiana, leaders have implemented new technology by establishing a web-based portal called "Serving Central."[12] There, under the "Find Your Fit . . ." tab, congregants can select from a long checklist skills that they possess and are interested in using in ministry. The search engine then produces a list of serving opportunities (at home and abroad) matched to those skills.[13]

Lifebridge Christian Church in Longmont, Colorado, has taken a similar approach. Congregants complete a volunteer interest form online that asks detailed questions about their vocational and avocational skills.[14] Staff and ministry leaders then review the information on the form and make recommendations to each member about relevant serving opportunities at the church or with one of its "glocal" partners (domestic and foreign agencies with which Lifebridge collaborates).

A second strategy for overcoming administrative obstacles involves rethinking traditional approaches to volunteer engagement. Many churches encourage members to serve on short-term missions trips abroad or at home. Beyond medical missions trips, though, few of these short-term experiences are deliberately designed by vocation. As a result, congregants send their bankers and architects out to paint houses and their artists and police officers to serve in Vacation Bible Schools. This isn't necessarily bad, and it can be a lot of fun. But some professionals in the pews are hungry for something different.

At Grace Community, Ed Fischer, a layman who has worked in the IT field for twenty years, has helped coordinate "geek trips" to the congregation's partner ministry, Nairobi Evangelical Graduate School of Theology. The seminary was eager to receive IT professionals who could teach short software classes as well as repair and upgrade computers and networks. Ed says he has loved coordinating the trips over the past several years. "Lots of times churches offer medical missions trips or serving in building projects," he says. "But there is a lot of value in creating vocational type trips. It's a great way to engage people that otherwise might not think of going on a short-term trip."[15]

Just as many congregations sponsor short-term missions trips, many host an annual ministry fair to expose congregants to volunteer service opportunities. With a little tweaking, this familiar event can become a vehicle for encouraging vocational stewardship along pathway two.

Leaders of a ministry fair could consider composing a vocationally oriented "Want Ads" booklet to pass out to congregants who attend. To create it, the fair organizer asks each ministry showcased at the fair to identify three or four serving opportunities *by skill set or occupation*. These are written up succinctly, such as "WANTED: Marketing or advertising professionals to help create new promotional brochure for our tutoring ministry" or "WANTED: Engineers or scientists with skills in water purification or wastewater technologies to help serve in our disaster relief efforts."[16]

To get maximum benefit from their ministry fair, church leaders would inform the congregation ahead of time that the booklet would be available and encourage church members to be thinking about specific vocational skills they might be interested in donating to a ministry.

A third strategy for overcoming obstacles in pathway two involves partnering with a local "volunteer clearinghouse" that can help the church match its professionals to serving opportunities. This is the approach Redeemer Presbyterian Church in New York City has taken through its close relationship with Hope for New York (HFNY).

Redeemer launched HFNY roughly twenty years ago. The church was teeming with young professionals in their twenties and thirties—energetic, career-focused singles excited by Pastor Tim Keller's vision of a church "for the city." Redeemer measures its success not just by church growth but also by the difference the congregation is making in the city. To facilitate that mission, Redeemer started HFNY to develop relationships with Christian nonprofits serving the city's poor and marginalized and then connect Redeemer congregants with them.

Over time, HFNY established relationships with over thirty affiliates. It supports these organizations through grants, coaching and its Professionals in Action program, through which Redeemer congregants donate their skills to build capacity in the nonprofits.

Elise Chong, HFNY's executive director, reports that "throughout the years, our affiliates have been constantly asking for professionals. Web developers are a fairly common request, or 'someone to do some marketing for me'—creating tools or marketing plans or a marketing brochure."[17] In response to these needs, HFNY's Professionals in Action program mobilizes volunteer teams with professional skills to complete short-term, pro bono projects for organizations serving the poor and marginalized.[18] Volunteers typically serve from one to three months. The team approach builds in accountability and ensures better results. "If Mary for some reason can't attend that night's meeting, at least Joe and Sally can do it," Chong explains. "So the project actually continues and completes, and you get a really good product at the end."

Fellowship Bible Church in Little Rock, Arkansas, has instituted the fourth strategy for encouraging vocational stewardship along pathway two: formal coaching. This congregation is interested in facilitating long-term serving investments by marketplace professionals from the church. To do so, Fellowship hired Bill Wellons as its "release pastor." Bill pours his life into high-capacity, middle-aged leaders in the church who are ready to free up considerable amounts of time to pursue service in the kingdom.

Bill describes his work as a coach to these congregants in detail in *Unlimited Partnership*, a flipbook he wrote with Lloyd Reeb of Halftime.[19]

Sometimes Bill's coaching involves cheerleading and encouragement. Sometimes it's about helping talented parishioners navigate church and ministry subcultures and bureaucracies. Sometimes it's providing spiritual care. Almost always, a key part of the coaching is helping marketplace leaders identify the transferable skills and knowledge they have.

Because of Bill's investment, several marketplace leaders from Fellowship have given themselves to intensive volunteer staff roles at the church or to deep engagements on behalf of organizations at home and abroad. For example, successful pharmaceutical sales representative James Saunders is giving ten hours a week as the lay leader of Fellowship's men's ministry. He has honed leadership skills for years in his industry, identifying talented individuals and mentoring them into successful salespeople. Motivating others and building teams energizes him. He uses these same skills now to recruit leaders for men's small groups and to enfold non-Christian business executives in the activities of the men's ministry.[20]

Overcoming fear with faith. Many church leaders fear that releasing congregants to agencies outside the congregation will leave the church itself bereft of the human and financial resources it requires. Leaders must conquer this fear if they are to implement vocational stewardship along pathway two. They will need to grow in trusting that God is able to ensure that all his work—inside and outside the four walls of the church—gets done when leaders are faithful to the equipping mandate he has given them in Ephesians 4:11-12. Clergy must believe that God will bless them for being open-handed with the talents resident in their congregation. It's a matter of banking on the promise Ecclesiastes 11:1 offers: "Cast your bread upon the waters, for after many days you will find it again." This text encourages generosity in the confidence that, by God's gracious design, it will produce return blessing.

This vision for producing open-handedness among pastors may sound unrealistic. But it can and has been done. Vernon and Charlene Armitage from Pleasant Valley Baptist Church are living demonstrations. They believe that members' gifts are not given solely for "church work," but for the kingdom. "Equipping is building the Body but also a kingdom thing," Vernon says. "A good healthy church ought to be serving the community."[21] His wife, Charlene, says, "We're not interested in people filling roles, but in roles fulfilling people." Their passion and strategic deployment may be outside the four walls of the church, but, she says, "we hold that up as extremely important."[22]

When asked if she was afraid that encouraging service out in the community would leave the church short on volunteers or money to fill its own needs, Charlene admits that she and Vernon did have those fears years ago. The turning point came in 2002 when Don Simmons visited Pleasant Valley to teach them on equipping. Charlene says that he persuaded them of the biblical vision for externally focused churches. She says she came to see that Pleasant Valley was being "selfish" by not sharing its talents with the community.

Since that time, Pleasant Valley has sent out hundreds of its people. For example, recently some master gardeners in the congregation launched a community gardens initiative. It now engages more than one hundred people in some seventy-five gardens all over the city, growing produce shared with the hungry and sold at affordable prices through community farmers markets. In addition, Charlene has mobilized educators from the church to serve local public schools. She herself serves on the school board. This arises from both her personal passion (she was an educator for thirty years) and her desire to model service in the community to her fellow congregants. "They need to see that that's just as valued as singing in the choir," she says.[23]

And what was the result for Pleasant Valley Baptist Church? "We discovered, the more we went outside the church, the more the inside of our church was taken care of," Charlene says. "That was not what we expected at all! It's just very much like what Jesus said: 'Get outside of yourself.'"

As Pleasant Valley engaged in more partnerships with parachurch ministries and participated in multichurch outreach efforts throughout the city, more unchurched people started attending the church. This energized the congregants—and made congregants more willing to serve inside the church, even in the nursery, to meet the needs of newcomers. Charlene adds, "The best way I know how to say it is, 'You go out of your self and your self will be taken care of.'"

At Fellowship Bible, the commitment to coaching high-capacity congregants for service *anywhere*—inside or outside the church—is facilitated by Senior Pastor Robert Lewis's "catch and release" philosophy. "Our people have a desire to do frontline ministry themselves, and they want their church to help them do it," he says.[24] Unfortunately, most pastors have a "catch and keep" philosophy, Lewis acknowledges. In the earlier days of his ministry, this was his approach. It only changed as he began to study more carefully the leadership modeled by Jesus. Lewis says that Jesus was a "catch-and-release fisherman. He would catch men and women with His gospel, and spend time with them to develop, season, and ground them in God's ways, but then He'd release them." He gave them over "to be salt and light, and to change the community."[25]

At Mariners Church in Irvine, Calfornia, Outreach Pastor Laurie Beshore has seen the Ecclesiastes promise of bread returning come true. She and other leaders at Mariners came alongside congregant Don Schoendorfer, a mechanical engineer who'd volunteered for years at the church's inner-city tutoring center. Don got passionate about the problem of immobility faced by millions of disabled people in the developing world. He believed his more than twenty-five years of experience as an engineer might offer a solution.

Don took on the challenge of creating a wheelchair that would be adequate to the demanding environmental conditions of Third World countries and that could be manufactured at an affordable price. He bought a bicycle and some white plastic lawn chairs at one of Southern California's big-box stores. After "tinkering in the garage" for several weeks, he'd constructed a sturdy, usable wheelchair. Today his wheelchair design has brought mobility to more than half a million people in the developing world.[26]

Laurie Beshore says that one of the highlights now on many Mariners short-term mission trips abroad is the opportunity to assemble and distribute wheelchairs. The experience deeply touches trip members and is often used by God to deepen their compassion for the poor, she reports. That affects their own walk with Christ and has led to stronger engagement at Mariners and its local ministries.

CONCLUSION: THE BLESSINGS OF PATHWAY 2

As we've seen, facilitating pathway two may require congregational leaders to make some changes in both their attitudes and their administrative structures. Change is never easy, and it doesn't happen without significant motivation. For those active in vocational stewardship along pathway two, the enormous benefits are well worth the effort.

Global and local ministries that receive the time and talents of pro bono professionals obviously benefit. This ought to be of some interest for pastors. But when pastors understand the benefits this pathway brings their own parishioners, that is even more meaningful and motivational. Such benefits are not hard to see.

The first benefit is the deep joy parishioners experience. They discover that it is profoundly rewarding to use their unique, God-given skills to serve others on the frontlines. Consider, for example, the experience of civil engineer Rod Beadle from Chicago. In spring 2010, Rod traveled to Haiti just after the massive earthquake in Port-au-Prince. Reflecting on his three weeks there, he said, "I was putting in clean water systems for some of the [displaced persons] camps and doing waste treatment. That was probably the coolest thing I've ever done professionally."[27]

Gordon Murphy of Barnabas Group says he has often witnessed "aha" moments when marketplace leaders grasp that their professional skills uniquely qualify them to offer service in a frontline ministry. He says, "When they actually get to use the gift that they are excited about, the gift of communication, the gift of marketing, the gift of whatever—when they get to use *that* gift—it significantly improves the 'wow' factor of the serving experience."[28]

Service along pathway two has also deepened some congregants' appreciation for believers whose skill sets are much different from their own. For them, it illuminates in fresh ways the truth of 1 Corinthians 12 about the value of all parts of Christ's body. Business consultant Kay Edwards reports that she has been abundantly blessed in this regard through volunteering with S.H.A.L.O.M. ministry, a grass-roots nonprofit in inner-city Milwaukee. She's amazed at the gifts and dedication of its staff. "[They] have no problem walking into a crack house at midnight on a weekend and pulling people out and saying 'Jesus loves you,'" Kay says. "I could *never* do that, never in a million years." Though she couldn't counsel drug addicts, the human resource management expert says, "I *can* run a board."[29]

Kay's service with S.H.A.L.O.M. has been so transformative she has launched her own initiative, Vesper Services Network, to make matches between professionals like herself and nonprofits who need their talents. "It's such an amazing experience" to rub shoulders with believers of diverse gifts, Kay says. "I wanted other people to have that experience."

Congregants who have donated their vocational skills to ministries also report that they've grown in their appreciation for the unity of Christ's body worldwide. Civil engineer John Rahe has served throughout the developing world on vocationally oriented short-term trips operated by Engineering Ministries International. His experiences have exposed him to the tremendous diversity of the worldwide church. "I've seen the exuberant worship of Africans in Kenya and Ghana, and then I've been to Bangladesh, where the men sit on the floor on one side of the church and the women sit on the other and they worship almost in silence," John says. "Just the richness of being able to see and experience the body of Christ is wonderful." A "dyed-in-the-wool evangelical," he explains that being married to an Orthodox Christian has given him a heart for promoting unity within the body. "We're called to love and respect each other," he says. "It's something God has put on my heart, and it's only become stronger through my association with ministry trips through EMI."[30]

Finally, and perhaps most importantly for congregational leaders, service along pathway two has sparked spiritual growth in some parishioners. Chicago executive Larry Mollner, who logged more than a million frequent flier miles during a high-powered career in international finance, says that his volunteer service has been the catalyst for making his faith genuine. After years of attending church somewhat mechanically, he now states simply, "I think I now practice my Christian faith in a way that is real and personal."[31]

Larry grew up Catholic and then attended various Protestant churches because his wife was Methodist. Over the years he volunteered at various churches, but the effect of that on him was minimal. Through vocational stewardship along pathway two, he has been able to utilize the outside-the-box thinking skills he honed during his career as director of the Futures Division at Morgan Stanley Dean Witter & Co. "Matching my experience and skill sets to the particular needs of the ministry seeking help is unique and effective," Larry says. "Together we are working for God's kingdom, and that is satisfying and very exciting."

Larry and his friend John Phillips, a retired real estate developer, have been matched through Barnabas Group with an inner-city ministry called Kids Off The Block. Diane Latiker, a resident of the Roseland community on Chicago's South Side, started this grass-roots outreach seven years ago. In a context where violence and gangs are commonplace, Diane welcomes youth into her modest home for a range of after-school activities and tutoring.

When Larry and John met Diane in 2010, the ministry still operated out of her home. "They'd cleaned out the living room/dining room area to make room for tables, chairs and some computers where kids could work," Larry says. It was clear that Diane needed organizational help and a better facility to bring the ministry to the next level. John drew on his professional network to locate rental space, and Larry has helped Diane with strategic planning.

Larry says he is no longer just writing checks to support others' outreach ministries. He's jumping into his car and driving to the city's South Side to help offer hope and vision to a generation of at-risk teenagers. He's building crosscultural relationships and contributing time, treasure and talent to benefit others. Larry says, "Helping others through these programs has changed my life. There are people in need and there are people who want to help. Putting them together is a joy. The results touch my heart. I want to do more. My Bible study has increased. My interest in knowing God has increased. It's all a part of what I call 'the new me.'"

Pathway 3

LAUNCH YOUR OWN SOCIAL ENTERPRISE

*The Mavuno Marathon is really the thing that has
managed to connect us to our mission here on earth. . . .
[We're] here to change society for the glory of God.*

KANJII MBUGUA

A third avenue of vocational stewardship that congregational leaders can consider facilitating is getting behind the entrepreneurial dreams of high-capacity congregants. Right now, your church may contain some talented marketplace leaders whom God is stirring in an exciting—and perhaps slightly scary—new way. They are actively thinking of leaving their "day job" (or at least carving out significant time in their schedule) to birth a new social enterprise. They dream of implementing a new kingdom endeavor to bless a targeted group or to provide a creative solution to a thorny social problem.

Right now in your congregation, there may be a successful businesswoman wondering if the time is now for her to exit corporate America and pursue her passion: launching a nonprofit agency to provide business coaching and start-up financing to inner-city entrepreneurs. Or perhaps an architect and a real estate developer in your church have dreamed together of doing something significant to address your city's affordable-housing crisis. In short, right now, God may be planting some big dreams in the hearts of your congregation's members—dreams that could rejoice your city and that many congregants could rally behind.

At a remarkable evangelical church in Nairobi, these sorts of social enterprises are being encouraged deliberately, as a centerpiece of the church's mission. Mavuno ("Harvest") Church's purpose is bold: "to turn ordinary people into fearless influencers of society." It does so through a carefully conceived, robust and unique discipleship program called the Mavuno Marathon.

THE MAVUNO MARATHON

Mavuno began roughly five years ago under the leadership of a young, articulate and dynamic pastor named Muriithi Wanjau. Pastor Muriithi was frustrated with much of what passed as discipleship in the evangelical church of Kenya. Borrowed from the West, its discipleship training was too individualistic, often compartmentalized and skewed away from praxis. Its information-oriented model didn't fit the African culture or produce believers whose lives truly changed. "I felt we were creating Christians who had become conformed to Christian culture on the outside but who were not transformed on the inside," Muriithi says. "So I'm in church, I know the hymns, I know the verses. I don't curse, I don't hit my wife— all the things that reduce Christianity to a bunch of 'don'ts.' But then it doesn't affect how I drive; it doesn't affect my political involvement, my concern for the environment, my living for something that is bigger than a nice house and a car."[1]

Muriithi wanted discipleship that was hands-on, interactive and *practiced*. He sought a kind of training that would combine biblical learning with real-life doing, all in a small-group format that would promote community. Its theology would emphasize Jesus' kingdom work, so participants would understand that faith is not only a matter of individual belief but also of actually *following* Jesus, deploying talents in the *missio Dei*. The form should be interactive, relevant and experiential. The initial result of Muriithi's thinking was Mizizi ("Roots").

"Mizizi is a very practical, hands-on course where you do the cognitive stuff at home," Muriithi explains. "Every week we went through the stuff that they'd read and I said, 'Now that you've read it, let's put your books down and practice it.'" So if the week's lesson concerned the how-tos of studying the Word, he'd send class members into quiet areas to examine a text alone for thirty minutes and then return to share their findings. When the lesson was on witnessing, he'd divide the class into pairs, and they would practice sharing their faith on a local college campus, striking up conversations with students. When the lesson concerned God's heart for the poor, he'd take the class to a prison. There they would serve the prisoners in whatever practical ways were needed, such as painting the library or delivering mattresses.

Muriithi watched Mizizi change people's lives. Seekers in the course became professing Christians. Individuals with troublesome habits they were trying to break—like smoking—achieved success. People who'd been Christians since their childhood felt their faith come alive. Small groups bonded; indeed, they didn't want to stop meeting once the course ended. Muriithi realized he needed to provide some next steps.

During this time, Muriithi and some other young leaders had been sent out by their mother church, Nairobi Chapel, to plant a satellite campus. Pastor Simon Mbevi and Pastor Linda Ochola Adolwa were on Muriithi's leadership team, and each had special interests. For Simon, it was prayer—he'd led multiple prayer crusades throughout the country. For Linda, it was justice—this had been a particular focus of her seminary studies. Muriithi encouraged his teammates to design experiential courses, akin to the style of Mizizi, on those themes. Eventually, the full picture of a sequenced discipleship program became clear to the team.

Mizizi was a great start, a foundations course to ground believers in the gospel of the kingdom. But to help participants maintain an "external focus," Muriithi knew they needed more. Simon designed Ombi ("Prayer") as a series of classes and hands-on activities that small groups that had originally formed through Mizizi could go through together. Meanwhile, Linda was hard at work writing a Bible study tracing the theme of God's heart for justice throughout the Old Testament. Her curriculum became the basis for a third course, Hatua ("Action").

These courses, as well as additional activities, are now together under the name of Mavuno Marathon. "If Kenyans are really good at one thing," Muriithi says with a smile, "it's marathon running." Everything about this discipleship track is focused on the goal of equipping Mavuno congregants for service in the world, as "fearless influencers of society."

In addition to the three courses described above, the Marathon includes an emphasis on serving and on leadership development. Mizizi

members remain with their small groups (called Life Groups) throughout
the process. "We recognize that many of the issues we face in our nation
are structural," Muriithi says. "You can't successfully face them as an individual, no matter how well intentioned you are. You have to have the
support structures to fight structural evil and injustice; you can't do it
yourself. So small groups are a very important segment of what we call
our Marathon."

After completing Ombi, individuals are expected to serve the church in
a variety of behind-the-scenes, often thankless tasks, such as assisting
with parking, ushering or nursery care. This part of the Marathon is deliberate: Muriithi believes it provides the environment for "high-capacity"
people to grow in character and humility. He says, "We realized that unless they turn to serving the church, there are dangers to serving in society.
[Those dangers] have to do with recognition. They have to do with integrity when you begin to attract attention," he explains. "So we're training
you all the time: 'How do you serve not because you're getting anything
out of it but because you're a Christian and you need to serve?'"

After a season, these individuals are invited to become part of Team
Mavuno. This group receives leadership training and coaching/mentoring
by the pastoral staff. They are educated about Nairobi's needs and tour
various parts of the city, learning about a variety of social, economic, spiritual and political issues. In this phase, group members are encouraged to
consider the ways they can use their particular gifts, assets and skills as
"fearless influencers" in one of six societal sectors identified by the church.
As Muriithi explains,

> One is politics and government. . . . We're encouraging many people to start
> initiatives in government. It might be lobby groups. It might be running for
> a seat as a city counselor or in parliament. We want people who are Chris-
> tians with integrity to go out and reform the politics of our nation. A sec-
> ond is media and the arts. That's big for us; media is such a huge tool for
> impact and we've seen that. A lot of the negatives that have come into our
> culture come in because of Hollywood and all of the associated media with
> it. So we are encouraging members to begin initiatives that create positive
> content and push that into society.

Other sectors include business, the family and education, health and the
environment, and church/missions.

In each instance, the church is committed to developing mature Christian believers who will launch "frontline initiatives" to address pressing issues in the various sectors. For example, Mavuno's first social entrepreneur in the health/environment sector is Mukuria Mwangi. He leads an effort called REFUGE (Restoring Forests for Future Generations) among indigenous tribal people in the Mau Forest. REFUGE assists tribal people in new beekeeping enterprises, which provide them with earned income and strengthen the pollination of this large forest, which is a critical ecosystem in East Africa. REFUGE has also started thirteen nurseries to aid in reforestation.

Simon Mbevi has now left the pastoral staff to launch Mavuno's first foray into the political/governance sector. He has created Transform Kenya, a nonprofit, to promote a nationwide prayer movement, raise up a generation of boys as leaders and create mentorship programs for Christians contemplating public service. In spring 2010, Transform Kenya launched a twelve-month discipleship and leadership-training course for believers who plan to run in the country's next elections for Parliament.

"It's not enough to just pray for good leadership, and then we sit back and all the wrong guys run for political office," Simon says. "We desire to raise up 120 Christian leaders who will go through a year of values-based training and prayer, who will covenant together so that when God gets us into political offices, we will glorify Jesus. . . . We believe that by 2012 we'll give this nation alternative leaders, people that they can feel good about voting for."[2]

Mavuno helps these frontline initiatives by promoting awareness of them among the congregation, gathering the various leaders for networking and training, providing prayer support and encouraging others in the church to participate in these endeavors (financially and by volunteering their skills). No staff members are allowed to launch frontline initiatives. Muriithi is passionate about *lay* ministry; he wants to resist temptations for "the church"—usually translated as the paid staff and clergy—to own the work. As he says,

> Our job is Ephesians 4:11-12, to *equip* people for works of service. So they are the ones to *do* the work of service; our job is to equip them. As a result, we've resisted the temptation to become a children's home or do a social justice ministry as a church because when we do that, we feel like we insti-

tutionalize it. Then people feel good that they're *giving* to one but don't feel any pressure to *begin* one. And our expectation is that every member of our church will actually begin a frontline ministry or join one.

"We call the people who have started frontline initiatives our 'premium potatoes,'" Muriithi says with a smile. "We say that they are our 'finished product' at Mavuno. For us, maturity is not based on what you know, but on what kind of impact you are having for the kingdom."

MAVUNO'S FRONTLINE INITIATIVES

Daisy Waimiri is one of those "premium potatoes." A thirty-three-year-old mother of two, Daisy initially resisted joining a Mizizi class. "I had a kind of 'elder brother syndrome,'" she admits. "I'd been a Christian for a long time, and I went in with an attitude of, 'I've been saved forever and there's nothing new these people can tell me.'"[3] But the experience was nothing like what she expected.

"I would say that my faith totally, totally changed," Daisy says. "It was like I became a new believer, you know? That was amazing. I was no longer tired of being saved. It was no longer this boring thing." She bonded deeply with her Life Group members, grew in her prayer life through Ombi and began considering more deeply what her particular gifts and passions were that could be utilized in the kingdom. Now, she reports, she has "a lifestyle of wanting to actually fulfill my destiny in God and actually wanting to do God's will, and watch him take me one step at a time."

A few weeks prior to her entering the Mizizi class, Daisy had been approached for small loans by her maid, Violet, and by a night watchman at a nonprofit where she volunteered. As a former community development major at college and as someone who'd worked in social enterprises as a young adult, Daisy was inclined to help. But she wasn't interested in providing mere handouts. She wanted to find a way to help low-income people like Violet and the watchman to start saving money; she hoped to provide capital for microbusinesses to help them generate additional income. She decided to offer these individuals an incentive to save: for every Kenyan shilling they put aside, she would add three more—as long as they agreed that they would use the money to purchase the means of some kind of income-generating enterprise.

The initiative was just "a little seed" at first, Daisy reports. However, through Mizizi and subsequent discussions with her Life Group and Muriithi, she became convinced that God was calling her to focus full time on the idea, and to grow it. "By the time I finished Mizizi," she reports, "I knew for sure that this was what I wanted to do. It was so clear. Nobody could talk me out of it!"

Daisy asked Violet to invite people from her church in the Kibera slum of Nairobi to an orientation meeting where Daisy would present the savings/microenterprise program. Violet brought her pastor and a small delegation from the church. "I made them a meal, and I told them that this is what I wanted to do," Daisy recalls. "I want you to save for three months. I'll triple your money, but it has to be for a business that you'll be doing, and then you'll be able to pay back." The delegation's response was enthusiastic.

Daisy then enrolled in a short-term course on microfinance from a non-profit in Kenya called ACOMA. When Violet and her church members returned with their savings—nearly one hundred people had decided to participate—Daisy divided them into groups of eleven, presented them with savings booklets and strategized with them about the raw materials they could purchase for launching new income-generating activities. Some chose to invest in purchasing charcoal for resale, others purchased ingredients for making foodstuffs for resale. "Before I knew it," she says with wonder, "we had three hundred members all in groups of eleven, and all [were] saving something."

As of this writing, her group has more than 450 members. Many have taken out and repaid multiple loans. One member has launched a beauty salon, another a grocery kiosk, a third a produce stand and another a business selling traditional hot foods. After prayer with her Life Group, Daisy decided she would not charge interest on the loans. Instead, to make the effort sustainable, she purchases the raw materials needed for the members' businesses at wholesale cost from vendors outside Nairobi. Then she sells the materials to the members at a higher price than she paid, but one that is still a bargain for them.

Members' profits from their enterprises have enabled them to improve their standard of living. For example, participating mothers tell of being able to afford children's school uniforms and to set aside savings for emergencies.

Daisy reports that Mavuno's support for her initiative has been invaluable. Her Life Group provides encouragement, counsel and prayer. Mavuno's promotion of her efforts has led to several tours of the Kibera slum to allow church members and their friends to meet firsthand the micro-entrepreneurs in Daisy's program. This has generated donations and volunteers. Mavuno has provided leadership training to Daisy and networked her with the other frontline initiative leaders. Most importantly, several other Mavuno congregants have joined her board of directors, each bringing unique vocational talents that are relevant to the endeavor:

> All of my board members are from Mavuno Church. They do different things. I have one who's a banker, so she really helps with the banking aspect of how to monitor all the accounts. . . . Then we have a lawyer from Mavuno and a lady who does a lot of our [grant] proposals. She works for a nongovernment organization. . . . When we did the data analysis on the businesses [in Kibera] that we should narrow down to, I did it with my board. They were very instrumental.

SEEING THE NEED UP CLOSE

Mavuno believes it is important to encourage its mostly middle-class, upwardly mobile parishioners to truly *see* their city and country, to experience its pain up close. Consumerism and the desire for material comfort is not something unique to Americans, Muriithi says. Kenyans, too, are easily caught up in the desire to accumulate. Thus, the Mavuno Marathon involves planned experiences to provide exposure to uncomfortable scenes and realities. These range from weekend social-justice retreats to city and slum tours to on-campus educational campaigns. Pastor Linda Ochola Adolwa says such campus-wide events are needed to help congregants grasp what is meant by "social transformation." She says she and other church leaders realized "it is a very big jump for people to move from saying, 'Praise God' to 'God has a heart for justice' to 'God wants us to do something about the society.' What does it actually look like for people to really engage in current issues in our context?"[4]

To make the concepts more concrete, Linda has helped lead two major campaigns. The first was an initiative to encourage Mavuno congregants with maids ("house helps") to sign them up for Kenya's national health insurance program—and pay the premium. As part of the campaign,

Linda preached a series of messages on the realities of the city. She showed a short video clip of a maid giving birth in her home in the slums—without any medical help, since she lacked health care. "Basically," Linda says, "we were helping the congregation to understand, number one, that this is not God's will; number two, that we can make a difference, since it doesn't even cost that much; and number three, this is your obligation." Not many middle-class Kenyans provide health insurance for their house help. But Linda tells them, "Righteousness means you do things differently."

Linda also designed a campaign to develop greater understanding within the congregation on the hot-button issue of land policy in Kenya. "This, of course, was very pertinent in light of the post-election violence and all of the challenges that Kenya is currently undergoing about equitable distribution of resources," she says. In the months leading up to the Kenyan people's vote on a new constitution, Linda and other Christians knowledgeable about the social, economic and political implications of land policy wanted to provide straightforward education to church members regarding proposed land-policy reforms in the draft constitution. These reforms sought to address problems such as expropriation of community land for political purposes, inadequate practices of land titling and a lack of transparency and accountability within government agencies charged with authority over land disputes. Added to these issues were tensions arising from the fact that some ethnic groups in Kenya have been favored historically in terms of land distribution by prior regimes.

The land policy issue is very complicated and controversial—one that perhaps many church leaders would prefer to ignore. Mavuno's leaders believe it is a vital, relevant, contemporary area where a biblically informed justice perspective must be brought to bear. Linda and her colleagues organized a seven-week course on the issue for church leaders in the capital as well as in Eldoret and Kisumu—cities hit hard by the 2007 post-election violence.

SOCIAL JUSTICE WEEKEND TRANSFORMS AN INTERNATIONAL BUSINESSWOMAN

In addition to the special, church-wide educational campaigns, congregants at Mavuno learn about social issues through the Mizizi course's "social justice weekend." Frontline initiative leader Anne Nzilani reports that the weekend was what God used to open her eyes to the needs of the poor and move her away from materialism.

Anne began attending Mavuno Church in September 2007 at the urging of her sister. She kept hearing good reports about Mizizi, and enrolled in the class in January 2008. Before Mizizi, Anne admits, she was happily working as a business consultant with a simply stated goal: "My vision was to make a lot of money." The Mizizi course challenged that. She learned that "God is really real," and that he had other priorities. "I learned about how God expects me to manage my money, and about social justice."[5]

God used the social-justice weekend retreat with her Life Group to turn Anne's life upside down. The group visited a refugee camp for internally displaced persons. They played with the children, and some members presented a workshop on business skills for adult residents. Anne sat in on this and was amazed at the talents and resiliency of the women who participated. "I realized there were so many women in there who could weave, make jewelry or make different kinds of products," Anne says. The problem was that with limited market exposure, their hard work would not generate much income. "So I thought, I can sit here and cry, or I can choose to do something about it."

In April 2008, just a few weeks after her graduation from Mizizi, Anne registered a new fair trade company called Bawa la Tumaini ("Wing of Hope"). Its mission is to market and sell products from marginalized producers, giving them the opportunity to make money from global markets. Such income would then allow these women to climb out of destitution.

The company beautifully capitalizes on Anne's vocational background and skills. The daughter of parents in the export business, she is widely traveled and knowledgeable about international trade. Her educational background is in product design, and she has worked with both design firms and design universities in Europe. Through her business consulting, she has built significant professional networks in the Netherlands, Austria, Finland, Australia, Spain, Germany and the United Kingdom. She also has wide-ranging contacts in various regions of Kenya that produce jewelry, handicrafts and soapstone crafts.

Mavuno's teaching on social justice and Anne's experience of getting up close and personal with poverty have set this talented businesswoman on a new, purposeful course. "The memory verse for the social justice lesson in

Mizizi was Matthew 25:40," Anne says. "'Whatever you do to the least of these, you do to me.' That is my inspiration. At the end of the day, that's what keeps pushing me at Bawa la Tumaini."

LESSONS LEARNED

Mavuno Church's model provides several lessons for congregations that wish to encourage social entrepreneurs. First, Mizizi provides the foundational kingdom theology that effectively undergirds a missional commitment. Second, the course includes a section inviting participants to identify and explore the unique passions and gifts God has given them. Third, Mavuno Marathon exposes congregants to the needs of the poor in their city and to contemporary issues of injustice. Fourth, as church leaders challenge congregants to take risks and do great things for God's kingdom, they also recognize that church members with natural gifts for doing so are the ones who could suffer from pride. So, in addition to affirming these people's talents and supporting their efforts to serve society, Mavuno challenges them to learn *and to practice* servant leadership. Fifth, the church helps high-capacity leaders to remember the foundational value of community and accountability, and expects them to be part of a Life Group. Sixth, it grounds these social entrepreneurs in the practice of prayer—for themselves, their initiatives, their city and their nation. As Linda says of the Ombi course, when you've completed it, "you fully understand that there can be no genuine social transformation except that which happens through prayer." Finally, Mavuno's model holds people loosely. It empowers the laity and sets these talented people free to minister *outside* the four walls of the church.

At Mavuno, in God's wonderful providence, leaders have found that the church's facilitation of members using their gifts well can end up blessing *both* the world "out there" and the internal community life of the congregation. This reality is particularly clear in the case of Mavuno Church's first frontline initiative leader, musician Kanjii Mbugua.

A MUSIC BUSINESS FOR THE CHURCH AND SOCIETY

Kanjii Mbugua first met Muriithi when both were in schools in California. They discovered that they shared a similar complaint about the church: it so often seemed irrelevant to young, educated adults. The two would joke about how Kanjii could be Muriithi's worship leader once Muriithi was a church planter, designing a new kind of congregation.

That joke became real life in 2005.

Kanjii had moved back to Kenya in 2004 after completing his education at the Musicians Institute in Hollywood and the Dallas Sound Lab in Texas. He renewed his friendship with Muriithi, just as the latter was preparing to launch Mavuno Church with the blessing of Nairobi Chapel. Kanjii reports that Muriithi told him, "We've complained about many things about the church and this is an opportunity for us to correct those things." Kanjii adds, "The biggest thing that stood out for me was the opportunity to write the story of what this church was going to be about."[6]

Both men knew they wanted Mavuno's morning worship service to be dynamic, attractive and culturally relevant. Kanjii and his band assumed leadership for worship arts, helping craft worship services with energetic music that rivaled what Nairobi's "yuppies" enjoyed in local pubs. With Kanjii's musical talent and Muriithi's preaching prowess, the new congregation began to grow rapidly.

Meanwhile, the core group at the church, including Kanjii, was going through Mizizi. Even though Kanjii completely understood that Mavuno's mission was "to put people in a system that would actually bring them to that place where they would use their God-given gifts to impact society," the vocational stewardship "aha" moment had not quite happened for him personally. Through Mizizi, Kanjii realized he had not yet adequately connected Sunday to Monday in his own life.

> I was very good at shifting the worlds—saying I lead worship on Sunday but on Monday I do my music business. But then I started realizing . . . that God had an intention for my gift to impact the world. This was a huge revelation because I'd never thought about life in that way. I'd always thought, *Okay, fine—business. We'll make money and then give money to the church, you know, and everyone's happy.* But then I saw God was showing us at Mavuno that church was not a *Sunday* thing. Church was a *life* thing and the gift that he had given me, he had given me to impact society.

Kanjii and other professional musicians in his Life Group, who'd completed Mizizi and begun Ombi, started making changes to become men of greater integrity in the music industry. Kanjii says,

The school of prayer was amazing for us guys. We've just really been challenged in church about being men of integrity and honor. So we discussed that we wanted to do something really audacious. [We decided] to do forty days of prayer—meeting at the office every morning at 5:00 a.m. Basically we asked God to tell us how we become men of honor in our workplace and in our families. And we've just operated very differently from then on.

Kanjii kept serving as worship leader throughout his participation in the Mavuno Marathon. Meanwhile, he and his colleagues at Kijiji Records were seeking God as to how to turn their music business into a culture-shaping frontline initiative.[7] In a particularly dramatic prayer time while on a layover in a Swiss airport, Kanjii felt he received clear guidance from the Lord: "God was saying that the mission of Kijiji is to take that medium of the arts and entertainment and use it to glorify him, to use it to bring about a restoration of his righteousness, a restoration of his values and a restoration of his moral code 'on earth as it is in heaven.'"

Excited, Kanjii and his coworkers started fleshing out what this could look like strategically. First, they would seek actual ownership of media outlets, or "mindshare" ownership, by producing music and music videos with positive values that would dominate secular radio. Kanjii says, "In any given year there are about thirty songs in the Kenyan music industry that make it to heavy rotation status. We've launched a 'Clean the Airwaves' initiative, and our goal for it this year is to produce twenty-five of those songs."

Kijiji also has produced new television shows to air on mainstream Kenyan stations. One is a reality show mimicking *American Idol*; it's a gospel music competition with ten artists. The difference is that none will be "voted off the island," as Kanjii puts it. Rather, each contestant will perform her or his music and also, throughout the competition, craft some kind of community-serving initiative using that musical talent. TV watchers will judge the contestants based on the creativity and effectiveness of their social projects as well as their songs. There will be one winner selected at the end of the season. Throughout the fifty-two-week show, which airs on prime time, the contestants (all Christians) will gain followings, Kanjii says excitedly. These musicians have agreed to share their talents at Mavuno's Sunday services and at high-school outreaches led by Mavuno teams. Kanjii expects this to affect attendance at church and the high school events positively, as fans seize opportunities to hear their favorite stars.

Second, Kijiji aims to sponsor attractive events and concerts with excellent Christian musicians offering a positive moral message. His group has already hosted numerous events at public high schools throughout the country. Here again Kijiji's outreach to the community collides brilliantly with the edifying-the-saints ministry of the church itself.

In conjunction with Mavuno, Kijiji Records has also implemented a major Spread the Love event for both church and community members. The concert offers a positive, family-oriented social event and an opportunity to showcase Mavuno's social-justice concerns. The last Spread the Love event raised awareness about poor conditions in Nairobi's prisons and generated revenue for a church-wide effort to purchase beds for prisoners in a jail where several Life Groups have been reaching out to inmates. Moreover, local radio and TV outlets cover these events, thus providing more "advertising" for Mavuno Church and drawing even more curious seekers to the Sunday morning services.

Muriithi knows that all these outreaches are contributing to the numerical growth of Mavuno. With that growth comes greater opportunities to draw people into the Marathon and greater resources for the church to pay its bills and pursue its mission.

REPAINTING THE PICTURE OF THE CHURCH:
BOLSTERING CREDIBILITY

Ken Oloo, a professional photographer, is another of Mavuno's frontline initiative leaders. The incident that prompted his social enterprise serves as a helpful metaphor to understanding much of Mavuno's own purpose and vision for advancing vocational stewardship.

A few years ago on a visit to Kampala, Uganda, Ken was moved by the sight of a small boy, three or four years old, naked in the street. "The most amazing thing," Ken says, "was that no one seemed to notice. So I took a picture of that boy."[8] Afterward he showed the photograph to a friend. The woman was so touched by Ken's picture that she rushed home to find clothes for the child. When Ken saw the little boy again four hours later, he was cleaned up and in fresh clothes. This was a mystery to him until he spoke with his friend later that day and learned of her actions. "I began thinking," Ken says, "if one of my pictures can make someone do that, then I want to use photography to communicate what happens in slums."

Back in Kenya, Ken has launched the nonprofit Filamujuani ("Films in the Sun") to do just that. It trains teens living in Nairobi's Kibera slum in photography and videography. Kids aged nine to eighteen have learned "how to shoot, how to edit and how to produce video," Ken reports. One group of his students produced a short documentary about life in Kibera that won a film competition against some fifty other contestants. For Ken, the ministry's value lies in how it is empowering these youth to tell their story accurately, to show what they are, beyond the too-limited impression that outsiders typically have of them:

> Basically . . . we train kids in the slum on how to communicate ideas. I think God creates them with a voice. [What] we're doing with media is helping them find their voice, giving them a platform to communicate their experience and share their stories. Most of us outside Kibera, all we can see are the dark and the filth. They show us stories that have happy endings, stories of joy.

Telling a better, more accurate story is what Mavuno Church does through its efforts to equip members to deploy their gifts for societal transformation. Among many middle- and upper-class Kenyans, the church is held in low esteem. It's ignored as irrelevant or ridiculed as emotionally immature or despised as hypocritical.

The post-election violence in 2007, in which Kenyans from different ethnic groups were attacked even inside churches, "brought the perception of Christianity to an all-time low," Muriithi reports. "It's not very pleasant what people think of the church. In the post-election violence, the church really acted like everyone else. They took sides. Church leaders fronted political candidates, and so they basically played a part in destroying the society. And the people noticed that." As a result, Muriithi says, "I feel like right now we're fighting a battle for credibility."

By encouraging its congregants to become "fearless influencers of society," Mavuno is trying to repaint the picture of the church. Muriithi believes it is possible to change the perception, since the church was once held in higher esteem:

Ten years, fifteen years ago it was different. We were ruled by a dictatorship then. The church was the one body that had the guts to stand up. Church leaders were very courageous; church leaders in our nation spoke out at the risk of their lives. And some of them did lose their lives. So as a result, the church had high credibility as an institution.

Today Muriithi wants to see Mavuno Church completely transform its members' lives. "Our business is about raising an army that will bring reformation in our generation." The Mavuno Marathon cultivates the personal and social righteousness that believers need in order to live as the *tsaddiqim* who rejoice the city. Mavuno's discipleship is helping members, as Muriithi puts it, "to grow to the place where they have confidence, assurance and such a heart for the society that they begin to lead their peers into effective responses to our society's problems. As church members take up roles of leadership . . . people will begin to say, 'We want what you have.'

"That really is the best advertisement a church can have."

Pathway 4

PARTICIPATE IN YOUR CHURCH'S
TARGETED INITIATIVE

*God doesn't just rely on preachers and pastors to bring
change to this world; he uses people in every domain of society
with the skills and conviction needed to advance
the Great Commission.*

REV. BOB ROBERTS JR.

Can you image a congregation that targets a particular community for
long-term, deep investment and then "plugs in" marketplace professionals
for meaningful and strategic service? The church's architects and real estate developers partner with residents in the targeted community to build
affordable housing—because safe shelter is a foretaste of the kingdom. Its
doctors, nurses, dentists, counselors, pharmacists and medical students
dream up creative ways to serve the members of the target community who
are without health insurance—because wholeness is a foretaste of the
kingdom. Its accountants set up free clinics so that the working poor of the
neighborhood have an alternative to the exploitive tax preparation companies that charge them exorbitant fees for "instant refunds"—because justice is a foretaste of the kingdom. And the church's artists and musicians,
photographers and graphic designers, videographers and dancers collabo-
rate with artistically gifted individuals in the neighborhood to provide a
robust arts program for local kids—because beauty is a foretaste of the
kingdom.

Or envision a slightly different story, one of a church that doesn't pick a particular *place* for radical, long-term engagement, but rather, a specific *issue*. The congregation hones in on the need to provide loving homes for children in the foster-care system or affordable housing for low-income families. Imagine targeted focus on issues like these providing all kinds of practical ministry on-ramps for lawyers, social workers, counselors, real estate agents, construction workers, architects, psychologists, appraisers, carpenters, parent educators, medical doctors, interior designers, lobbyists, researchers, communications specialists, landscape architects—and many others—to ply their vocational talents.

All this sounds wonderful in theory, but it begs an obvious question: *Are any churches actually doing these sorts of things?* An honest answer is, well, not many. But there are some.

In Brooklyn, New York, for example, St. Paul Community Baptist Church has been at the center of the Nehemiah Housing initiative that has brought new, affordable homes to more than two thousand working families.[1] In Fort Lauderdale, Florida, Calvary Chapel has literally transformed the foster-care system through its efforts to mobilize and train many new foster and adoptive families in southern Florida.[2] So it is possible for a church to establish and execute a specific, sustained focus on a critical issue and make a measurable difference.

Moreover, in the Sandtown neighborhood of inner-city Baltimore, in the Lawndale and West Garfield neighborhoods of inner-city Chicago, in the Ravendale neighborhood of Detroit and the Summerhill neighborhood of south Atlanta—and dozens more places—congregations committed to deep, comprehensive, long-term community development have produced visible transformation.[3]

The notion that real-life churches actually rejoice their cities is not fiction.

In this chapter, we'll look in detail at two congregations—Southwood Presbyterian Church (PCA) in Huntsville, Alabama, and Crossroads in Cincinnati, Ohio—that are testing out, in the real world, kingdom-oriented transformational initiatives that involve vocational stewardship. One has targeted a specific neighborhood in its city; the other, a specific issue. Both have been at their labors for several years; neither is anywhere near finished. Their stories offer us much by way of inspiration and instruction.

The two churches are quite different. Southwood is traditional in many ways, a denominational church with an almost homogenous membership, in a relatively small city (population 180,000). Crossroads is anything but traditional. It's nondenominational, diverse and huge—with 12,000 attendees—and it's in a city of more than two million.

But the two have some things in common when it comes to mission. Both are externally focused. Both believe that a narrow and deep outreach ministry focus is far more effective than the mile-wide, inch-deep approach that characterizes many congregations. Each has committed to long-term investment. Additionally, at both Southwood and Crossroads, church leaders had to be captured by the missional call of the gospel of the kingdom before they could launch into their impressive initiatives. And leaders and congregants at both congregations had to experience punched-in-the-guts compassion. At both churches, attention to mobilizing congregants for service according to their specific skill sets and passions has evolved over time.

Let's take a closer look at their stories.

SOUTHWOOD PCA AND LINCOLN VILLAGE MINISTRIES

Southwood's journey into robust, holistic community development ministry in its city began with painful repentance. Roughly three years into his pastorate, Mike Honeycutt became convicted that Southwood had "become a church very much inward-focused . . . and not really reaching our community very well."[4] Through much prayer and a personal retreat, Honeycutt came to see that the congregation had "lost zeal for the Great Commission." It was devastating to see that he'd failed in his leadership in this way, but he was convinced that God shows his shepherds these painful truths not to condemn them but to change them.

Returning from his retreat, Honeycutt gathered his vision committee to begin the long, hard process of helping the church change course. He took the group outside to look at Southwood's sign, where he pointed out that it didn't provide information for passersby about when the church met for services. He told them, "This is what we've done by facing inward: we've stuck our rear end out to the community."

Honeycutt began preaching on Acts, trying to place the vision of a more missional, externally focused church before his parishioners. "Rather than living primarily for ourselves," he told his flock, "we must begin to identify ourselves, by word and deed, as servants of our community."[5]

While a majority of the congregation embraced the new message, there were detractors. A few worried that the turn meant Honeycutt had bought into liberal, "social gospel" theology. Others simply didn't like change. And still others didn't like Honeycutt's leadership and saw this transitional time as an opportunity to voice their displeasure. When all was said and done, forty-five to fifty people, including a few elders, left Southwood. But many of the church's leaders "immediately came on board, wanting to get started." And many new people joined, wanting to be part of a church with an externally focused vision.

Shortly into the new journey, Honeycutt recruited Mark Stearns—a longtime Southwood member with a decade of experience working among the poor through a local ministry called Harvest—to be the church's director of Mercy Ministries. Mike Stanfield, a good friend of Mark's and an elder at Southwood at that time—recalls telling his fellow elders, "If you're hiring him to sit in an office, you're wasting your time. You've got to turn him loose and let him get out into the community."[6]

That's just what Honeycutt did.

Mark began exploring Lincoln Village, an old mill community of cramped houses in poor condition that bore all the visible signs of poverty and despair, that is an eight-minute drive from Southwood. He had driven by this neighborhood daily when he was working with Harvest. He recalls feeling a tug to enter the community to learn more about its residents. During one visit, Mark was invited into a home. Its decayed condition overwhelmed him. "I remember there was a little girl there, sitting on the floor. Everything she slept [among] was around her. I noticed [bugs] on the walls and holes in the floor, and my first thought was, 'Oh my God. I cannot believe this child is living in a situation like this.'"[7]

In an effort to begin connecting Southwood to the community, one day in 2002 Mark walked into the principal's office at the Lincoln Elementary School and introduced himself to Principal Christy Jensen. He asked her what needs the school had that the church might assist with. Taken aback—and somewhat skeptical—Jensen put Mark off politely, telling him she would think about that. He returned a few days later and repeated the query. Nonplussed, Jensen asked him to wait a moment and stepped out to consult with her secretary. She couldn't believe Mark had returned, and she didn't know quite what to do with him. The secretary mentioned that some teachers had been complaining about the wretched condition of the school's overhead projectors and suggested that Jensen ask Mark if the church could assist with that. So she proposed this to Mark.

A few days later, five projectors arrived. "I'd wondered," Jensen says, "whether this guy was for real. I didn't know if I'd ever see him again."[8] With the credibility of five overhead projectors behind him, Mark returned to the school, and told Jensen about his desire to see Southwood Church partner meaningfully with the community. She then took him on a tour of the school, sharing her passion for its students and educating Mark on the uphill battle they faced. Almost 95 percent of the students were from low-income families. Many children were being raised in single-parent homes or by their grandmothers. Together Mark and Jensen began dreaming of what a partnership between the school and the church could become.

Mark knew it would be a stretch getting Southwood's congregants engaged hands-on in the distressed Lincoln neighborhood. He knew he'd need support from the pulpit. So he took Honeycutt on a home visit to one of the families from Lincoln. The house "reminded me of something from a Third World country," Mark recalls, noting that the plumbing was broken and the stench was awful. A few minutes into the visit, it became clear to Mark that the odor bothered Honeycutt. "I remember praying that he would suffer," Marks says with a chuckle. Honeycutt says, "I was just overwhelmed by the fact that six miles north of our nice middle/upper-middle class suburb where our church is we've got incredible poverty, as bad as anything you'd see in the Appalachian Mountains."

After they concluded the visit and walked outside, Honeycutt turned to Mark and declared, "This is where the kingdom of God needs to be."[9]

THE "BEFORE" PICTURE

The challenges ahead were great. While Huntsville's poverty rate was 12.8 percent citywide, in Lincoln Village it was more than 57 percent. Signs of drug use and crime were clearly visible. According to 2000 U.S. Census data, the number of adults in Lincoln Village with a high school diploma was 47 percent. Three-quarters of residents rented their homes, and more than 40 percent of those rentals were in neglected condition, some lacking working plumbing or kitchen facilities. "It was really run-down housing," remembers Liz Clemons, longtime director of the local Boys and Girls Club.[10] Close to half of the houses were defined by the census as unaffordable—that is, rent consumed more than 33 percent of a renter's annual income.

Meanwhile, at Lincoln Elementary, 96 percent of students were enrolled in the free lunch program, showing the wide extent of poverty. Reading scores on the standardized Stanford Achievement Test (SAT10) were in the twentieth or thirtieth percentiles.[11] The writing scores were in the red zone, well below state standards. The prevalent belief among most teachers was that the curriculum had to be "watered down" for high-poverty students.[12]

MOBILIZED AS A "DRINK OFFERING"

After Honeycutt's first visit to Lincoln Village, he and Mark met with the vision committee and then all the church's officers to share their thoughts about targeting Lincoln Village for significant investment. Shortly afterward, Honeycutt challenged Southwood's members from the pulpit to be "poured out like a drink offering" for this community.[13] The following week, Honeycutt invited Mark to preach, asking him to inform the congregation about the needs there.

"I had taken a lot of pictures," Mark recalls. "I had them blown up and I stood up [by them]. And for the next two or three months I would speak in a Sunday school class or preach about our responsibility and what God has called us to be about."[14] He told fellow congregants that the Lincoln Village community, though distressed, had been "made in God's image and had value."

Church leaders began strategizing about how to address the Lincoln Village community holistically—its spiritual, emotional, physical and educational needs. "We set goals and objectives, and we had to decide how we would implement those goals," Mark recalls. "We really had to sit down at first and say, 'How will we attack [the problems]?'"

From the outset, three things were clear. First, Honeycutt says,

> When we started in Lincoln Village, Mark and I both knew that we would
> need to make a long-term commitment to the community. Not only did we

understand that the work would be slow and would require years of service, but we also were aware of some of the cynicism/skepticism that is often present in communities like this where ministries come and go, never staying long enough to really become part of that community.

Shari Henry Jones, who worked at Southwood as assistant Mercy Ministries director in the early years of its involvement with Lincoln Village, remembers, "We really thought we needed to stick with it for a generation."[15]

Second, relationships and holistic ministry would have to be the hallmarks of the ministry. "We are working to reach the whole person," Jones told a local newspaper reporter in 2005, and then added, "We are really focusing on relationships here. We want our volunteers to not only put in hours here, but to really get to know the kids and the families. They have a lot to offer us."[16]

Third, other churches had to be invited into the process. Mark explains: "Early on I said, 'We will never plant our flag [in Lincoln Village]—ever.' Because that [would] push away other people. It would say we are territorial, and we are not territorial at all. We need the whole body of Christ to do what needs to be done."

At Southwood, Mark emphasized to the large fellowship that "everybody had the responsibility of being part of the solution to the problems in the community." Although he never used the term "vocational stewardship," recruiting people according to their skill sets and passions was on Mark's radar screen from the beginning.

I talked about every area [of need] I saw—because I was walking the streets and spending time with the families. So I knew that there were medical problems, that we needed doctors [and] dentists. [We needed] lawyers to represent these women being battered by their husbands. We needed people who knew something about real estate. [We needed] teachers who were retired who wanted to come back. . . . When I'm talking to people, I ask, 'What is your passion? What has God gifted you at?' And we try to plant them down in an area they can flourish in.

"Mark would ask people that wanted to help, 'What are you good at? What do you like to do?'" Honeycutt remembers.

For his part, Honeycutt worked to "help people get over the sacred/secular split."

One of the things that I began to do was, in a general way, push very intentionally the idea of vocation and calling, and recognizing that all these
[secular] callings are valid before the Lord. . . . Every ability and gift that
they had could be used to glorify God. . . . People started seeing that [their
skills] were valuable not only at work but also [could] be used for specific
missions in a project like Lincoln Village.

Congregational response was tremendous. By 2005, Jones reported that
half or more of the flock had been involved in some way in Lincoln
Village.[17]

ADOPTING LINCOLN ELEMENTARY SCHOOL

Initial efforts focused on Lincoln Elementary. Southwood began recruiting tutors, and Mark began visiting pastors from a variety of churches,
inviting their participation. Together with other congregations, the newly
named Lincoln Village Ministry refurbished the school's library with a
state-of-the-art computer lab and scores of new books. It renovated an old
greenhouse attached to the school to enable Lincoln students to take hor-
ticulture classes.

In the school's old, disused gymnasium, the ministry built a giant science lab, complete with a terrarium and a salt-water aquarium. Most im-
pressively, its two-thousand-square-foot black-painted ceiling boasted
huge hanging replicas of the planets. Frank Six, an astrophysicist at
NASA's Marshall Space Flight Center in Huntsville, got involved early on
in the science lab project after hearing Mark explain his vision to get the
kids dreaming. "That got me going," Frank says.[18]

"My role," Frank says, was in asking, 'What can NASA do to help?'"
He learned from teachers at Lincoln that furniture, equipment and attractive visuals were needed. "I found that NASA transfers surplus equipment
to a government warehouse." There Frank was able to find tables, chairs
and a mobile platform.

Then Frank recruited Marshall's graphics arts group to help. He spoke
with the manager, Janice Robinson: "I said, 'Janice, you have *got* to see what
is going on at Lincoln Village.'" Frank drove Janice out there one day at
lunchtime, and one of the Lincoln Village Ministry staff gave her a briefing
on what they were doing. She got quite excited. "So I told her, 'I am going
to need some help here.' And she said, 'You just tell me what you need.'"

The graphic designers "did their wizardry with their computers," Frank says, and found all kinds of images. "Then they let me come over and pick out the ones that were fitting for biology, astronomy, physics, chemistry and so forth," he says. "I picked out three-dozen or so of those, and they made posters of them, and I took them over to the teacher, and we hung them around the walls."

These material aids were not the most important expressions of the ministry's core values. The best gift to the school was caring adults. Church members began volunteering as room mothers and field trip chaperones. Over time, more than half of Lincoln's 212 students were enjoying personal, one-on-one mentor/tutoring, thanks to volunteers from Southwood and other congregations.

The people investment began to pay off. Melinda Clark, curriculum specialist at Lincoln Elementary reports, "Since Southwood and the other churches have come on board, just the presence of the mentors and the volunteers and having the kids matched with those mentors . . . has brought lots of love into the building, lots of excitement into the building."[19]

The excitement spilled out into the community as well. Church volunteers slowly forged relationships with students' parents. After the first two years of Lincoln Village Ministry's involvement, a thrilled Principal Jensen reported that attendance at the PTA meetings had skyrocketed from about a half a dozen to more than one hundred. "We pack out the place usually. And I think that part of that is that [the tutors] have helped the parents see the importance of parent involvement."[20]

Educators from Southwood have played key roles at Lincoln Elementary. Margaret Powell trained as an English teacher, and before she had kids, taught in a middle school. When she and her husband began raising their family, she decided to homeschool. That kept her busy over the next eighteen years. Along the way, she longed for the opportunity to serve other, more needy children. Her mom reassured her that "this season would come," Margaret says.[21]

When Margaret's daughter hit her teen years, the two of them began tutoring children together at Lincoln Elementary once a week. When her daughter entered public high school, Margaret found she had additional time available. She joined Lincoln Village Ministry's after-school program, called The Linc, and volunteered at the school in its Camp Success tutoring program. When Lincoln Elementary had to shut that program down, Margaret continued to show up at the school, helping anywhere she could.

For a while, Margaret served as an assistant in the science lab. Then she had an opportunity to do what she loves best: work one-on-one with a child struggling to learn to read. Eventually, the school asked her if she'd be willing to get her certification as a substitute teacher (which she did) and then invited her to serve as an intervention specialist. "Basically it means I'm to intervene with kids who are continuing to fall behind despite the best efforts in the classroom," she explains.

For the next few years, Margaret volunteered at Lincoln Elementary for twenty hours per week, working with small groups of children on reading and math. While that level of investment may sound burdensome, Margaret describes it as a joy:

> What I'm doing now is the fulfillment of something I've always known God was calling me to. Earlier, when I asked him about it, I felt he was saying, 'Yes—but not now.' By giving me the privilege of teaching my own children, I knew God was going to use the things I was learning to help me teach children who did not have the opportunities that my children had. So working at Lincoln Elementary is an answer to a vision I have had for a long time. The work is fulfilling, not because I once thought I'd be "good" at it . . . but because I beg God every day to help me finish the work he's prepared me to do.

Margaret serves in her vocational sweet spot, and she says that helps explain why she's been able to sustain her high level of commitment. "I don't know," she says, "God just wired me to be a teacher. Not so much on a grand scale, but more of a one-on-one. . . . This is something I've always dreamed of doing."

Relationships with the kids and families informed church volunteers of significant unmet physical needs. So Southwood and other churches banded together to establish a food and clothing pantry, providing such basics as coats, shoes and meals. Such services are a huge help to the school, Principal Jensen explains. "For teachers to be able to teach and the child to learn, you have to meet basic needs. Lincoln Village Ministry has helped us address our students' fundamental needs—medical, clothing, food, dental, vision and more. If there is a need, they will find a professional who will willingly give the services for free."[22]

LEGAL ADVOCACY

As Mark Stearns got to know neighborhood families, one critical need that surfaced was for legal services. He turned to Derek Simpson from Southwood, who had been primed to respond positively—both because of his longstanding friendship with Mark and because he was familiar with the challenges faced by the poor. Just after graduating from law school at the University of Alabama, Derek had worked many cases for indigent court-appointed clients.

Derek reports that he remembers well the Sunday several years ago when Mark posted huge, blown-up photographs from Lincoln Village in the sanctuary and preached a powerful word about the congregation's need to respond. Derek immediately agreed to be part of a committee to work toward establishing the new ministry and then provided the legal counsel needed to shepherd Mark through the process of incorporating Lincoln Village Ministries as a nonprofit. But Derek says his real "aha" moment in terms of vocational stewardship didn't come until that first time Mark called him asking legal advice on behalf of a resident he'd befriended in Lincoln Village. Derek explains,

> I remember all these friends of mine that were doctors and would go on these mission trips, and how great they thought it was that they could use their skills. I would think, *How in the world [can] a lawyer go into the mission field?* That was really a challenge. How can we *all* advance the kingdom of God in our different professions? I didn't really know if I could or not. But Mark called me, and he asked me a question about somebody who was in the Village. I told him to have them call me and I could help them. Then it just grew from there. I thought, *Oh my gosh, this is just a whole other opportunity to help.*[23]

Over time, Derek has been able to assist about twenty Lincoln Village residents. "What they think is a huge problem is often a small problem that can be taken care of very quickly," he says. "They might get a ticket, and then a 'failure to appear.' And it just keeps growing and growing, and then they run from the law. And what I can do is bring them in, and we can take care of everything all at once."[24]

"There is so much joy out of letting people know, 'Hey, these problems are taken care of,'" Derek says.[25] He has helped people get their driver's licenses renewed, clear up back fines or get into subsidized housing when their applications were initially denied. He has also helped a woman in a domestic violence situation to secure a protection order and has assisted single moms in obtaining child support.

Derek recalls with a laugh the year he served Southwood as a second-grade Sunday school teacher. "I just dreaded it—I had no joy!" Contrasting this with his current role, he says that he "gets a ton of joy" out of serving as a lawyer: "God blessed me and enabled me to be a lawyer. And it's almost like . . . you learn certain things and you can speak a certain language, and the people you're helping don't speak that language. . . . Just by the grace of God, I can speak the language that they need."[26]

IMPROVING HOUSING CONDITIONS

About six months into Southwood's new partnership with Lincoln Elementary, Mark took his friend Mike Stanfield on a home visit in Lincoln Village. "We met a family that was living in a two-room hovel with no electricity or running water," Stanfield remembers. Mark said to him, "We're trying to reach these kids in school, but this is what they're coming home to. So we're having a hard time helping them."

Mike's heart was captured. "I'm thankful for the blessings I have," he says, "and that increases my feeling of responsibility to give back." He was ready to serve.

When asked why Mark came to him to lead a new housing initiative, Mike, an engineer with a long history of leadership in the church, replied that it was probably a combination of his strong friendship with Mark and the skills he could bring to the table for such an effort. "I'm a pretty good strategist," Mike says, "organizing, setting goals and laying out a plan on how to accomplish those goals." He adds quickly,

> I'm the first to recognize that I'm *not* good at a lot of stuff. So the board that I recruited includes a real estate developer. It includes a lawyer who handles all our legal aspects. It includes a man who owns a construction company, so he handles all our construction issues for us. So I guess that's a skill set I have: to see what's needed and then to pull it all together to make something happen.

Stanfield and his team established the Lincoln Village Preservation Corporation (LVPC) in May 2003 with the mission of purchasing homes in the Village, refurbishing them with volunteer labor and assisting renters in becoming homeowners. To date, LVPC has purchased forty-two housing units and provided new or renovated homes for twenty-eight grateful families. Given LVPC's relative youth, Michelle Jordon, head of Huntsville's Department of Community Development, says, "Those are very impressive statistics."[29]

Residents see the difference LVPC is making in the community. As one said simply, "I've seen a lot of changes. The houses are looking better, the yards are."[27] Liz Clemons from the local Boys & Girls Club agrees: "Words cannot describe how they've lifted up this community. They've come in with a group of people and rebuilt the community. . . . The improvements that they've made in the Lincoln Village area are phenomenal."[28]

Several real estate professionals from Southwood have donated their skills to the LVPC. Mickey Plott, a forty-five-year-old real estate broker who owns his own company, has been completing property appraisals for LVPC since its inception. This is the first time he has been able to use his professional skills to benefit a nonprofit ministry. He recently spent a week completing appraisals on several homes in Lincoln Village.

Due to stringent bank regulations, Mickey is not allowed to offer his services for free. However, he charges one hundred dollars for each appraisal, instead of his normal four-hundred-dollar fee. He has also been able to help The Village Church, the church plant Southwood started in Lincoln Village a few years ago. Through his company, Mickey purchased a property that included two portable classrooms. These he donated to the new church to use as Sunday school space.

Mickey says, "I want to help people," and he loves how he's getting to use his skills for the ministry. "I've never been a real hands-on type person; I'm no good with a hammer," he says, laughing. But he can bring his real estate expertise to the table. Mickey was able recently to negotiate with a bank on LVPC's behalf so it would not have to complete appraisals on every property in a group of similar ones that had been refurbished. This has "really helped to keep their costs down," he reports.[30]

For Sam Yeager, a commercial real estate developer from Southwood, involvement with Lincoln Village Ministry gives him an opportunity to do two things he loves: come alongside frontline ministry leaders as an encouraging friend and business counselor, and ply his gift for "doing deals." He likes to say his biggest contribution is just "being Mark's helper, more than anything."[31] But the "soft skills" Sam has honed over many years in the world of commercial real estate development have also helped LVPC:

> What I do here is put deals together. I raise money for things and help put partnerships together. And I keep people together, and we work out problems and issues, and we think about what it takes to get something done and who you need. That's my biggest vocation . . . and that's what I bring to this [endeavor]. In the world of debt and budgets and raising funds—that's where I bring my expertise.[32]

Sam's knowledge of navigating the zoning permits process and his relationship with the City of Huntsville have also been a big boon to LVPC.

A FORETASTE OF HEALTH AND WHOLENESS

Medical professionals from Southwood have also been part of Lincoln Village Ministry's multifaceted work in the community. Physician Brian Cost, pediatrician Eloise Alexander and dentists Brian Beitel and Al Willis have all donated free care to kids and adults in need in the neighborhood. For several years, Alexander volunteered significant hours at the HEALS clinic at Lincoln Elementary. (HEALS is a local nonprofit aimed at providing health care to the city's poor; it sponsors clinics in several locations in the city.) Ray Saunders, a social worker at the HEALS clinic at Lincoln Elementary, reports that "Southwood . . . has made a tremendous difference in providing services that we at HEALS could not provide for the families that we serve."[33]

THE "AFTER" PICTURE

Southwood's work in Lincoln Village—and that of the many other congregations involved in Lincoln Village Ministry—is not finished. But after seven years of strategic and compassionate investment, real change has unfolded. With LVPC's efforts in the housing arena, the neighborhood's appearance, at least in the vicinity immediately adjacent to the school, has visibly transformed. "It's night and day," Mark says. "It's peaceful, quiet. You see kids playing together. You see neighbors talking to each other." He reports that there is no longer the same drug traffic as once characterized these streets.

"When people drive through here, they see that this place has been cleaned up," he says. When an unfamiliar vehicle enters, [residents] notice it—and they watch the driver turn around and leave, looking for a more dilapidated area to "get hooked up." Mark sums it up: "The community is more neighborly, hopeful, safe. It feels like it's going in a different direction." At the same time, he emphasizes that there is still a long way to go. "I can go two blocks from here and it's just a completely different story."

Underneath the easily visible external improvements is a current of new hope—hope that arises when people find that they are not alone, that someone cares about them and is *for* them. Dale Bowen from LVPC says,

> So much hope has come into the school. I think that translates back into the neighborhoods we haven't been able [yet] to touch housing-wise, because those kids are getting medical, dental, food, clothing. The Boys & Girls Club is in our vicinity. They have so much hope now compared to ten years ago, because they have an influx of people coming to assist them and come alongside of them.[34]

The single most impressive transformation, however, was acknowledged in 2010 when Lincoln Elementary was selected as one of the winners in the Panasonic National School Change Awards competition, which honors six schools nationwide that have significantly changed for the better.

At the end of the 2003 school year, Lincoln's fourth-graders scored 63 percent proficiency in reading and 60 percent proficiency in math on the Alabama Reading and Math Test (ARMT). By the end of 2005, this had improved to 86 percent proficiency in reading and 100 percent proficiency in math.[35] The next school year, 2006-2007, Lincoln Elementary was named a "Torchbearer School" by the State Department of Education, in recognition of the achievement and progress of all students.[36]

Faculty and administrators at the school give Lincoln Village Ministry much of the credit for the amazing transformation. Fifth-grade teacher Joy Downing says,

> If Lincoln Village Ministry wasn't involved here, we would feel the pressure of having to meet the basic needs of our students. I taught in Title 1 schools in Georgia, and it was difficult. It's hard to reach them academically when you're concentrating on reaching them emotionally. Here the ministry volunteers work with our children, encourage them, show them love.[37]

Principal Jensen sums it up simply: "I believe LVM was a godsend to us and to this community. Our success would not have happened without lots and lots of support and compassion for these children."[38]

CROSSROADS AND THE JUSTICE MISSION

At Crossroads in Cincinnati, the central focus of the church's inch-wide, mile-deep outreach is not on a particular neighborhood, but on a pressing cause: promoting justice in the face of the evil of international sex trafficking.

Given the vast resources Crossroads seeks to deploy into this justice mission, it has had to discipline itself to avoid diffusing its outreach efforts. "From the very beginning [of Crossroads], we tried to exalt the word *no*," says Pastor Brian Tome.[39]

> There's a lot of good ideas out there, there's a lot that God is calling to, but there's very few things that God is calling *us* to. And so to do that you've got to say no to a lot of good things. If you don't, you're going to have a default to having fifty or sixty things that you support for fifty dollars a month, or if you're a smaller church, thirty things that you support at twenty-five dollars a month. And that kind of stuff we saw from the very beginning as just not very effective. So we want to do very few things very well.

One thing Crossroads desires to do very well is promote justice for victims of sex trafficking domestically and in India through a strategic partnership with International Justice Mission (IJM). Crossroads's journey on the justice mission began in 2005, primarily through former teaching pastor Brian Wells's encounter with Gary Haugen's writings (Haugen is the founder of IJM). "Reading *Good News About Injustice* really challenged me," Wells says. He'd digest Haugen's interpretation of a text, then check the verses in his Bible. "I'd read it in context and I'd be like, 'That point he's making—it's exactly right!'" Wells recalls. "How come I've never stopped and really read that before?"[40]

"It really messed with me," he says. "I came back from that experience and met with some of our leaders at Crossroads. And I said, 'You know, I just want to confess, I've been preaching an incomplete gospel.'"

Crossroads leadership felt God was saying something to the church through Wells. When he indicated a desire to meet with Haugen in Washington, they sent him off with a twenty-five-thousand dollar check to

IJM. "I told Gary personally, 'I believe you are a prophet. You've given the church a word that we need to hear,'" Wells says. "'Now how can we help without getting in the way?'"

Crossroads's journey on its justice mission had begun. It took them first to Sri Lanka, where it sent a team of researchers, lawyers and business-people because IJM was considering establishing a new field office. The team completed a comprehensive briefing over seven months, but IJM's plans were stymied when civil war broke out in the country. Undaunted, the Crossroads team continued dialogue with IJM. Together, they concluded that the church's efforts should focus on victim aftercare. "IJM had developed significant success criteria on the legal and interventions fronts, but there needed to be more attention and a lot more resources put toward aftercare," Wells says.

Since 2006, Crossroads has invested more than half a million dollars helping IJM's various aftercare partners to provide high-quality residential counseling and vocational rehabilitation for children and women rescued from sex trafficking in Mumbai. More than one hundred volunteers from Crossroads have gone onsite, doing everything from painting murals and making repairs at the facilities to researching gaps in the aftercare system to leading photography workshops with teens rescued from brothels.

Predictably, some in the church began wondering whether there were human trafficking issues in Cincinnati that the church should also be addressing. Christine Buchholz, the first justice director at Crossroads, began attending meetings of the local Rescue and Restore Coalition, called End Slavery Cincinnati. The relationship grew deep, and eventually Crossroads partnered with End Slavery Cincinnati on the first major study on human trafficking awareness in the city. More than twenty-five volunteers from Crossroads, led by attorney Deborah Leydon, conducted research and interviews to assess both the extent of the trafficking problem regionally and the adequacy of existing laws addressing it.

Deborah had been part of the Crossroads team that wrote the Sri Lanka briefing for IJM. She hadn't been aware of the extent of sex trafficking until she read *Good News About Injustice*. Family circumstances prevented her personal involvement in Crossroads's Mumbai work, but she responded eagerly to the opportunity to help End Slavery Cincinnati.

Deborah not only drew on her own talents as a lawyer but also leveraged her institutional assets. As a partner at Dinsmore & Shohl LLP she
was able to designate pro bono hours to the work and engage a number of
the firm's paralegals in the effort. Today Deborah continues to contem-
plate how to leverage her position for the church's justice work: "Our firm
keeps getting bigger and I keep thinking, *I should stay here and take advantage of the resources I have.* I mean, certainly with my staff and other attorneys and paralegals and others who are interested in these kinds of topics
as well. You know, we're standing by ready to help."[41]

MOBILIZING BY SKILL SET AND PASSION

With Crossroads's dual focus on the massive aftercare needs in India and
local work with End Slavery Cincinnati, staff were concerned that congregants could become paralyzed by the bigness and complexity of this
issue. So they began implementing a structure to mobilize volunteers. Andrew Peters, who took over as justice director from Christine Buchholz in
2009, says,

> We've basically created four "buckets," and they are the main ways that
> we've identified that the Lord has gifted people for engagement. And so
> we have a research bucket, a planning bucket, a prayer bucket and a com-
> munications bucket. I'm using the term *buckets*, but we don't talk about
> that publicly. What we say to folks is, "You know what? It's not like you
> have to make a decision between the girl being raped on the side of the
> street [in Cincinnati] or the girl being raped overseas. It's how do *you*
> uniquely engage?[42]

So, Andrew explains, an artist would likely be assigned to the communications bucket, since "all of our initiatives at some point and time are going
to have needs [to] communicate the reality of God's heart for justice creatively and with excellence." Parishioners from professions in which research is required are assigned to the research team. They might write a
fact sheet on bonded labor in India for a small-group leader to use in educating his fellowship. Or a Crossroads small-group leader might request a
speaker from the communication team to give a presentation to her group
about the situation in India or locally. The presentation might involve
multimedia, so the "communications bucket" members with graphic design, PowerPoint or videography skills might also contribute. "It's really

practical engagement that's right in people's sweet spot," Andrews says, "but it's around justice."

Crossroads member Mark Pruden, a mental health counselor, contributes his skills by conducting a formal orientation for participants in the emotionally intensive short-term trips to the aftercare homes in Mumbai. Mark also makes himself available for post-trip debriefings or small-group or individual therapy. Sometimes people—especially those with abuse in their own backgrounds—need help processing their experience in India, as it can trigger painful memories.[43]

Jamie Elkins, a 2006 political science graduate from Miami University in Ohio, is employing her talents onsite in Mumbai as a full-time intern with the IJM field office. Previously a paralegal with an immigration law firm, Jamie was first involved with Crossroads's justice work on the communications team. Now she's deploying her administrative, organizational and writing skills on behalf of the community relations team at IJM-Mumbai. She is helping to write a curriculum for local churches to aid pastors in educating their members about injustice. She's also assisted with the implementation of three educational conferences for Indian church leaders, focused on teaching them how to fruitfully engage their congregants.[44]

David Masys, a corporate salesman whose "personality, disposition and skill set" render him an effective communicator who can quickly establish rapport with a wide variety of people, serves by leading the communications team.[45] One of its recent projects was traveling to Mumbai and putting on a fun, relaxing and meaningful retreat for the IJM field staff. "Normally the [local] administrative staff has to handle all the details of the retreat," explains Don Gerred, former head of IJM-Kolkata. "This time they didn't have to work. They were able to rest, and that's a big deal. People in these offices need to be able to decompress."[46]

Linda Averbeck, a tax lawyer who heads up the research bucket, has about thirty-five Crossroads members from a variety of professions she can draw on (counselors, attorneys, business leaders, social workers and a prosecutor). The team has written a manual for leaders of future short-term trips to India. Now they're musing about a new local project. "A lot of people at the church want to work on the local [problem] of trafficking because they know it happens here in Cincinnati like it happens everywhere," Linda says.[47]

Nonprofits like End Slavery Cincinnati are already doing the important work of educating police officers and first responders (such as paramedics and emergency room staff) on the issues. Consequently, members of Linda's team see a potential role for Crossroads to "focus on the people who are vulnerable to being trafficked," she says. The idea is to partner with nonprofits that work with individuals, such as immigrants or runaways, to identify risk factors and perhaps do preventive education with potential victims.[48]

The justice team's lay mobilization efforts are being further honed and strengthened now with the addition of a talented engineer, Roberta Teran, who is providing leadership and a significant amount of time to oversee the four buckets. At her day job, Roberta manages global logistics and projects for Procter and Gamble. Her involvement with the justice work at Crossroads began three years ago when she led the church's first team trip to Mumbai. Her management skills and international experience well suited her to this role, where she coordinated people and timelines and troubleshot problems.

Under Roberta's leadership, Crossroads has established a clear pathway for engagement for parishioners wishing to join the justice work. The communications team has now designed regular informational meetings and briefings for congregants who want to learn the basics about the church's work in India. On Crossroads's website, interested parties can get information about the work and the four buckets, as well as complete a skills inventory. A spreadsheet documenting the skills of each potential volunteer is then produced.

Roberta agrees that vocational stewardship is a critical strategy for effectively deploying Crossroads's pool of talent and achieving the aims of the justice team:

> We track people based on what they say their unique skills are. So, for example, if someone says, "I am a nurse," we would say, "Okay, we want to do a [small-team] trip to India, and we want it to be medically based." [Another] example would be, we want to do an art-therapy class for the girls in India, or a nutrition class. We would go through that spreadsheet and see who was interested in that.[49]

In February 2010, the justice team sent a "SWAT" team to Mumbai. "That involved a series of workshops [at the aftercare homes]," Roberta says. "One of them involved health and hygiene. Several people [on] that work team had experience in health care; one was a nurse." Crossroads had had good experience with SWAT trips, which gather a small group of professionals from the same occupation for a short overseas trip to accomplish particular objectives.

At one point, Crossroads sent huge, diverse teams to Mamelodi, South Africa. But then South Africa missions director Rob Seddon came to see that the church would accomplish more by recruiting people by their professional talents and deploying them in smaller groups. The church began sending teams of musicians to work with schoolchildren; teams of business experts to help Africans with job training and entrepreneurial start-ups; and teams of educators to come alongside African teachers in Mamelodi.[50] The church's justice team has imitated this approach and plans to use more of these SWAT teams in the future. The next one in the pipeline is a short-term trip for police officers from Crossroads. The goal is to match this team with IJM's in-country investigators to share ideas and best practices through training sessions.

There will be continued focus also on putting individual congregants into roles best suited to their expertise, Roberta says. For example, one Crossroads justice volunteer indicated on her skills assessment that she was good at marketing. So this woman was matched with I-Sanctuary, a nonprofit that partners with aftercare homes in Mumbai to sell jewelry that rescued girls make. In another instance, a woman from Crossroads asked Roberta, "I am an administrator at work and I love it. Can I be an administrator for some work with [the] justice [team]?" There was indeed a need for this—and this volunteer has removed a considerable part of the paperwork load from Roberta and from Don Gerred.

"We've just got to figure out how to get more people involved with meaningful work and accountability, to feel like they're doing something valuable," Roberta says. "For me, the whole piece [is] around getting people linked in with their skills to the justice [ministry] to enable the overall vision."

LESSONS LEARNED FROM SOUTHWOOD AND CROSSROADS

Though neither the leaders of Southwood nor those of Crossroads would ever claim to have figured everything out, and though the missional journey of both churches is still young, their stories are instructional as well as inspirational. Let's look at several lessons they've learned.

First, leaders at both churches recognize the importance of preaching and leading with an emphasis on the kingdom—on the church's external focus for mission in the community and the world. Crossroads's lead pastor, Brian Tome, says,

> I view the weekend experience and the teaching not just as knowledge dissemination but really as a rallying cry inside of a locker room. . . . So it's a major shift from coming into a classroom model, or coming into a stage performance model, or coming into a "Shekinah-glory-room" model or something. I look at it as people coming into a locker room where they should be reclarified about what their mission is and have a sense of energy going back out.

Southwood's former pastor, Mike Honeycutt, says, "As we brought specific change initiatives to the congregation, we rooted them in the overarching vision of becoming a *missional* church. We also tried to state the vision in a way that is easily understood and difficult to forget." He came up with simple, short phrases to describe the heartbeat of the church's vision: "discipleship that faces outward" or "discipleship that faces the world." He says, "That statement did two things: it addressed congregational concern that we were abandoning our calling to build up the body of Christ, and it kept us moving in the right direction—outward."[51]

A second lesson from these churches is that a narrow and deep strategy makes sense not only because it is more effective in terms of tangible results for the people or communities served; it also makes progress more visible. And *that* contributes to the ongoing motivation of the congregation. Tome explains that when you put all your eggs into very few baskets, the effects are deeper: "What happens is that you actually start putting up wins on the board, and your church gets excited because they can see tangible change that's happening." Honeycutt agrees: "One of the great things about our involvement is that we can see transformation visibly taking place."[52]

Third, the stories of these churches reveal that success requires significant financial commitment. To mobilize such commitment, intentional leadership and directed preaching were required. Former Crossroads justice director Andrew Peters explains how the congregation raised over 200,000 dollars for investment in aftercare:

We did a series here called Consumed, and it was all about breaking free from materialism. Like how does the Western consumer mindset influence how you spend your money? So it was a six-week series, very intense, and basically out of that we saw a tremendous [result]—folks just experienced a freedom in financial giving in February of '08 in amazing ways.[53]

At Southwood, Honeycutt and others had to be bold and matter-of-fact about the costs urban renewal and church planting in Lincoln Village would require. Southwood pays Mark's salary and that of Pastor Alex Shipman at The Village Church. It also provides four thousand dollars per month to Lincoln Village Ministry and recently pledged twenty thousand dollars to pave The Village Church's parking lot. "We didn't get a lot of pushback" on the finances, Honeycutt gratefully remembers. Its situation was helped by a few unique factors, though: a few individuals from Southwood and others from the Huntsville community made very large gifts, and other congregations came on board to provide funds and volunteers to Lincoln Village Ministry.

A fourth lesson learned is that, while both churches strongly affirm the value of mobilizing congregants by their skill sets, they do not see vocational stewardship as their *exclusive* method of lay mobilization. There is a call for everyone to serve, for all to take responsibility. And there are many opportunities for service that require no particular professional training or experience. In short, there's a place for everyone, not just white-collar professionals. As Dale Bowen from LVPC explains, "As Mark cast a vision [at Southwood], he told them there is an area of work for every person. People felt like they had something to contribute [even] if they weren't a doctor or a dentist. It was put out there to everybody, knowing that there was something out there across the board for everybody."[54] Tome from Crossroads emphasizes that the first task in lay mobilization is simply getting *any* kind of involvement. He believes that serving based on one's particular gifts can then unfold over time:

On the front end, the most important thing is simply to get in the game. . . . [Church members] need to just get in the game in any grunt-level position or anything that pushes the kingdom forward. Then as time goes on we trust to the Holy Spirit's whispering [that] they'll refine themselves and get to a place that may be more customized for who God has them to be. But the most important thing is getting people engaged.

Finally, this pathway, particularly as expressed in neighborhood-targeted ministry, requires a mindset of mutuality. When a church of largely middle- or upper-middle-class congregants, many of them white-collar professionals, gets engaged in a low-income neighborhood, the risk of paternalism is high. Church leaders must work hard to help their highly talented laity to see their *own* poverty and need. A great way of doing so is to teach the biblical definition of poverty, namely, "the absence of shalom in all its meanings."[55] Poverty is not only material; it is relational and spiritual as well. Given the universal implications of the Fall, all humans—including those materially non-poor—are poor in one way or another.

This understanding can help congregants who are not economically poor to avoid considering themselves as superior. It also can help congregants find places of commonality with the members of the target community. Southwood's Alan Judge, a real estate attorney, says for example, that the residents of Lincoln Village are no different from the middle-class folks at Southwood: "They deserve to have the dignity of having an opportunity to own a home" just as much as his peers do.[56]

The mutuality of ministry is not only about the fact that both parties give and receive. It's also about the reality that they are jointly envisioning and creating a better future together. A great beauty of pathway four is the opportunity for the targeted community or people affected by the targeted issue to come together with servants from the church and imagine *together* what a new future could look like. Then, as God's Spirit works, they can rejoice together over the new foretastes of shalom their mutual labors bring into reality.

Conclusion

REJOICING THE CITY

*The claim of the Bible is that not only does Jesus come
to do his project of remaking the world into shalom;
he comes to make us participants in that building.
That is part of the intrinsic purpose of his coming.*

REV. GREG THOMPSON

Sometimes stories can be simultaneously inspirational and immobilizing. We hear the account of someone—perhaps like the someones in this book—and think, *What they've done is pretty amazing. I loved hearing about it. But I don't think I could ever do something like that.*

Maybe this has been your reaction to the stories told here. As a church leader or an individual parishioner, perhaps your heart sped up a bit when reading these accounts—but then doubts crept in. You wonder whether you have the energy or creativity, the latitude or fortitude, or the capacity or competency to live missionally through your work (or to lead your congregation in doing so). This vision of vocational stewardship for the common good is attractive, you concede, but perhaps not attainable. You're just not sure, as a church leader, that you could move your flock in this direction. You're just not convinced, as an individual worker, that you could imitate the sorts of actions you've read about here.

It's true that, in a sense, the individuals and congregations showcased in this book are extraordinary. In a context where so many individuals lack vision for effectively wedding their faith and work, the examples of people like Perry Bigelow and Daisy Waimiri and Tom Hill III are noteworthy. In a context where most congregational leaders never talk about vocation, the accounts of churches like Mavuno and Christ Community and The Falls Church are rare.

At the same time, though, what the individuals and church leaders profiled in this book have accomplished is not outside the realm of possibility. These are people like you; these are congregations like yours. What they have done, you can do.

The stories I've told about them are true, but space constraints made it impossible to give a full accounting. Consequently, my anecdotes run the risk of making vocational stewardship sound simple. And since that could be discouraging to readers who wonder, "Why haven't I been more adept at this?" let me share a few additional details. These serve as reality checks about the way the journey of vocational stewardship typically unfolds. It is not a mechanical, simple or straightforward process. The people and the churches profiled in these pages have struggled, questioned, gotten frustrated and taken missteps along the way. They're ordinary folk like you and me. They didn't have this all figured out.

Coming to clarity about the specific actions you can take to advance the kingdom in and through your profession takes time—time to muse, to pray, to consult, to read, to discuss, to question, to debate. Wendy Clark, the young business owner of Carpe Diem Cleaning whom we met in chapter ten, estimates it took her about *ten years* to understand how to advance foretastes of the kingdom through her business. In the early days, a lot of her attention went simply to keeping the company afloat. Perry Bigelow (chapter two) didn't read Zechariah 8's beautiful vision of a neighborhood where the children play safely in the streets while the old folks chat on their porches one day and then go out and build HomeTown Aurora the next. Wendy and Perry read a lot of books, went to conferences, discussed matters with trusted friends.

Tim Schulz (chapter seven) reports that ReVive Industries is a dream that he's been kicking around for three years or more. For even longer than that, he's wrestled with how his various passions—about recycling, homelessness, unemployment and art—should or could fit together coherently. He's debated and discussed these things with his wife, his family members and spiritual mentors. Now he has the vision clearer, but he's only just begun the implementation phase. A big question for him is whether and when to quit his regular job to run ReVive Industries full time.

Finding the vocational sweet spot is typically a process with plenty of trial and error in it. Coke executive Bonnie Wurzbacher (chapter ten) didn't start out as a business major in college. Nor was her first job in business. She spent five years as a teacher before coming to the realization that it wasn't the right fit and that she'd have to have the courage to try something else. Margaret Powell (chapter thirteen) longed for years to teach at-risk kids, but had to wait until her own child-rearing responsibilities lessened before she could take on the role she now has as an intervention specialist. And remember that before Tom Hill III lent KimRay employees to the city, he'd almost lost his business and laid off many workers because of his unwise decisions.

Waking up to all the different possibilities there are for serving God through our vocational skills also takes time. For a while, Derek Simpson, the attorney from Southwood (chapter thirteen), could see how his doctor friends could serve the kingdom but not how he could as a lawyer. Moreover, sometimes vocational stewardship takes on unexpected forms. For example, Val Shean (chapter one) didn't go to Uganda with a clear vision of being a peacemaker. She went as a veterinarian. While there, God expanded her influence and reputation, and she had to strategize well on how best to capitalize on those dimensions of her vocational power.

All the individuals whose stories I've told eventually found their vocational sweet spot and have experienced great joy in deploying their talents to advance the kingdom. None of them, though, think they have vocational stewardship down to a science. For most, the journey to where they are now, with what they are doing now, has required much effort, intentionality and perseverance. The way has not always been linear.

Similarly, the churches mentioned in this book also hit bumps along the road. They weren't perfect. They have their struggles just like every congregation. Mavuno Church (chapter twelve) is wrestling with how to adequately support all its entrepreneurial frontline initiative leaders as that group expands. As a young and very fast-growing congregation, it also sometimes lacks mature leaders for all its Mizizi small groups.

Duke Kwon from Grace DC (chapter ten) reports that although their vocationally oriented small groups thrived for a year, and some still continue, others have fizzled. This small church emphasizes involvement in Community Groups (their word for weekly home fellowships), and some parishioners can't commit to simultaneous membership in those *and* a vocation group. Consequently, today Grace DC is trying to discern how to infuse the Community Groups with more emphasis on vocation and how to provide further support to members in wedding faith and work effectively.

Crossroads (chapter thirteen) plans no departure from its commitment to an inch-wide, mile-deep ministry strategy, but finding enough serving on-ramps to meet the demand from its thousands of members is a challenge. Meanwhile, leaders at Southwood (chapter thirteen) face a different problem: some of the initial enthusiasm for Lincoln Village Ministries has dampened over time now that this urban ministry is no longer the "bright new thing" at the church.

GOD PROVIDES OUR HAMMERS

Pursuing the journey of vocational stewardship as a church is not about "three easy steps and you're done." It's an evolving process that looks different at different times and contexts. And it's not one-size-fits-all. Moses enjoyed a very clear call from God (not many of us get a burning bush experience!). But he also had to endure a very long season of preparation for his work. Even when he was in his vocational sweet spot, things weren't easy. Besides outside opposition, he faced trouble from his own team members. Or consider Joseph. It took him a long while to develop the mature character needed to manage the gifts and power he had been given. Sometimes he enjoyed a context where he could really bloom (think of his influence and platform as vice regent in Egypt) while at other times his circumstances were more constrained (such as when he was in prison).

No matter what our particular season or context, though, what we can be utterly confident about is God's promise to help us on this exciting but messy journey. After all, he is the one who has called us into it. He is the one who issues us the breathtaking invitation to join him on his mission to restore all things. He's the one who has prepared good works in advance for us to walk in and who handcrafted us for them (Eph 2:10).

My pastor, Greg Thompson, tells a story about his dad, Bruce, a gifted carpenter and handyman. Bruce's favorite Saturday routine was a morning spent on some kind of home-improvement project, followed by an afternoon of college sports on the tube. While Greg's brothers spent Saturdays playing football, he liked to stay home and "help" dad on projects. A father himself now, Greg recognizes the sacrifice his dad made to bring him into those Saturday morning projects. Over the years, Greg and his dad repaired many things together.

One morning, Greg noticed lying next to his father's hammer—the one with the initials BT carved into the handle—a second hammer. When Greg looked closely at it, there were the initials GT—for Greg Thompson. "The hammer," Greg says, "was an invitation, and it was assurance that my participation in his work was not only tolerated, but desired, and not only desired, but anticipated, and not only anticipated, but provided for."[1]

And that, Greg assured us, is what Jesus does for us.

In all the spheres where we work—education, business, government, media, law, arts and more—we are agents of restoration. Talk about a heady job title! The contentions of Christian doctrine are bold: the work we do *matters* and it *lasts*. In an age of *Dilbert* and *The Office*, which assert that modern work is all about futility and absurdity, these are astonishing claims.[2] We might even be tempted to think that they are a fantasy—except that, as we've seen, real people in real churches are living them out. Not perfectly, and not without struggle, of course. But they've made progress in the journey of vocational stewardship because God has supplied them with the hammers. He called them into his work and made provision for them to carry it out. He will do the same for you and me.

REBUILDING THE WALL, REJOICING THE CITY

The book of Nehemiah tells the story of God's people working together to rebuild the city wall around Jerusalem. Residents of the city were vulnerable to attack from enemies and wild beasts. In the ancient world, an unwalled city was a place of despair. Knowing how poor the quality of life was in such a place, Nehemiah wept bitterly when a countryman from Jerusalem visited Babylon and informed him of conditions back home (Neh 1:4). So moved was Nehemiah by the groans of the Jerusalemites that he determines to take action. God granted him favor before his Babylonian boss, and Nehemiah traveled to Jerusalem. There he mobilized the people and inspired them to work together diligently to rebuild the city walls and gates.

Nehemiah 3 is sometimes overlooked, since it reads a bit like the "begat" passages—those mind-numbing chronicles of genealogy in the Old Testament. It's a listing of all the folks who labored on the wall and which sections they worked on. It even tells a bit about their occupations. Some of the wall builders were priests; others were public officials. Some were perfume makers, one was a security guard, some were goldsmiths, and several were merchants.

Everybody had a part to play. They worked on different sections of the wall and they brought to their labors their own individual talents. Together they used their gifts to bring about the common good.

Pastor Scott Seaton of Emmanuel Church in Arlington, Virginia, notes that vocational stewardship looks a whole lot like this. He explains that without a strong city wall, Jerusalem was not a place of shalom. "Walls and gates helped create a safe environment for a prosperous community," he says, "not just economically, but socially, educationally and spiritually."[3] Moreover, the Hebrew words used in Nehemiah 1 indicate that the Jerusalemites felt ashamed of their city and situation. Today we don't have physical walls around our communities. Instead, other features provide strength and identity: our economic systems, our schools, the arts and nonprofit sectors, our governing structures, our neighborhoods, the media, the legal system, the health-care system and the like. Each of these sectors is like a section on the city wall, and all must be strong and flourishing if people are to enjoy tastes of shalom.

The book of Nehemiah makes clear that the work of rebuilding the city wall wasn't easy. The laborers faced threats from enemies who opposed the project. And the work itself was grueling; after all, the wall had lain in ruins for 141 years! But Nehemiah was a very wise leader. He let people work on the section of the wall closest to where they lived. In other words, they did the parts of the work that they were most passionate about. This, too, is a lot like vocational stewardship. We persevere best when our labor is focused on what we do well and enjoy, and when we've found the place on the wall that corresponds to the passions and gifts God has placed inside us.

The book of Nehemiah also reveals the profound joy that arises from participating in rebuilding the wall. When the task was completed, the people gathered for a huge assembly and celebration. Individually they could rejoice in the role they had played. Collectively, they danced jubilantly in their newfound security. Tastes of shalom broke into the city, and the response was one big party.

Vocational stewardship that produces community transformation brings that kind of joy.

Sometimes the joy is first a quiet, internal experience. Believers who participate intentionally, thoughtfully, strategically and creatively in the *missio Dei* through their daily work taste more deeply of God. They learn more about his character as they participate with him in the things he is passionate about. Their work lives gain deeper meaning and purpose. They realize that God is accomplishing his "creational order" work through them. That is, they're able to see the intrinsic value of their farming or their "lawyering" or their artistry or their managing or their teaching. Through such professions, they realize that God is doing his work—through them!—of providing for, sustaining and governing his world.

Believers who take vocational stewardship seriously also see their reliance on the Holy Spirit become more authentic, more of a daily practice. They lean hard into prayer, seeking heavenly wisdom for decisions. They offer up their workday, each day, as worship to God. They look for new ways to serve their neighbors near and far through their work. Along the way, they begin to feel as though they have stopped being mere spectators and have become active players in the work King Jesus is doing to push back the curse and push in the kingdom of shalom. And all of this brings rejoicing.

As we take up our place as agents of restoration, we also become instruments through which our neighbors taste more of God's goodness. As we faithfully do our part on the section of the "wall" we've been called to, we promote the common good. Depending on our circumstances, our efforts to steward our vocational power can cause transformation at a variety of levels—among individuals, within local organizations or neighborhoods, or throughout institutions and different sectors of society.

Sometimes those we'll serve through our vocational stewardship are part of our own fellowships. Musician Craig Pitman (chapter seven), for instance, is a *tsaddiq* bringing a foretaste of healing to fellow parishioners in grief. Graphic designer/illuminator Jessie Nilo (chapter one) has been a *tsaddiq* for believers who've needed a deeper, richer taste of God's beauty.

Sometimes those we serve are part of our own workplaces. Insurance agent Bruce Copeland (chapter two) was a *tsaddiq* to female employees in his firm during a time of institutionalized discrimination, offering them a fresh taste of justice. Businesswoman Wendy Clark (chapter ten) is a *tsaddiq* to her employees who need a taste of compassion as they struggle to balance work and family.

Other times we serve those in our cities. Educator Margaret Powell (chapter thirteen) has been a *tsaddiq* for the children of Lincoln Village who needed to see that school success was possible. Gardeners Mark and Courtney Williams (chapter one) are *tsaddiqim*, giving Pittsburgh teens from a distressed inner-city neighborhood a taste of hope. Business owners Tom and Beth Phillips in Memphis (chapter one) are *tsaddiqim*, offering economic opportunities to some of America's poorest citizens. Mayor Don De Graff (chapter one) is a *tsaddiq*, bringing his racially diverse community greater foretastes of unity.

Sometimes we'll bring a foretaste of shalom to neighbors very far away. Paper chemist Dan Blevins (chapter ten) has been a *tsaddiq*. By contributing to new livelihoods for squatters in Manila through his work with Village Handcrafters, he has helped prompt their rejoicing. Solicitor Matthew Price (chapter one) has been a *tsaddiq* to illegally detained prisoners in Uganda, who through his efforts have tasted rescue. Photographer Ken Oloo (chapter twelve) is a *tsaddiq* to teens in Kibera, giving them a taste of economic sufficiency. Bonnie Wurzbacher (chapter ten) is a *tsaddiq* whose work at Coke helps that international company bring jobs and economic development to communities throughout the developing world.

And sometimes our work can contribute to reformation in our particular vocational sectors. Perry Bigelow's example of and advocacy for unconventional suburban development methodologies are contributing to change in the way homebuilding happens in Illinois. Through her teaching at Harvard University and her model home in Colorado, interior designer Cynthia Leibrock (chapter six) is a *tsaddiq* promoting the value of accessibility in her field, encouraging designers to adopt aging-in-place strategies. Through her work with Act One, screenwriter Barbara Nicolosi (chapter one) is trying to seed Hollywood with artists who bring a deep theology of Fall and redemption to their work in film.

Through their efforts to disciple believers who will apply their vocational talents in the media, government, education, health care and business sectors, Mavuno Church leaders are trying to repair sections of the "city wall" in Nairobi. Meanwhile, Southwood Presbyterian and its partner congregations are trying to do the same on a smaller scale, in a neighborhood that needs greater tastes of shalom.

Today many in our world are groaning, because "city walls" are in disrepair. Our neighbors near and far are hungry for greater experiences of reconciliation, beauty, health, peace, justice and other kingdom foretastes. This broken world is waiting for the unveiling of believers who will live as the *tsaddiqim*, deploying their talents to rejoice the city. King Jesus has many hammers ready—inscribed with the names of his people. Now it's time for church leaders to nurture their members and for those members to take up those hammers and live missionally in and through their work.

Then, many dances of rejoicing will begin.

Afterword

You say grace before meals. All right. But I say grace before the
concert and the opera, and grace before the play and pantomime,
and grace before I open a book, and grace before sketching,
painting, swimming, fencing, boxing, walking, playing,
dancing and grace before I dip the pen in the ink.

G. K. CHESTERTON

I have a good friend who is a businessman, or perhaps more accurately, an entrepreneur. From his undergraduate days on, he has had eyes to see opportunities and then found ways to capitalize on his insight. Over time he has had his fingers in all sorts of things, and it is literally impossible for the average person to live life without interacting with his work. We live with and by his entrepreneurial imagination; his ideas have had legs.

A few years ago we were having lunch, and he asked me if I knew why he wanted to talk. Quite candidly, I didn't, even though there is affection and respect between us that grows out of years of history. Over the table he said to me, "You think that what I do matters. You think that my work as a businessman matters. That my work itself matters. That the work of business matters. I've been in the church my whole life, and have been in and around the parachurch for years, and you know what? Both see me in the same way. When I walk into the room it's as if a big checkbook walked in. That's all I am. Nobody cares what I have done to make money."

If my friend's story were isolated, one among a thousand, it might be different. But sadly, his experience is the experience of most Christian people who spend their lives in the marketplaces of the world, hoping as they do that there is some honest connection between what they do and the work of God in the world. They yearn to see their vocations as integral, not incidental, to the *missio Dei*.

Sorrowfully, most of the time the church teaches the opposite. Catholics, Orthodox, Protestants—we all stumble over this, more often than not offering instead that our vocations are incidental, on the sidelines of what God really cares about and is doing—as my friend the entrepreneur has painfully discovered.

For many years I have traveled across America, taking up the question of vocation. Over the miles I have visited seminaries from the East Coast to the West Coast, asking deans and presidents, "How do you understand vocation? How is it taught to your students?" Sometimes that question has grown out of an hour's conversation in an office, sometimes over a day with the seminary's faculty. Eerily, I have heard the same words most everywhere I have gone; that is, "What you're saying is our theology, but we don't teach that here."

Because of the history woven into those conversations, there is always a common ground of honor and hope. I don't enter in to end a relationship; rather, I always want to deepen a friendship and to find a way to do something together. Sometimes I have said in response, "But I wonder who you imagine your students will pastor? Most people in most congregations spend most of their lives in their vocations—and you have no time to address that reality in the years you have them here?"

If the story ended there, it would be one thing. But as ideas have legs, so does a curriculum. Not a week goes by that I don't talk to someone whose life is immersed in the marketplace—and here I am using the word to cover a range of vocations, from business to politics, from agriculture to education, from journalism to medicine, from law to the arts, from building trades to architecture, and on and on and on. Everywhere I go I hear the longing folks have to see the work of their hands as integrally connected to the work of God. And usually that longing is bound up with the sadness that the church doesn't seem to understand, and, even more pointedly, that pastors don't seem to understand.

One man I talked with this past year told me something of his life. For decades he has labored away in the business world, working hard, taking up increasingly complex tasks that involve people and money. Over the years he has given himself with honest humility to service in the churches where he has lived, and is a kind, loyal, thoughtful man (my reading of him, not his description of himself). With some pain, he said, "I've never had the sense that the pastor thought of someone like me when he was preparing his sermon. It always feels more like he imagines that people live in the church, not the world."

What are we to do? I refuse to be a cynic, and with Bono I believe that "tearing a corner off of the darkness" is a good life. We can all be glad that Amy Sherman has passions and commitments that have taken her into this question with remarkable theological richness. Always attentive to both the biblical vision and the challenges of ordinary life for Everyman and Everywoman, she has set forth a vision of vocation that is profoundly formed by the reality of the kingdom of God, telling stories of men and women from all over the world who see their lives and labor as callings, as integral to the *missio Dei*.

My hope is that we will never again pray "Your kingdom come, your will be done on earth as it is in heaven" without remembering Dr. Sherman's very good work, calling all of us as she does to see our work as kingdom callings.

Steven Garber
The Washington Institute

Appendix A

KEY THEOLOGICAL THEMES UNDERGIRDING VOCATIONAL STEWARDSHIP

1. The Gospel of the Kingdom

To steward their vocations well, Christians need to have a big conception of God's redemptive work. At the heart of the gospel is the glorious message of new life in Christ, made possible by the atoning sacrifice of our Savior Jesus, who lived the life we ought to have lived and died the death we deserved for our sins. Yet this good news is even bigger: God's salvific work is not limited to individual salvation but concerns his mission of restoring the whole of the created order (Col 1:19-20; Eph 1:9). The gospel of the kingdom is about making *all* things right. It's about the creation of the new world—what Revelation 21:1 calls "a new heavens and a new earth"—a place without suffering, pain, tears, war, hunger, oppression and death.

Jesus' kingdom has been inaugurated and is *now* in definite ways because of his life, ministry and resurrection (Lk 4:21, "Today this scripture is fulfilled in your hearing"). As Christians, we have entered this kingdom and become citizens in it, and that citizenship is to shape us in every way—including in our work lives.

Why this matters for vocational stewardship.

1. Because it helps us avoid the mistake of thinking that the only important vocations are "full-time Christian ministry" (pastors, missionaries and so on).

2. Because it helpfully directs our attention to God's "short list" of priori-

ties (preach the gospel to the poor, bring recovery of sight to the blind, set the oppressed free—that is, evangelism, compassion ministry and justice mission).

3. Because it offers us the general goal—relevant to all vocational work—of doing that which serves as sign and foretaste of the coming kingdom.

2. GOD'S TELOS: "BEHOLD, I AM MAKING ALL THINGS NEW"

This is obviously related to number one above. Jesus' resurrection shows his plan for restored life. We anticipate new bodies and a new earth, the very re-creation of God's creation. These truths should lead us to reject gnostic dualism and affirm the goodness of creation, for God does not plan to send the planet to the trash heap, but to redeem and renew it. Thus the afterlife is not disembodied, and salvation is not spiritual only.

Why this matters for vocational stewardship. Because we are called and invited to join God's reclamation work *now* . . . and our participation in that will *last*. In short—our work *matters*. The great resurrection chapter ends with this: "Therefore, my dear brothers, stand firm. Let nothing move you. Always give yourselves fully to the work of the Lord, because you know that your labor in the Lord is not in vain" (1 Cor 15:58). Because of Jesus' resurrection, our work is not in vain. It won't be thrown out at the consummation. God's reclamation work extends as "far as the curse is found"; he is renewing and reconciling all things under his headship.

God's high charge to humankind—to serve as vice regents over creation—was not rescinded after the Fall; it remains our destiny in the New Jerusalem (Rev 5:10). Thus, the work faithful Christ-followers do in the present, whether that involves art or business or writing or nursing or engineering or urban planning or any of the other myriad professions, lasts into God's future. As Lesslie Newbigin wrote, "All who have committed their work in faithfulness to God will be by Him raised up to share in the new age, and will find that their labor was not lost, but that it has found its place in the completed kingdom."[1]

3. THE HEART OF PERSONAL DISCIPLESHIP

Christ calls us to follow him. He seeks obedient disciples submitted to his cosmic lordship. He expects us increasingly, by the power of his

Spirit, to conform to his character (displaying the fruit of the Spirit); to believe and order our lives by his truth; to embrace his passions and priorities; and to join him on his mission in the world. Like him, we are "sent ones."

Why this matters for vocational stewardship. Because it affects the "what" of personal and corporation mission: what we *do* matters, not just our character. Although there is no sacred/secular divide, not all secular vocations are created equal, and we should make wise choices about investing our lives in the things God is passionate about. Why give yourself and your vocational talents to firms that invent new flavors of cat food and new colors of lipstick? To the greatest extent possible, Christians should avoid the trivial and seek career opportunities that focus on the deeply significant: human flourishing, public order, creation care, justice and beauty.

4. Our General Vocation (the Cultural Mandate)

Although fallen and under the groans of the curse, creation is ordered, revelatory, meaningful and cherished by God. The Father calls his children to be stewards/vice regents of his creation (Gen 1:28). He gives us the gifts of both nature and culture, and calls us to imitate him as creative beings, both tending (protecting) and working (developing) the Garden. This cultural mandate calls us to recognize that "the Earth is the Lord's and the fullness thereof" (Psalm 24:1 ESV) and to gladly serve as stewards of the bounty God has provided us for the meeting of our own needs and the world's.

Why this matters for vocational stewardship.

1. It means that we all get to participate in this vocation, regardless of our specific jobs (which may be tedious or permit little or no room for creativity). We can also live this general vocation through our avocational interests, hobbies and volunteer work, as well as through the non-work spheres of our lives, such as family life and recreation.

2. It means we are called to be culture makers, and it gives us guidance for that work.

3. It legitimizes so-called nonspiritual pursuits like art and science (and many others).

4. It means God has shared his power and authority with us; he has given us real responsibility in this world. We have a high calling.

5. It means the environment matters and we should focus on creation care and be "green" in and through our vocations.

5. A Proper View of Human Nature

We need to embrace both our fallenness/sinfulness *and* our glory as people made in God's image and as Christians who are now redeemed and in Christ, with the Spirit living inside us. As John Eldredge put it in *Waking the Dead*, "I daresay we've heard a bit about original sin, but not nearly enough about original glory, which comes before sin and is deeper to our nature."[2]

The Bible begins with Genesis 1, not Genesis 3. We need both the humility that acknowledges our sinfulness fully ("the heart is deceitful") and the courage to affirm that God's divine power is alive in us through his Spirit. There are dangers in both a too-high view of ourselves *and* in a too-low view.

A biblical view of human nature also teaches us that we are made for community. The only thing that was "not good" in paradise was that Adam was alone. We are made for God, and for relationship with one another.

Why this matters for vocational stewardship.

1. Because our work matters in God's redemptive purposes. We—though frail and always in need of his work to make us adequate (2 Cor 3:5-6)—are part of God's plan. As St. Augustine wrote, "God without us will not, as we without God cannot." Astonishingly, the apostle Paul calls us God's coworkers (2 Cor 6:1). If we think of ourselves only as hopeless worms that sin constantly and have nothing to offer, we won't believe ourselves capable of fulfilling our calling as God's coworkers who have been designed by him for good works (Eph 2:10).

2. Because we should seek to advance healthy, just community through our work. We are not created only for work—this idea is the root of workaholism. We are called to relationship and charged to live and act as the new humanity, displaying in and through our community life the beauty of Jesus whose Spirit indwells us.

6. Appropriate Sobriety About "the World, the Flesh and the Devil"

Our culture is shaping us in all kinds of ways that we are often unaware of or inattentive to. Evangelicals sufficiently schooled in a robust biblical worldview may be equipped to recognize evil or unbiblical ideas. But the same Christians can sometimes fail to see evil or unbiblical cultural forms and patterns. Reformed theologian David Wells has shown how evil tendencies are embedded and affirmed in our public institutions—and these manifestations of worldliness can affect us to an even greater degree than the behaviors traditionally associated with worldliness (drinking, promiscuity, gambling and so on).

Why this matters for vocational stewardship.

1. It encourages us to be sober about how very difficult it actually is to change the world.

2. It reminds us that prayer is fundamental.

3. It warns us (in terms of our culture making) about fighting only in the realm of ideas and not in the realm of institutions.

7. We Are Aliens and Strangers in This World and Are to Live Accordingly

Why this matters for vocational stewardship. This obviously affects the "how" of our work: we are to be certain kinds of bosses and employees, acting on biblical virtue and rule, which is different from the way the world operates. But it also should shape the *ends* of our work and creativity. Vocationally we want to be about the work of helping people to flourish, but we need a biblical definition of "human flourishing" rather than the world's definition.

8. A Biblical Understanding of Power—and of Blessing

Power is a gift (one that is often abused, but that is not inherently evil, as some Christians think). God grants us power—and charges us to use it responsibly. He has also blessed us richly. We need to know the purpose for which God has given us power and blessings.

Why this matters for vocational stewardship. We American Christians have relatively more power, wealth, opportunity and privilege than most of the rest of the world. Especially those in the academic and professional disciplines have great opportunity to contribute to human flourishing (more than do the world's destitute who struggle simply to survive). Since we are the recipients of such power and privilege, we are especially accountable for its right use ("from the one who has been entrusted with much, much more will be asked," Lk 12:48). Our vocational opportunities—the fact that we have vocational choice—is a gift, a privilege and a form of power, one that we must take very seriously and be very intentional about.

9. A BIBLICAL UNDERSTANDING OF STEWARDSHIP—AND OWNERSHIP

In the Bible, being stewards is fundamental to our human nature and our general vocational calling. Stewardship is about devoting all that I am and all that I have to God, recognizing him as the ultimate owner of everything (ourselves, our lives, our time, our money). As members of one body, as humans created for community, God calls us to fight the ingrained selfishness with which we all struggle and to recognize that his gifts are given to all for the common good.

Why this matters for vocational stewardship. For some Christians, it seems that stewardship is only about the use of our money. We need basic teaching on whole life stewardship. People need to know that they are accountable for how they steward their work life and vocational abilities.

10. GOD'S HEART FOR THE POOR, THE ALIEN, THE WIDOW, THE OPPRESSED AND THE ORPHAN

God's passion for the poor and his hatred of injustice are two central divine character traits. He goes so far as to say that there is no true worship without doing justice (Is 1); that "religion that God our Father accepts as pure and faultless is this: to look after orphans and widows in their distress and to keep oneself from being polluted by the world" (Jas 1:27); that caring for the needy and doing justice are central to what it means to know God (Jer 22:16); that the kingdom of God "belongs" to the poor (Lk 6:20); and that we can even find Jesus in the face of the poor (Mt 25:45).

Why this matters for vocational stewardship. While we are called to do many diverse things through our vocations (such as making scientific discoveries, creating beauty and defending truth), God does have a special emphasis on justice and compassion for the poor, and that priority of his should influence our vocational stewardship in some way.

11. COMMON GRACE

God gets his work done not only through his church, but also through a wide variety of other created institutions and through nonbelievers of goodwill. As John Calvin argued, nonbelievers have achieved significant works of insight in many fields. We Christians are to note such achievements as praiseworthy and as coming from God, who left gifts in human nature "even after it was despoiled of the true good."[3] In his graciousness, God also restrains evil through common grace, working to maintain order in social life.

Why this matters for vocational stewardship. Because it means that Christians, and churches, can legitimately partner with those outside the church in pursuing the common good. God can advance his sovereign purposes—for beauty and justice, wholeness and peace—through secular institutions, and we must discern all the places where he is at work.

12. THE ONE CHURCH

The Apostles' Creed affirms that Christians believe in "the holy catholic church." The apostle Paul used the image of one body to describe God's church and instructed us never to undervalue a part of that one body that is different from us. We are interdependent (1 Cor 12:21, "The eye cannot say to the hand, 'I don't need you!'"). We *belong* to one another (Eph 4:25).

Why this matters for vocational stewardship. Because in our efforts to deploy our parishioners for vocational stewardship, we should be mindful of the efforts of our brothers and sisters in other congregations toward similar ends. We should be ready to partner, to listen and to learn from other churches that are also seeking to advance God's sovereign, good purposes in the world.

Appendix B

A DISCUSSION GUIDE FOR
CONGREGATIONAL SMALL GROUPS[1]

The dictionary defines *vocation* as "a strong feeling of suitability for a particular career or occupation." The term is virtually synonymous with *calling*, as it comes from the Latin *vocare* ("to call"), the sense of being drawn into a particular field. Thus, a vocation is not simply a job; indeed, your current employment may or may not align with a deeper calling. Further, you may not be getting paid for your vocation: you may be studying in some kind of program, volunteering in your field of interest or not drawing any income. The defining aspect of a vocation is an inward sense that you were "made for this," as increasingly confirmed by your affinity and skills, and by other people and opportunities.

Not only has God created us to worship him and live in community with others; he has shaped within us a need to work with dignity and purpose. Our work stewards and cultivates the treasures of creation as part of what theologians call our "cultural mandate." Though a fallen world sullies the inherent dignity of work—through what the Bible calls "thorns and thistles"—God's mandate continues. And perhaps most amazing, what we do for Christ will be enjoyed forever.

We want to consider these issues in community, to help each other sort through what it means practically to live out our callings. One format would be for community groups to make this a focus once per month, beginning with a meal together. After the meal, have a group member share responses to some or all of the questions below, raise related themes they want to address or take questions from the group. It is best to identify this person at least a week in advance, to give them time to prepare. Be sure to end the discussion with prayer for the group member and his or her vocation.

1. **Overview**. In a few minutes, tell the group about your vocation. What do you do? Who do you work for? What does a typical day (if there is such a thing) look like? Who do you work with? What related training or education did you receive?

2. **Calling**. When and how did you begin to feel drawn to this area? To what degree have you thought about your job as a calling from God, part of a larger "cultural mandate"? It's OK to be honest! For many people, a job is something you do to pay the bills, or something you seemingly fell into. Thus, an underlying sense of calling may seem nebulous at best. Share honestly how you look at your vocation.

3. **Image**. Part of what it means that you are made in the image of God is that you "image" God to creation, similar to how a portrait portrays a person. In a fallen world, we are but marred images, but what attributes of God (e.g., mercy, care, order, justice, creativity, beauty) does your vocation particularly reflect to others?

4. **Idolatry**. Any good thing raised to an ultimate thing becomes an idol—something that we primarily look to for our identity, security and meaning. In what ways do you see your vocation serving as an idol, either to yourself or others?

5. **Community**. Do you have Christian community within your vocation, that is, people who speak the language of your calling and can offer insight, encouragement or feedback into what you do? If so, what does that look like?

6. **Scripture**. What biblical passages have you found particularly helpful as inspiration or guidance in your field?

7. **Articles**. Are there any short articles on the intersection of faith and your vocation that you've found helpful? If so, feel free to summarize them or even share them in advance with the group to include in the discussion.

8. **Worldview**. A worldview helps explain the world we live in, answering such basic questions of life as Why are we here? How do I explain the problems in my life and the world? What is the solution to those problems? Where are we ultimately going, and does what I do now relate?

Everyone has spoken or unspoken answers to those questions. The Bible proclaims these:

- *Creation*: God created us in his image, giving us inherent dignity and worth, for the purpose of glorifying him, not ourselves.

- *Fall*: We are naturally alienated from God, such that everything we do is tainted by some form of selfishness: pride, ambition, greed, envy, malice, prejudice, lust, etc.

- *Redemption*: In ourselves, we are unable to overcome our sinful natures and remove our guilt and shame. Yet at the cross, Jesus' life was graciously exchanged for ours.

- *Restoration*: One day God's kingdom will come in fullness, but it has already begun in our hearts and lives. What we do now in faith for Christ will be enjoyed forever.

Your vocation likely has explicit or implicit answers to some or all of the above questions. How do they compare with a Christian worldview? Do they conflict in such a way as to bring any professional or social pressure on you?

9. **Artifacts**. In *Culture Making* Andy Crouch encourages Christians to help shape our world not simply by *condemning, critiquing, copying* or *consuming* culture but through *creating* "artifacts"—cultural goods, whether chairs, language, laws, art or even omelets. What vocational artifacts have you considered creating that in some small way help create culture?

10. **Influence**. James Davison Hunter in *To Change the World* calls most Christian attempts at cultural engagement inadequate, concluding they have mostly served to marginalize the church, with little impact on culture. Instead, he calls us to "faithful presence" in our fields, at whatever level. Though this would include living moral lives as a biblical witness to others, Hunter calls us to participate in, identify with and humbly influence the existing structures of society. What might that look like for you in your vocation? In your field, what makes you passionate/angry/excited enough to call you to be a positive influence? What dilemmas might you face? Brainstorm ways you could work with other Christians in your vocation toward a common purpose.

Appendix C

FOR FURTHER INFORMATION

Readers can find a number of helpful follow-up resources at www.vocationalstewardship.org. This is a sampling:

RESOURCES FOR PASTORS AND CHURCH LEADERS

1. Ten Ways to Encourage Vocational Stewardship at Your Church

2. Eight Steps for Starting a Pathway 2

3. An Introduction to Business as Mission (BAM)

RESOURCES FOR INDIVIDUAL BELIEVERS

1. Annotated bibliography of books on vocational issues

2. Additional profiles of Christians engaged in vocational stewardship along each of the four pathways

3. "Personal Manifesto/Vision for Work" worksheet from Harbor Presbyterian Church North County

Appendix D

INDEX OF PROFILES BY VOCATION

Agriculture — Jacob Schenk, p. 164; Courtney and Mark Williams, p. 38

Animal Therapy — Helen Bach, p. 124

Antiques — Martha Rollins, p. 138

Architecture — Jill Sorenson, p. 108

Art — Lisa Marten, p. 35

Astrophysics — Frank Six, p. 206

Athletics — Danny Wuerffel, p. 35

Business — Wendy Clark, p. 159; Tom Hill III, p. 151; Dave and Demi Kiersznowski, p. 154; Justin Kitch, p. 56; Milt Kuyers, p. 162; Larry Mollner, p. 181; Stanley Tam, p. 34

Chemist — Dan Blevins, p. 169

Civil Engineering — Rod Beadle, p. 180; John Rahe, p. 181

Construction — Tim Schulz, p. 127

Culinary Arts — Tim Hammack, p. 122

Dance — Jeanine Lacquement, p. 161

Dentistry — Brian Beitel, p. 212; Al Willis, p. 212

Education — Margaret Powell, p. 207

Entertainment — Carlos Oscar, p. 163

Environmental Science — Mukuria Mwangi, p. 187

Fashion Design — Bora Aksu, p. 164

Finance — Daisy Waimiri, p. 188

Government — Pia Cayetano, p. 163; Don De Graff, p. 40; Simon Mbevi, p. 187

Graphic Design   Jessie Nilo, p. 35

History   Anne C. Bailey, p. 160

Home Design/Building   Perry Bigelow, p. 59

Human Resources   Kay Edwards, p. 180

Insurance   Bruce Copeland, p. 56

Interior Design   Cynthia Leibrock, p. 110

IT   Ed Fischer, p. 175

Journalism   Russ Pulliam, p. 123; David Aikman, p. 125

Law   Deborah Leydon, p. 215; Matthew Price, p. 29;
                              Derek Simpson, p. 209

Law Enforcement   Doug Call and Dennis Wittman, p. 32

Lobbying   Rich Nymoen, p. 31

Management   Roberta Teran, p. 218; Bonnie Wurzbacher, p. 156

Marketing   Anne Nzilani, p. 191

Mechanical Engineering   Don Schoendorfer, p. 179

Medicine   Eloise Alexander, p. 212; Simon Chiu, p. 123;
                              Brian Costa, p. 212; Andy Macfarlan, pp. 37,
                              124; Barry Sorrells, p. 58

Mental Health Counseling   Mark Pruden, p. 217

Music   Craig Pitman, 126; Kanjii Mbugua, p. 193

Nursing   Susan Beeney, p. 39

Oceanography   Jorge Vazquez, p. 43

Photography   Ken Oloo, p. 196

Paralegal   Jamie Elkins, p. 217

Property Appraisal   Mickey Plott, p. 211

Real Estate Brokering   John Phillips, pp. 123, 181

Real Estate Development   Sam Yeager, p. 211

Sales   David Masys, p. 217; James Saunders, p. 177

Screenwriting   Barbara Nicolosi, p. 57

Veterinary Medicine   Val Shean, p. 41

Notes

Introduction

[1]D. Michael Lindsay, *Faith in the Halls of Power: How Evangelicals Joined the American Elite* (New York: Oxford University Press, 2007), p. 226.

[2]Ibid., p. 192.

[3]Ibid., p. 130.

[4]For example, Greg Newman, a San Francisco venture capitalist, has provided start-up funds for a candle company in Thailand that employs women recovering from sexual abuse. Full-time philanthropists Dennis and Eileen Bakke have established the Harvey Fellows program to encourage smart evangelicals to study at Ivy League schools. William Inboden used his positions in the upper echelons of government to craft the International Religious Freedom Act of 1998. He describes himself as one who wants to shape the culture, not just follow it.

[5]Timothy J. Keller, "Creation Care and Justice," sermon delivered at Redeemer Presbyterian Church, New York, January 16, 2005.

[6]Ibid.

[7]*Shalom* is the rich Hebrew term conveying the idea of peace with God, peace with self, peace with others and peace with the created order. *Peace* here refers not simply to the absence of hostilities but to deep wholeness.

[8]I'm indebted to Rev. Jeff White of New Song Harlem Church in New York City for this insight.

[9]To be sure, Jesus also clearly taught that the kingdom is also "not yet." We wait and long in our still-broken world for its full consummation. Our efforts alone will not and cannot inaugurate it. We are permitted a big God-sized vision for our labors and our hopes, but we are not allowed Utopianism. The kingdom will arrive in fullness only at the return of the King.

[10]Don Simmons, president, Creative Potential Consulting and Training, telephone interview with the author, August 5, 2010.

[11]The term is Bill Hybels's from his book *Holy Discontent: Fueling the Fire That Ignites Personal Vision* (Grand Rapids: Zondervan, 2007).

[12]I spend a disproportionate amount of time on pathway one, "Bloom Where You're Planted," because it is the most important and most common expression of vocational stewardship. It's also the pathway that every church—regardless of size or limited resources—can and should emphasize.

[13]Lisa Belkin, "Time Wasted? Perhaps It's Well Spent," *New York Times*, May 31, 2007 <www.nytimes.com/2007/05/31/fashion/31work.html?spc=19&sq=&st=nyt>.

Chapter 1: What Does a Rejoiced City Look Like?

[1]The passages studied are Ps 46:9; 72; Zech 8:4-13; Is 2:2-5; 11; 25:6-9; 26:1-12; 32:1-8; 35; 42:1-4; 49:8-21; 51:3-6; 54; 61–62; 65:17-25; Jer 23:5-6; Ezek 34:11-31; Joel 3:17-18; Amos 9:11-15; Mic 4:3-4; Zeph 3:14-20; Zech 8:3-17; 14:6-21; Rev 21.

[2]There are likely more than three dimensions, but our investigation here must be limited.

[3]The Hebrew word for "do justice" in Micah 6:8 is *mishpat*. As Tim Keller notes, it occurs over two hundred times in the Old Testament and connotes the ideas of punishing wrongdoing and giving people their rights (*Generous Justice* [New York: Dutton, 2010], pp. 3-9). Christians in a variety of professions can play important parts in the work of rescue. Law enforcement officers and undercover detectives locate victims and document the presence of abuse. Prosecutors and judges bring perpetrators to account. Social workers, mental health workers and professionals using music, art and dance therapy can bring healing to victims. Investigative journalists and other communications professionals (graphic designers, editors, photographers, videographers, screenwriters, film producers) can raise awareness by publicizing the stories of oppression worldwide. Human rights advocates, diplomats and public officials can work to craft and implement legislation criminalizing trafficking, bonded labor and other forms of abuse. Public relations specialists and professional fundraisers can deploy their talents to raise resources for nonprofit organizations conducting rescue operations and for aftercare homes.

[4]Matthew Price, missionary with BMS World Mission, "Prayer Letter," April 2009, and personal correspondence with the author, July 5, 2011.

[5]A classic text on the problems of concentrated poverty neighborhoods is William Julius Wilson's *The Truly Disadvantaged: The Inner City, the Underclass, and Public Policy* (Chicago: University of Chicago Press, 1987).

[6]Rich Nymoen offered his skills as a lobbyist and attorney in the fight for equity. Christians in other occupations, such as public administrators, politicians, public policy researchers, economists, experts in policy evaluation and political scientists, can also advance this kingdom value through their work.

[7]Rich Nymoen, "ISAIAH's Land Tax Campaign in Minnesota," *Groundswell* (March/April 2004) <http://commonground-usa.net/isaiah04.htm>.

[8]Ted Grimsrud, "Biblical Basis for Restorative Justice," address to the Center for Justice and Peacebuilding, Eastern Mennonite University, Harrisonburg, Va., December 1, 2008.

[9]Multiple professions offer opportunities for working to bring about restorative justice: working in prison administration; serving as a mediator or counselor; working for victim assistance units of criminal justice agencies; being involved in advocacy to promote restorative justice approaches; teaching restorative justice principles in law schools and conflict resolution programs.

[10]As quoted in Howard Owens, "The Genesee Justice Story," *The Batavian*, November 26, 2010 <http://thebatavian.com/blogs/howard-owens/genesee-justice-story/22423>.

[11]Paul Mrozek, "MHA Salutes Dennis Wittman," Restorative Justice Online (May

20, 2010) <www.restorativejusticeonline.net/RJOB/mha-salutes-dennis-wittman/>.

[12]Cornelius Plantinga Jr., "Educating for Shalom: Our Calling as a Christian College," Calvin College <www.calvin.edu/about/shalom.htm>. Emphasis in original.

[13]This is not an exhaustive listing of kingdom marks. Additional ones include truth, joy, solidarity, accessibility, community, creativity and service.

[14]All quotes from Danny Wuerffel are from a telephone interview with the author, October 5, 2010.

[15]Art also serves "horizontal" purposes. Artists of all sorts create works that feed the aesthetic hunger of our souls. We need beauty, for God made us with senses and placed us in a sensory world. Environment matters. The landscape architect's efforts to beautify the city, the engineer's work to clean up abandoned lots and the city planner's establishment of a new public park—these are all kingdom endeavors.

[16]All quotes from Jessie Nilo, founder and director, VineArts, are from a telephone interview with the author, September 1, 2010. In addition to the ways VineArts artists promote beauty in worship, they've also deployed their artistic talents to bring beauty to troubled individuals. Artists from VineArts visit nursing homes and a local crisis pregnancy center, facilitating art projects by the elderly and by teen moms-to-be. The art helps draw people out from their anxieties and sadness, Jessie reports.

[17]Lisa Marten, owner, relevatorart, telephone interview with the author, September 1, 2010.

[18]All quotes from Andrew Macfarlan, MD, Albemarle Square Family Healthcare, Charlottesville, Va., are from an interview with the author, March 6, 2011.

[19]All quotes from Courtney Williams, Community Gardening Coordinator, Lots of Hope Garden, The Pittsburgh Project, are from a telephone interview with the author, August 27, 2010.

[20]Mark Williams, Community Outreach Coordinator, The Pittsburgh Project, telephone interview with the author, August 27, 2010.

[21]Ibid.

[22]Ibid.

[23]From James Montgomery's 1821 hymn "Hail to the Lord's Anointed."

[24]Thyda Duong, "New Hope, 'New Normal,'" Long Beach Business Journal, October 14-27, 2008, posted on New Hope Grief Support Community <www.newhopegrief.org/newnormal.htm>.

[25]"South Holland, IL," Encyclopedia of Chicago <www.encyclopedia.chicagohistory.org/pages/1173.html>.

[26]Unless otherwise noted, all quotes from Don De Graff, mayor, South Holland, Ill., are from a telephone interview with the author's assistant Kelly Givens, March 3, 2011.

[27]"2010 CommUNITY Dinners," Village of South Holland <www.southholland.org/index.php?page=events/commdinners>.

[28]"Cattle, Guns, and Murder . . . or Peace?" Christian Veterinary Mission <www.cvmusa.org/Page.aspx?pid=3049>.

[29]Rob Cullivan, "Boring Church Works on Uganda Peace Making," *Portland Tribune,* July 22, 2010 <www.portlandtribune.com/news/story.php?story_id=1279322751240 29100>.

[30]Ken Sande, "Cattle Rustling, AK-47s, and Peacemaking," Peacemaker Ministries (April 29, 2010) <http://bookstore.peacemaker.net/blog/?m=201004>.

[31]Al Tizon, Ron Sider, John Perkins and Wayne Gordon, "Business on a Mission," *Prism*, November/December 2008, p. 9.

[32]Ibid., p. 10.

[33]Ibid., p. 9.

[34]Dr. Jorge Vazquez, "Inspiring Scientist—Dr. Jorge Vazquez," Jet Propulsion Laboratory, California Institute of Technology <http://stardustnext.jpl.nasa.gov/Insp_ people/vasquez.html>.

[35]"Jorge Vazquez," Jet Propulsion Laboratory, California Institute of Technology, <http://science.jpl.nasa.gov/people/Vazquez/>.

[36]The creed closes with "And we look for the resurrection of the body, and the life of the world to come." The Nicene Creed, Creeds of Christendom <www.creeds.net/ ancient/nicene.htm>.

[37]For example, 2 Cor 4:18; Col 3:2; Heb 11:10.

Chapter 2: What Do the Righteous Look Like?

[1]As we take up this topic of righteousness, some readers may be puzzled by a conundrum. On the one hand, the Bible constantly holds up the challenge to be righteous while, on the other, it makes it crystal clear that "there is no one righteous, not even one" (Rom 3:10). How do we hold these things together? We start by recognizing that God alone is perfect in righteousness. We are sinners, and we rely for salvation on the imputed righteousness of Christ for our salvation. So, as I use the word *righteous* throughout this chapter, I'm not claiming that we can be perfect.

Additionally, nothing that I say in this chapter should be construed as meaning that Christians, through our own "righteous" conduct, can earn salvation. The righteousness I discuss here is not the same thing as the total sanctification that awaits us in the new earth. Righteousness is what we possess as saved sinners whom God calls "saints." His Spirit lives in us and has made us—and is making us—"new creations." The call to live as a *tsaddiq* is not the same thing as a call to live as a perfect, sinless person. We Christians aren't perfect. No, far from it. But we have been made anew and we've decided to follow Jesus as Lord. Now his Spirit resides in us, empowering us to be his disciples. Looking backward from the cross of Christ, we understand that the righteous are those who trust God, follow him, love him and seek his purposes—though not perfectly.

[2]Given how often I use these terms in the book, it may be useful to know how to pronounce them. *Tsaddiq* is pronounced "tsad-deek" and *tsaddiqim* is "tsad-de-keem."

[3]N. T. Wright, "Righteousness," in *New Dictionary of Theology*, ed. David F. Wright, Sinclair B. Ferguson and J. I. Packer (Downers Grove, Ill.: InterVarsity Press, 1988), pp. 590-92.

[4]Timothy Keller, *Generous Justice: How God's Grace Makes Us Just* (New York: Dutton, 2010), p. 10, emphasis in original.

[5]Jerome F. D. Creach, *The Destiny of the Righteous in the Psalms* (Atlanta: Chalice Press, 2008), p. 18.

[6]Douglas J. Schuurman, *Vocation: Discerning Our Callings in Life* (Grand Rapids: Eerdmans, 2004), p. 123.

[7]Miroslav Volf, *Work in the Spirit: Toward a Theology of Work* (New York: Oxford University Press, 1991), p. 100.

[8]Ibid., p. 119.

[9]Creach, *Destiny of the Righteous*, pp. 34-36.

[10]Doug Sherman and William Hendricks, *Your Work Matters to God* (Colorado Springs: NavPress, 1987), p. 97.

[11]This is a central message in Mark Labberton's insightful book *The Dangerous Act of Loving Your Neighbor* (Downers Grove, Ill.: InterVarsity Press, 2010).

[12]Creach, *Destiny of the Righteous*, p. 29, 37. Notice the similarity of Creach's and Keller's definitions of the righteous.

[13]Ibid., p. 38.

[14]Tim Keller, "Creation Care and Justice," sermon delivered at Redeemer Presbyterian Church, New York, January 16, 2005.

[15]Justin Kitch, "The Fourth Priority," CEO Unplugged (September 20, 2006) <http://ceounplugged.homestead.com/philanthropy>. Note: Kitch sold Homestead.com in 2007 to Intuit, but did so after saying no to eighteen other offers. The yes to Intuit came because Kitch was confident the merger would allow Homestead's values and community-blessing practices to continue.

[16]Copeland's story is told in James E. Liebig's *Business Ethics: Profiles in Civic Virtue* (Golden, Colo.: Fulcrum Publishing, 1990), pp. 139-51.

[17]"Who We Are," Act One <www.actoneprogram.com/about-us/who-we-are>.

[18]John Romanowsky, "Christians Behind the Screen: An Interview with Barbara Nicolosi," *Godspy* (November 10, 2005) <http://oldarchive.godspy.com/reviews/Christians-Behind-the-Screen-An-Interview-with-Barbara-Nicolosi-by-John-Romanowsky.cfm.html>.

[19]All quotes from Barry Sorrells, retired orthopedic surgeon, are from a telephone interview with the author, March 14, 2011.

[20]In 2009 two students in the course objected to a reference that was made to Christianity. This led to the cancellation of the program. However, Sorrells met with the Christian Medical and Dental Association, and it decided to implement the LifeSkills Institute as part of its on-campus programs, which reach 80 percent of the medical schools in the nation.

[21]Dallas Willard, *The Great Omission: Reclaiming Jesus's Essential Teachings on Discipleship* (New York: HarperOne, 2006), p. 7.

[22]Ibid., p. 24.

[23]Perry Bigelow, "The Builder-Developer As Steward of God's Resources: Bringing God's Kingdom to the Marketplace and the Inner City," in *Faith Goes to Work*, ed.

Robert Banks (Washington, D.C.: The Alban Institute, 1993), p. 61.

[24]Perry Bigelow, interview with the author, June 28, 2010.

[25]Ibid. The current recession has been such a huge hit on the housing sector that Bigelow Homes has had to make some cuts. Perry calls this current climate "the Great Depression" in housing.

[26]Bigelow, "The Builder-Developer," p. 61.

[27]Ibid., pp. 61-62.

[28]Bigelow Homes also sponsors the annual "House for Hope" project. It donates land on which to build a house and then encourages members of its professional network of trade partners to donate the necessary labor and materials for construction. Then Bigelow sells the house and donates the profits to Hope International, a Christian nonprofit, which uses it to support microenterprise loans in the developing world.

[29]Perry Bigelow, "Think Differently, Think Creatively" (address to the Metropolitan Mayors Caucus Housing Task Force, February 8, 2006), Bigelow Homes <www .bigelowhomes.com/Why_Bigelow/Think_Differently>.

[30]Ibid. "The assessed value per acre at Bigelow's subdivision HomeTown Aurora (HTA) is 2.25 times higher than that of other area developments." This is a function of the relatively high density of the HTA subdivision combined with the high price per square foot of the small, premium-quality homes.

[31]I am indebted to Steve Hayner, president of Columbia Theological Seminary, for this insight.

Chapter 3: Why We Aren't the *Tsaddiqim*

[1]Michael Cassidy, *This Passing Summer: A South African's Response to White Fear, Black Anger, and the Politics of Love* (Oxnard, Calif.: Gospel Light Publications, 1990), p. 252, emphasis added.

[2]This was the conclusion of some of the contributors to the Christian Vision Project, a Pew Charitable Trust–sponsored initiative of Christianity Today International, from 2007 to 2009. The project raised three fundamental questions in an attempt to assess the state of American evangelicalism. In 2008 the query was, "Is Our Gospel Too Small?"

[3]In 2008, a survey by *Leadership Journal* of nearly 700 evangelical pastors on views of gospel and mission did offer some hopeful news about slowly changing perspectives. It reported that "[a] consistent theme emerging from the survey is the belief that previous descriptions of the gospel were incomplete." Slowly, pastors are embracing a fuller gospel of the kingdom. The article quoted Birmingham, Alabama, pastor David Platt as representative: "We have emphasized that you pray a prayer and you're saved, to our detriment." Increasingly, the survey reported, justification is seen as the beginning of the journey rather than whole gospel message. Relatedly, the survey showed changes in pastors' understandings about the kingdom of God. One third said they believed the kingdom was a present as well as future reality. While this reveals that this view is still not the dominant one, evidence from the survey reveals that a shift has begun. For 58 percent said that ten years ago they believed the king-

dom was a future reality only. (See Helen Lee, "Missional Shift or Drift?" *Leadership Journal*, November 7, 2008 <www.christianitytoday.com/le/fall/7.23.html>.)

[4]Joan Huyser-Honig, "Keith Getty on Writing Hymns for the Church Universal," Calvin Institute of Christian Worship (September 1, 2006) <www.calvin.edu/worship/stories/getty.php>. In some ways, in fact, bad theology in our songs can be more damaging than bad theology in our sermons. For we *participate* in singing; our senses and bodies are engaged. People are more likely to remember the words of the worship songs they sing than the preacher's words they hear. As anyone who has ever had the experience of not being able to "get that darn song out of my head" can testify, lyrics to choruses stick with us. Yet songs containing powerful truth can also unify and sustain us in the life of righteousness. Consider the vital role of music in the American civil rights movement; truth in song animated bravery and perseverance.

[5]Dick Staub, "My Rant Against CCM," *Christianity Today*, December 20, 2005. Staub's views echo other CCM critics, including singer-songwriter and producer Charlie Peacock. Peacock was one of the first Christian music insiders to raise red flags about the industry. Back in 1998, he lamented that "it is not uncommon for songwriters to perpetuate a truncated kingdom view in their lyrics. And it's out of this small, insufficient picture of the reality of kingdom life that Christian music gets categorized, the good news of Jesus gets trivialized, and authentic faith in him gets caricatured." Charlie Peacock, *At the Crossroads: Inside the Past, Present, and Future of Contemporary Christian Music*, exp. ed. (Colorado Springs: Shaw Books, 2004), p. 72.

[6]Brian McLaren, "An Open Letter to Worship Songwriters," *Worship Leader Magazine*, March/April 2005, <www.brianmclaren.net/archives/lettertosongwriters.pdf>.

[7]Tori Taff, *100 Greatest Songs in Christian Music* (Nashville: Integrity Publishers, 2006). The list of the top one hundred songs was compiled via a survey. Fifty percent of survey respondents were CCM industry professionals and 50 percent were from a random sample of the magazine's 2,500 subscribers. This list included songs from the past few decades, thus identifying songs that have had "staying power." In 2007, *CCM Magazine* (*Contemporary Christian Music Magazine*) changed its name to *Christ Community Music Magazine*.

[8]Our ratings were admittedly subjective, and a few songs were nearly impossible to rate at all since they were about family relationships (for example, "Butterfly Kisses" by Bob Carlisle) or marriage (for example, Steven Curtis Chapman's "I Will Be Here"). We also compiled all the song lyrics into one large document and conducted a mechanical count of the number of times certain words appeared in the songs. We had two grouping of words. One set included *I, me, myself, mine, forgive* (and *forgiven, forgiveness*), and *atone* or *paid*. The other set included *justice, hungry, poor, oppressed, needy, serve, restore, heal, compassion, community* and *neighbor*. We found 1,623 uses of the words in the first set and only 29 uses of words from the second set.

[9]Others include *Christ's Call to Discipleship* by James Montgomery Boice; *The Divine Conspiracy: Rediscovering Our Hidden Life in God* by Dallas Willard; *Spiritual Disci-*

plines for the Christian Life by Donald S. Whitney; *The Cost of Discipleship* by Dietrich Bonhoeffer; *How Now Shall We Live?* by Charles W. Colson; *A Long Obedience in the Same Direction: Discipleship in an Instant Society* by Eugene H. Peterson; *Celebration of Discipline: The Path to Spiritual Growth* by Richard J. Foster; *The Master's Plan for Making Disciples: Every Christian an Effective Witness Through an Enabling Church* by Win Arn; *The Reason for God* by Timothy Keller; *Discipleship Essentials: A Guide to Building Your Life in Christ* by Greg Ogden; *Taking Discipleship Seriously: A Radical Biblical Approach* by Tom Sine; *The Great Omission: Reclaiming Jesus' Essential Teachings on Discipleship* by Dallas Willard; *The Kingdom That Turned the World Upside Down* by David Bercot.

[10]There were some important exceptions. For example, Rick Warren's *The Purpose Driven Life* is an all-time bestseller, and he preaches a holistic gospel. Tim Keller's *The Reason for God* has been extremely popular, and he's one of the best gospel-of-the-kingdom preachers around today.

[11]James Davison Hunter, *American Evangelicalism: Conservative Religion and the Quandary of Modernity* (New Brunswick, N.J.: Rutgers University Press, 1983), pp. 142-43. The eight publishing houses were Bethany, Gospel Light, Moody, Revell/Spire, Scripture, Tyndale, Word and Zondervan. Five years later, Hunter published a study of evangelical college students called *Evangelicalism: The Coming Generation* (University of Chicago, 1987), noting that among this population there was an "accentuation of subjectivity and the virtual veneration of the self, exhibited in deliberate efforts to achieve self-understanding, self-improvement, and self-fulfillment" (p. 65).

[12]David Wells, *No Place for Truth, or Whatever Happened to Evangelical Theology?* (Grand Rapids: Eerdmans, 1993), pp. 130-31.

[13]Ronald J. Sider, *The Scandal of the Evangelical Conscience* (Grand Rapids: Baker, 2005), pp. 59-61.

[14]Ibid., p. 58.

[15]Dallas Willard, *The Great Omission: Reclaiming Jesus's Essential Teaching on Discipleship* (New York: HarperOne, 2006), p. 4.

[16]Ibid., p. 62.

[17]N. T. Wright, *Surprised by Hope: Rethinking Heaven, the Resurrection, and the Mission of the Church* (New York: HarperOne, 2008), p. 19.

[18]Ibid., p. 5.

[19]Ibid., p. 19. Hymns like John Keble's "Sun of My Soul, Thou Saviour Dear," for example, teach us about "losing ourselves in heaven above"—an idea far better suited to Buddhism than orthodox Christianity. In other hymns, we sing of Jesus coming to take us home—*away* from earth to heaven. By contrast, a hymn like James Montgomery's "Hail to the Lord's Anointed" directs attention to Christ's eternal kingship and the flourishing that will unfold in the New Jerusalem.

[20]Randy Alcorn, "Bodily Resurrection: Don't Settle for Less," Eternal Perspective Ministries (March 4, 2010) <www.epm.org/resources/2010/Mar/4/bodily-resurrection-dont-settle-less>. Alcorn is the author of the extensive book *Heaven*, a 560-page tome on the afterlife (Tyndale House, 2004).

[21]Wright, *Surprised by Hope*, p. 19.

[22]Ibid., p. 211.

[23]A word on 2 Peter 3:10-12 may be in order here. There the apostle talks about the world being consumed in fire. We need to recall that fire in Scripture typically means a refining fire. It's more often about purification, not annihilation. More to the point, Peter himself speaks in 2 Peter 3:13 of "a new heaven and a new earth." The word *new* there is *kainos* (new in nature or quality) not *neo* (new in time or origin). Therefore, Peter means "new" in the sense of *renewed*, not brand new.

[24]Wright, *Surprised by Hope*, p. 193, emphasis in original.

[25]Ibid., emphasis in original.

[26]Ibid., p. 208.

[27]Ibid., p. 211. Wright continues: "This will of course be radically different from the kind of work we would engage in if our sole task was to save souls for a disembodied heaven or simply to help people enjoy a fulfilling relationship with God as though that were the end of the matter. It will also be significantly different from the kind of work we might undertake if our sole task was to forget any God dimension at all and try simply to make life better within the continuation of the world as it is."

[28]D. Michael Lindsay, remarks at the Following Christ conference, Chicago, Ill., InterVarsity Christian Fellowship, 2008.

[29]D. Michael Lindsay, *Faith in the Halls of Power: How Evangelicals Joined the American Elite* (New York: Oxford University Press, 2008), p. 191.

[30]Ibid., p. 221.

[31]Ibid., p. 130.

[32]Ibid., p. 192.

[33]D. Michael Lindsay, "A Gated community in the Evangelical World," *USA Today*, February 11, 2008. Available at <www.rev.org/article.asp?ID=2991>.

[34]This was the finding of South African scholar Charles Villa-Vicencio and the personal experience of Beyers Naude, one of the most prominent white conservative Christians to join the resistance movement. By "real encounter," Villa-Vicencio meant that white Christians had become personally acquainted with the real-world living conditions of blacks under apartheid, and they had developed peer relationships with blacks (critical since at that time most whites dealt with blacks only in master-servant relationships). See *Resistance and Hope: South African Essays in Honor of Beyers Naude*, ed. Charles Villa-Vicencio, Beyers Naude and John W. de Gruchy (Grand Rapids: Eerdmans, 1985).

[35]Cassidy, *This Passing Summer*, p. 224.

[36]Ibid., p. 227.

[37]Ibid., p. 473.

[38]Ibid., p. 239.

Chapter 4: How the Gospel of the Kingdom Nurtures the *Tsaddiqim*

[1]See Michael Card's song "The Promise," *The Promise* (Brentwood, Tenn.: Sparrow, 1991).

[2]James Choung, *True Story: A Christianity Worth Believing In* (Downers Grove, Ill.: InterVarsity Press, 2009).

[3]Ibid., p. 198.

[4]Darrow L. Miller, *Servanthood: The Calling of Every Christian* (Phoenix: Disciple Nations Alliance, 2009), p. 95.

[5]Michael Frost and Alan Hirsch emphasize that our sentness is tied to our discipleship to Jesus: "Jesus defines us totally. . . . Our connection with the Trinity is through its Second Person. This has many implications, but for one it means that we can never get beyond the fact that we are disciples and therefore people directly connected to the messianic purposes in the world." *The Shaping of Things to Come* (Peabody, Mass.: Hendrickson, 2003), p. 113.

[6]Dietrich Bonhoeffer, *Life Together: The Classic Exploration of Faith in Community* (New York: HarperCollins, 1954), pp. 43-44, emphasis added.

[7]Ryan Bell, "Witnessing to God's Reign," *Spectrum*, August 4, 2008 <www.spectrummagazine.org/print/845>.

[8]The apostle John wrote, "The reason the Son of God appeared was to destroy the works of the devil" (1 Jn 3:8 esv).

[9]Jesus charged the original disciples with such labor: "One day Jesus called together his twelve disciples and gave them power and authority to cast out all demons and to heal all diseases. Then he sent them out to tell everyone about the Kingdom of God and to heal the sick" (Lk 9:1-2 nlt).

[10]Frost and Hirsch, *The Shaping of Things*, p. 115, emphasis added.

[11]N. T. Wright, *Surprised by Hope: Rethinking Heaven, the Resurrection, and the Mission of the Church* (New York: HarperOne, 2008), p. 200, emphasis added.

[12]"There's a riddle in the Talmud that goes like this, 'If God intended man to live on bread, why didn't he create a bread tree?' . . . The answer is that, in fact, God . . . prefers to offer us a grain and invite us to buy a field and plant the seed. He prefers that we till the soil while he sends the rain. He prefers that we harvest the crop while he sends sunshine. . . . Why? Because he would rather we become partners with him in creation. Of course, God could simply supply our every need and solve our every problem. But our God invites us into a creative partnership with him. He supplies the earth, the air, the water, the sun, and our strength and then asks us to work with him." Frost and Hirsch, *The Shaping of Things*, p. 159.

Chapter 5: Integrating Faith and Work

[1]Doug Sherman and William Hendricks, *Your Work Matters to God* (Colorado Springs: NavPress, 1987), p. 16. Sherman's organization did a survey of two thousand Christians. Ninety percent had *never* heard a sermon relating biblical principles to their work life.

[2]Nancy Lovell, "An Interview with David Miller," FaithInTheWorkplace.com <www.christianitytoday.com/workplace/articles/interviews/davidmiller.html>, emphasis added.

[3]Pete Hammond, R. Paul Stevens and Todd Svanoe, ed., *The Marketplace Annotated*

Bibliography: A Christian Guide to Books on Work, Business, and Vocation (Downers Grove, Ill.: InterVarsity Press, 2002). This extensive literature review includes several hundred books, but a significant number do not specifically address the question of integrating faith and work.

[4]Seminars in Christian Scholarship, "Business as Ministry: Exploring the Issues, Patterns, and Challenges," Calvin College, July 16-17, 2007 <www.calvin.edu/scs/2007/seminars/business>.

[5]The Fellowship of Christian Graduate Students lists thirty-eight such professional associations on its website. See <www.bgsu.edu/studentlife/organizations/fcgs/christprof.html>.

[6]David W. Miller, *God at Work: The History and Promise of the Faith at Work Movement* (New York: Oxford University Press, 2007), p. 6.

[7]Ibid., p. 5. Douglas J. Schuurman's book *Vocation: Discerning Our Callings in Life* (Grand Rapids: Eerdmans, 2004) offers an accessible summary of the thought of Luther and Calvin.

[8]Ibid., p. 129.

[9]Ibid., p. 131, emphasis added.

[10]Ibid., p. 192, n. 18.

[11]Ken Walker, "It's Time for Marketplace Ministry," *Charisma*, May 31, 2003 <www.charismamag.com/index.php/features2/234-unorganized/7624-its-time-for-marketplace-ministry>.

[12]Miller, *God at Work*, p. 135.

[13]Ibid., p. 139.

[14]The fifteen were Blackaby Ministries International—Marketplace Ministries, Fellowship of Companies for Christ International, Kingdom Companies, Breakthrough Fellowship, Businessmen's Fellowship USA, International Fellowship of Christian Businessmen, Christians in Commerce, His Church at Work, C12 Group, Christian Businessmen Connection, Kiros, Life Chasers, Marketplace Network/Made to Matter, International Christian Chamber of Commerce, and Needle's Eye Ministries.

[15]Fellowship of Companies for Christ International, "Vision and Mission" <www.fcci-online.org/about-us/vision-mission>.

[16]Ibid. Breakthrough Fellowship, the International Fellowship of Christian Businessmen and the Christian Businessmen Connection also state as their main objectives evangelism and personal discipleship. Businessmen's Fellowship USA encourages businessmen to share Christ in their workplace and offers a variety of events where Christians can tell their testimonies publicly. All these groups tend to limit their attention to ethical matters to those concerning individual behavior, as opposed to the mezzo- and macro-level ethical issues described by Miller.

[17]See Blackaby's Marketplace Ministries webpage for current Bible study dates <www.blackaby.org/resources/bible_study>.

[18]D. Michael Lindsay found that these business leaders were strongly committed to personal ethics and that many sponsored workplace Bible studies or hired corporate

chaplains. He also met business leaders who expressed concerns about guarding their firm's public self-presentation. Some corporate executives he interviewed noted that one way their faith shaped their work concerned their decisions about company spokespeople. They worked to ensure that such spokespeople, including celebrities, shared the faith values the evangelical executives held. Jockey CEO Debra Waller made a decision that in the underwear company's advertisements that showed both men and women, the actors would wear wedding bands. In this way Waller "publicly link[ed] evangelical faith with corporate decision-making." *Faith in the Halls of Power: How Evangelicals Joined the American Elite* (New York: Oxford University Press, 2008), p. 179.

[19]The Business As Mission (BAM) movement offers hope for a more robust integration of faith and work that advances foretastes of the kingdom. Readers wanting to know more about this important and encouraging development can read an overview of BAM on <www.vocationalstewardship.org>.

[20]The twenty-three were Christian Engineering Society, Christian Dance Fellowship, Christian Educators Association International, Christian Medical and Dental Associations, Affiliation of Christian Geologists, Artisan, Gegrapha, Christians in the Visual Arts, Christian Legal Society, Association of Christian Economists, Christians in Political Science, American Scientific Affiliation, Christian Pharmacists Fellowship International, Association of Christians in the Mathematical Sciences, Association of Christian Librarians, Christian Sociology Society, Christian Association for Psychological Studies, Christian Veterinary Mission, Christians in the Theater Arts, Affiliation of Christian Biologists, North American Association of Christians in Social Work, Christian Foresters Fellowship, and Nurses Christian Fellowship.

[21]"Purposes of the ACMS," ACMS Online <www.acmsonline.org/beliefs/index.html>.

[22]Christian Neuroscience Society <http://cneuroscience.org>.

[23]Timothy R. Tuinstra, "Applying the Reformational Doctrine of Christian Vocation to our Understanding of Engineering as a Sacred Calling," presented at the Christian Engineering Education Conference, June 22, 2006. See <http://people.cedarville.edu/employee/tuinstra/bio_.htm>.

[24]CIVA has updated its mission statement since then, to be called to creative work, devoted to the church and present in culture. See "Mission," Christians in the Visual Arts <www.civa.org/about/mission>.

[25]Christian Medical and Dental Associations, "About Our Organization" <www.cmda.org/WCM/CMDA/Navigation/About/About_CMDA.aspx>.

[26]James Davidson Hunter, *To Change the World* (New York: Oxford University Press, 2010), p. 235, emphasis in original.

[27]Doug Spada, founder, WorkLife, Inc., telephone interview with the author, November 9, 2010.

Chapter 6: Inspiration

[1]Doug Spada, "Founder's WorkLife Vision," YouTube <www.youtube.com/watch?v=r-tDaFcsVdo>.

[2]All quotes from Tom Nelson, senior pastor, Christ Community Church, Leawood, Kans., are from a telephone interview with the author, October 21, 2010.

[3]Robert J. Banks, ed., *Faith Goes to Work: Reflections from the Marketplace* (Eugene, Ore.: Wipf & Stock, 1999), pp. 22-26.

[4]Ibid., p. 24.

[5]Lesslie Newbigin, *Signs Amid the Rubble: The Purposes of God in Human History* (Grand Rapids: Eerdmans, 2003), p. 47.

[6]Frederick Buechner, *Wishful Thinking: A Seeker's ABC* (New York: HarperOne, 1993), p. 119.

[7]Evangelical scholars John Bernbaum and Simon Steer assume a blunt position on this issue. They argue that "all jobs are not of equal worth in God's sight. A biblical perspective on work suggests that work is a God-ordained activity and that labor is of value as we serve as stewards and co-creators in God's world. But cultural worth is another criterion of Christian teaching about work. If we are called to be servants, the work that we do must bring benefit to others—benefit that has significance. We should avoid not only jobs that are harmful by definition (gambling and prostitution, for example), but also work that results in no useful service. Using our abilities to develop, make, or sell people luxury items or articles that can be harmful is not a biblically sound choice of a career. That is not God's desire for us." *Why Work* (Grand Rapids: Baker, 1986), p. 87.

[8]Unless otherwise noted, all quotes from Jill Sorenson, sustainability advisor, Rebuild Consulting, are from a telephone interview with the author, July 29, 2010.

[9]Unless otherwise noted, all quotes from Cynthia Leibrock are from "The Secrets to Aging Beautifully" (audio file) <http://agingbeautifully.org/tape1.mp3>.

[10]Joyce Wadler, "A Colorado Home Is Ready for Its Owners' Old Age," *New York Times*, February 19, 2009.

[11]Ibid.

[12]"Rehabitat Fund: The Carpenter's Helpers," Aging Beautifully <http://agingbeauti fully.org/volunteers.html>.

[13]In part three, I outline four pathways of expressing vocational stewardship. Jill and Cynthia demonstrate how believers can live out more than one pathway at a time. Both are examples of pathway one (blooming where you're planted). Additionally, Jill's volunteer work abroad is an example of pathway two (donating skills). Cynthia's Rehabitat initiative is an example of pathway three (launch your own social enterprise).

[14]Jill Sorenson, "Beyond the Walls," *JILLM: Searching for Beauty in the Everyday* (February 19, 2007) <http://jillm.com/2007/02/19/beyond-the-walls-2>.

[15]Douglas J. Schuurman, *Vocation: Discerning Our Callings in Life* (Grand Rapids: Eerdmans, 2004), pp. 130-31.

[16]Unless otherwise noted, the following quotes are from Adam Hamilton, "@ Work," sermon delivered at Church of the Resurrection, Leawood, Kans., July 19, 2009.

[17]"GEAR for Sports® Joins Fair Labor Association," June 19, 2000, press release <www.gearnosweat.com>.

Chapter 7: Discovery

[1]Pastor Armitage retired from his role as senior pastor at Pleasant Valley in late 2010.

[2]Church Community Builder (CCB) is a sophisticated program that enables congregations to build and manage profiles of members' involvement. CCB's "Positions" feature, for example, helps church leaders match service opportunities with individuals best suited to fill them based on their gifts, passions, skills and leadership style. The software also allows congregants to search online and apply for service opportunities that fit them well.

[3]All quotes from Charlene Armitage, director of equipping, Pleasant Valley Baptist Church, are from a telephone interview with the author, August 24, 2010. (She retired from this church position in late 2010.)

[4]Quotes from Sue Mallory, assistant stated clerk of the session, Brentwood Presbyterian Church, and author of *The Equipping Church*, are from a telephone interview with the author, August 11, 2010.

[5]All quotes from Don Simmons, president, Creative Potential Consulting and Training, are from a telephone interview with the author, August 5, 2010.

[6]On a more encouraging note, though, these few are among the most popular. According to Erik Rees at Central Saddleback Church, some fifty thousand congregations have used the SHAPE assessment. Originated by Saddleback Church in California, SHAPE helps people identify not only their spiritual gifts but also their heart passions and personality type, as well as experiences that have shaped them. Servants by Design, created by Fellowship Bible Church in Little Rock, Arkansas, is perhaps the best assessment tool in terms of its breadth of coverage. It combines a spiritual gifts questionnaire with a behavioral assessment and numerous questions about abilities and skills. Halftime, a Christian ministry helping successful marketplace leaders make the shift from "success to significance," recommends this tool. Servants by Design is also used in the curriculum for the Christian parachurch ministry Men's Fraternity, "for men to determine how they interact in vocation and serve outside of their job." According to Ann Blair from Fellowship Bible Church, more than fifteen thousand groups of men attend a weekly Men's Fraternity meeting globally.

[7]Don Simmons agrees. He says the publishers of the assessment tools hardly ever include suggestions for people to deploy their gifts outside the four walls of the church. This, he thinks, is because those publishers know that this internally focused approach sells better. Many church leaders, he laments, are far more interested in getting members to do church work than externally focused mission.

[8]From Dorothy Sayers's essay "Why Work?" *Creed or Chaos* (New York: Harcourt Brace, 1947), as quoted in Douglas J. Schuurman, *Vocation: Discerning Our Callings in Life* (Grand Rapids: Eerdmans, 2004), p. 134.

[9]Tim Hammack, "Gourmet Giving," *Guideposts*, October 2010, p. 61.

[10]Ibid., p. 62.

[11]John Blackstone, "Former High End Chef Now Feeds the Homeless," *CBS Evening*

News (November 25, 2009) <www.cbsnews.com/stories/2009/11/25/eveningnews/main5777661.shtml>.

[12]Hammack, "Gourmet Giving," p. 64.

[13]Stan Grossfeld, quoted in "The Pulitzer Photographs: A Glimpse of Life," produced by the Newseum, Washington, D.C.

[14]Ronald J. Sider et al., *Linking Arms, Linking Lives: How Urban-Suburban Partnerships Can Transform Communities* (Grand Rapids: Baker, 2008), p. 127.

[15]John Philips, real estate developer, interview with the author, Chicago, June 28, 2010.

[16]Unless otherwise noted, all quotes from Helen Bach, administrative supervisor, Olive Crest, are from a telephone interview with the author, September 23, 2010.

[17]Kevin Brennfleck and Kay Marie Brennfleck, *Live Your Calling: A Practical Guide to Finding and Fulfilling Your Mission in Life* (San Francisco: Jossey-Bass, 2005), pp. 36-39.

[18]Craig Pitman, "The Christian Artist in Ministry," ArtsReformation.com (April 12, 2006) <www.artsreformation.com/a001/cp-ministry.html>.

[19]"Our Impact," Carson Scholars Fund <http://carsonscholars.org/content/about-csf/our-impact>.

[20]Brad Bell, "A Dislocated Heart," sermon delivered at The Well Community Church, Fresno, Calif., September 5, 2009 <http://thewellcommunity.org/podcast/the-feed-sermon-podcast/1/dislocated-heart-nehemiah-11-4/220>.

[21]All quotes from Tim Schulz, founder, ReVive Industries, are from a telephone interview with the author, September 2, 2010.

Chapter 8: Formation

[1]I'm indebted to Tim Keller for this insight.

[2]Rabbi Michael Strassfeld, "Avodah: Vocation, Calling, Service," My Jewish Learning <www.myjewishlearning.com/practices/Ethics/Business_Ethics/Themes_and_Theology/Value_of_Work/Work_as_Calling.shtml>.

[3]Kenton Beshore, *Rooted: Connect with God, the Church, Your Purpose* (Irvine, Calif.: Mariners Church, 2010), p. 108.

[4]Ibid., p. 104.

[5]Mark Labberton, *The Dangerous Act of Loving Your Neighbor: Seeing Others Through the Eyes of Jesus* (Downers Grove, Ill.: InterVarsity Press, 2010), p. 96.

[6]Ibid., p. 67.

[7]Ibid., p. 182.

[8]Ibid., p. 184.

[9]Tim Keller, "A New Kind of Urban Christian," The Christian Vision Project (June 15, 2006) <www.christianvisionproject.com/2006/06/a_new_kind_of_urban_christian.html>.

[10]Gary Haugen, *Just Courage: God's Great Expedition for the Restless Christian* (Downers Grove, Ill.: InterVarsity Press, 2008), p. 18.

[11]Ibid., p. 20, emphasis added.

¹²Ibid., p. 38.

¹³Brad Pellish, associate pastor, Bethany Bible Church, interview with the author, Phoenix, December 3, 2009.

¹⁴Dallas Willard, *The Great Omission: Reclaiming Jesus's Essential Teachings on Discipleship* (New York: HarperOne, 2006), pp. 16-17.

¹⁵Steve Gillen, campus pastor, Willow Creek North Shore Community Church, telephone interview with the author, September 7, 2010.

¹⁶As vice regents, our stewardship responsibility is to *develop* the creation (that's the Hebrew word *abad* in Genesis 2:15, where it says Adam was to work the garden) and to *protect* it (that's the Hebrew word *shamar* in Genesis 2:15, translated as *tend*).

¹⁷I'm indebted to Andy Crouch for this insight.

¹⁸Andy Crouch, *Culture Making: Recovering Our Creative Calling* (Downers Grove, Ill.: InterVarsity Press, 2008), p. 230, emphasis added.

¹⁹Quoted in Amy L. Sherman, *Being There: Faith on the Frontlines—Successful Models of Faith-Based, Cross-Sector Collaboration from the 2006 Partners in Transformation Awards Program* (Indianapolis: Sagamore Institute for Policy Research, 2006), p. 41.

Chapter 9: Deploying Vocational Power

¹Tim Keller, "Cultural Renewal: The Role of the Entrepreneurs and Intrapreneurs," Center for Faith and Works, Entrepreneurship Forum 2006 <www.faithandwork.org/2006_ei_forum_page3037.php>.

²Steve Garber, president, Washington Institute, personal conversation with the author, October 13, 2010.

³Kim S. Phipps, "Prologue: Campus Climate and Christian Scholarship," in *Scholarship and Christian Faith: Enlarging the Conversation*, ed. Douglas Jacobsen and Rhonda Hustedt Jacobsen (New York: Oxford University Press, 2004), p. 174.

⁴James Davison Hunter, *To Change the World: The Irony, Tragedy, and Possibility of Christianity in the Late Modern World* (New York: Oxford University Press, 2010), p. 252.

⁵See Howard Gardner, *Frames of Mind: The Theory of Multiple Intelligences* (New York: Basic Books, 1993).

⁶Andy Crouch, *Culture Making: Recovering Our Creative Calling* (Downers Grove, Ill.: InterVarsity Press, 2008), p. 67.

⁷Brian Fikkert and Steve Corbett, *When Helping Hurts: How to Alleviate Poverty Without Hurting the Poor . . . and Yourself* (Chicago: Moody Press, 2009).

Chapter 10: Pathway 1

¹All quotes by Hill are from Matthew Myers, "CEO Profile: Tom Hill, President, Kimray Incorporated," Christ @ Work <www.christatwork.com/data/PDFFiles/Tom%20Hill%20interview.pdf>.

²Rev. Dr. John Yates, "Seek the Welfare of the City: A Vision for Pastors and Pastoring," Commencement Address at Covenant Theological Seminary, St. Louis, Mo., May 16, 2008.

[3]"Faith and Work Ministry," Harbor Presbyterian Church—Downtown (San Diego) <www.harbordowntown.org/get-involved/faith--work-ministry>.

[4]All quotes from Duke Kwon, former associate pastor, Grace DC, are from a telephone interview with the author, November 3, 2010.

[5]Davida Foy Crabtree, *The Empowering Church: How One Congregation Supports Lay People's Ministries in the World* (Herndon, Va.: The Alban Institute, 1989), p. 6.

[6]Additionally, every Labor Day, Yates invites a lay member to preach a sermon on faithfulness in vocation.

[7]Visit <www.vocationalstewardship.org> for a copy of Church of the Savior's "Service of Ordination."

[8]Tom Nelson, senior pastor, Christ Community Church, telephone interview with the author, October 21, 2010.

[9]Susan Olasky, "An 'Integral Life' at Work," *World*, November 29, 2008 <www.worldmag.com/articles/14692>.

[10]Ibid.

[11]Ibid.

[12]"Work Life at Peachtree," Peachtree <www.peachtreepres.org/Worklife.aspx>.

[13]Victor Pentz, "Soli Deo Gloria: Calling of Peter and the Fisherman Disciples," Sermon Series: Vintage Jesus (August 31, 2008) <www.peachtreepres.org/downloads/sermons/20080831sermon.pdf>.

[14]All quotes from Bonnie Worzbacher, senior vice president for Global Customer and Channel Leadership, The Coca-Cola Company, are from a telephone interview with the author, August 25, 2010.

[15]Center for Faith and Work <www.faithandwork.org>.

[16]All quotes from Katherine Leary Alsdorf, director, Center for Faith and Work, Redeemer Presbyterian Church, are from a telephone interview with the author, February 6, 2009.

[17]Fashion Industry Group, Center for Faith and Work <www.faithandwork.org/fashion>.

[18]"Entrepreneurship Initiative: The Competition," Center for Faith and Work <www.faithandwork.org/the_competition_page1234.php>.

[19]Winners have been diverse. Threads Theater Company, a 2007 winner, aims to "start inclusive conversations about faith and contribute to cultural renewal." A 2009 winner, Alphabet Scoop Ice Cream, provides job training and mentoring in an ice cream shop for at-risk youth. Entrepreneurship Initiative has also helped jump-start initiatives to provide legal aid to those in extreme poverty, jobs in the toy-making industry in Honduras, holistic health care for the underserved on Staten Island and a safe house for victims of sex trafficking.

[20]Duke Kwon, former associate pastor, Grace DC, telephone interview with the author, November 3, 2010. Grace Church launched twelve groups, creating the categories for them inductively based on congregational responses. These included groups for artists, educators, businesspeople, engineers, health care professionals and Capitol Hill staffers, among others.

[21]All quotes from Wendy Clark, owner, Carpe Diem, are from a telephone interview with the author's assistant Sally Carlson, September 27, 2010.

[22]James Davison Hunter, *To Change the World: The Irony, Tragedy, and Possibility of Christianity in the Late Modern World* (New York: Oxford University Press, 2010), p. 257, emphasis in original.

[23]Anne C. Bailey, plenary address, Following Christ Conference, Chicago, 2008 (audio file) <http://media.intervarsity.org/mp3/AnneCBailey.mp3>.

[24]Gordon Govier, "InterVarsity Alumni—Anne C. Bailey," InterVarsity (October 16, 2008) <www.intervarsity.org/news/intervarsity-alumni--anne-c-bailey>.

[25]Ibid.

[26]Jeanine Lacquement, founder and director, Children of the Light Dancers, telephone interview with the author, May 16, 2010.

[27]Timothy Stoner, "Milt Kuyers: Redefining Success," in *My Business, My Mission*, ed. Doug Seebeck and Timothy Stoner (Grand Rapids: Partners Worldwide, 2009), p. 23.

[28]Ibid.

[29]Milt Kuyers, former owner, Star Sprinklers, telephone interview with the author, August 25, 2010.

[30]All quotes from Carlos Oscar, professional comedian, are from a telephone interview with the author, August 10, 2010.

[31]Information about Pia Cayetano here is taken from her blog at <www.mydailyrace.com> and website at <www.senatorpiacayetano.com>.

[32]"Interview with Philippines' Senator Pia Cayetano," *The World of Parliaments*, July 2005, p. 4 <www.ipu.org/PDF/wop/18_en.pdf>.

[33]"Profile: Bora Aksu," *Artisan*, vol. 1 <www.artisaninitiatives.org/Publisher/Article.aspx?ID=75333>.

[34]Bonnie Alter, "People Tree Goes Designer," Treehugger (May 10, 2007) <www.treehugger.com/files/2007/05/people_trees_ne.php>.

[35]Ibid.

[36]This account is based on the profile of Schenk in *Entrepreneurs in the Faith Community: Profiles of Mennonites in Business*, ed. Calvin W. Redekop and Benjamin W. Redekop (Scottdale, Penn.: Herald Press, 1996), pp. 18-38.

Chapter 11: Pathway 2

[1]Unless otherwise noted, information and quotes from Dan Blevins are from a telephone interview with the author, September 16, 2010.

[2]"Finishers Project Mission Statement," Finishers Project <http://finishers.org/index.php?id=75>.

[3]Quoted in Daniel Blevins, "Baby Boomer Finds New Calling," *American Family Association Journal* (October 2009) <www.afajournal.org/1009default.asp>.

[4]"Volunteering," Mt. Pisgah Methodist Church (Johns Creek, Ga.) <www.mountpisgah.org/Mission/Volunteering.cfm>.

[5]PLACE, a discovery tool that assesses congregant's gifts, talents, skills, life experiences and passions, was developed by Jay McSwain. See <www.placeministries.org>.

[6]Taking the artist-waitress as an example, the first biblical counsel to heed comes from Colossians 3:23-24, about doing all our tasks "as for the Lord." The waitress should ask for God's help in offering excellent customer service and in being a punctual, hardworking and honest employee. She should seek to love and serve her co-workers. She could also brainstorm with friends as to how, despite her modest position, she could advance kingdom values—such as peace, beauty, justice, sustainability or community—in and through her work. For example, if the restaurant is small and family owned, she may be able to talk to the owners about buying local produce as an expression of environmental stewardship. If it is part of a large chain, her boss may not have a lot of scope for making such a decision. In this instance, the waitress might suggest a different sort of activity, such as a training session for wait staff in effective ways to deal with nasty customers. Perhaps a counselor, or a person with conflict resolution skills, from the waitress's home congregation, could be invited in to give a short presentation on this topic. In this small way, the waitress can contribute to promoting the kingdom value of peace at her workplace.

Meanwhile, since her true calling is as an artist, she might consider what actions she could take to promote beauty in the way the food is presented or the manner in which the restaurant is decorated. Or she may be able to volunteer her services to decorate the restrooms or brighten up the landscaping outside the restaurant. Perhaps she could even convince the restaurant's owner to allow her to use the facility occasionally, when it is closed, to give art classes to disadvantaged children.

[7]Aaron Hurst, "Making the Most of a Wave of Volunteers," *The Chronicle of Philanthropy*, June 4, 2009 <http://philanthropy.com/article/Making-the-Most-of-a-Wave-of/57445>.

[8]Mark A. Hager, "Volunteer Management Capacity in America's Charities and Congregations: A Briefing Report," Urban Institute, Washington, D.C., 2004, p. 19.

[9]Sue Mallory, assistant stated clerk of the session, Brentwood Presbyterian Church, Los Angeles, telephone interview with the author, August 11, 2010.

[10]Gordon Murphy, managing partner, The Barnabas Group Chicago, telephone interview with the author, April 7, 2010.

[11]William Diehl, *Thank God, It's Monday!* (Philadelphia: Fortress, 1982), pp. 191-92.

[12]"Serving Central," Grace Community Church <http://gracecc.org/serve/serving-central>.

[13]I found two parachurch ministries that also deploy this sort of technology. Mission Finder has this model on its "Vocational Missions Opportunities" page. See <www.missionfinder.org/level2.htm>. (A drop-down menu allows a user to select his or her vocational skill area. The site then generates a list of nonprofit ministries looking for volunteers with that or a similar skill.) Serving in Mission uses a similar approach on its site, at a page labeled "Missions By Your Career." See <www.sim.org/index.php/career>.

[14]"Glocal: Externally Focused Ministries," Lifebridge Christian Church <http://lbcc.org/externallyfocused>.

[15]Ed Fischer, telephone interview with the author, September 2, 2010. Other churches too have started implementing vocationally based short-term missions trips. The River Church in San Jose, California, sends professional teams to support Paz y Esperanza, a Peruvian ministry active in fighting child sexual abuse. "We try to bring over people who have best practices in law enforcement, criminal prosecution, the psychology area and Christian community activism," coordinator Pete Snell reports. Last year, for example, the team included four forensic nurses, an ex-cop, some interpreters and a businessman. (Pete Snell, telephone interview with the author, August 31, 2010.) Northwood Church in Keller, Texas, sponsors numerous vocationally based short-term missions trips to its partners in Vietnam and Mexico. Its 2011 trips calendar included specific opportunities for medical professionals, educators, businesspeople, athletes, carpenters and people with expertise in the care of special-needs children. Northwood's senior pastor Bob Roberts Jr. has written about such efforts in his book, *Real-Time Connections: Linking Your Job with God's Global Work* (Grand Rapids: Zondervan, 2010), p. 123. See also the "Glocal" section of the church's website at <http://northwoodchurch.org/glocal_ministry.php?id=13>.

[16]Alternatively, the fair coordinator could collect all the want ads and then cluster them by skill set, and create several one-page sheets (in different colors) by vocational skill. For example, one sheet would list all the ministries (with their booth numbers) that had indicated a need for people with various sorts of business skills. Another sheet would list all the ministries that indicated they had serving opportunities for people in the creative arts. A third would list the ministries that indicated some kind of need for communications professionals.

[17]Unless otherwise noted, all quotes from Elise Chong are from a telephone interview with the author, July 14, 2010.

[18]"Professionals in Action," Hope for New York <http://hfny.org/volunteer/professionals-in-action>.

[19]Bill Wellons and Lloyd Reeb, *Unlimited Partnership: Igniting a Marketplace Leader's Journey to Significance* (Nashville: B & H Publishing, 2006).

[20]Ibid., pp. 60-61.

[21]Vernon Armitage, "Defining Moments: Volunteerism," audio CD produced by Willow Creek North, July 2009.

[22]Charlene Armitage, director of equipping, Pleasant Valley Baptist Church, telephone interview with the author, August 24, 2010.

[23]This and the following quotes from Charlene Armitage are from personal correspondence with the author, November 28, 2010.

[24]Robert Lewis, "What to do with Talented People," *Innovation 2007: Connecting Innovators to Multiply* (Leadership Network, 2007), p. 42 <http://leadnet.org/resources/download/innovation_2007>.

[25]Ibid., pp. 43-44.

[26]Don Schoendorfer, founder and president, Free Wheelchair Mission, interview with the author, Irvine, Calif., July 8, 2009.

[27]Rod Beadle, president and founder, Engineering Resources Association, telephone interview with the author, July 21, 2010.

[28]Gordon Murphy, managing partner, The Barnabas Group Chicago, telephone interview with the author, April 7, 2010.

[29]All quotes from Kay Edwards, president and CEO, Vesper Services Network, are from a telephone interview with the author, August 13, 2010.

[30]John Rahe, president, Rahe Engineering, telephone interview with the author, July 22, 2010.

[31]All quotes from Larry Mollner are from an interview with the author, Glencoe, Ill., June 30, 2010.

Chapter 12: Pathway 3

[1]All quotes from Muriithi Wanjau are from an interview with the author, Nairobi, January 20, 2010.

[2]Simon Mbevi, director, Transform Kenya, presentation at Mavuno Church, Nairobi, January 22, 2010.

[3]Unless otherwise noted, all quotes from Daisy Waimiri are from an interview with the author, Nairobi, January 20, 2010.

[4]All quotes from Linda Ochola Adolwa, associate pastor, Mavuno Church, are from an interview with the author, Nairobi, January 20, 2010.

[5]All quotes from Anne Nzilani, founder and CEO, Bawa la Tumaini, are from an interview with the author, Nairobi, January 20, 2010.

[6]All quotes from Kanjii Mbugua, CEO, Kijiji Records, are from an interview with the author, Nairobi, January 20, 2010.

[7]I've included Kanjii's story in this pathway three chapter because it emerged out of Mavuno Church. However, in Kanjii's case, the influence of the Mavuno Marathon didn't result in a new social enterprise; they did not create a new organization. Instead, they created new programs within their business. In this way they've acted as what Tim Keller has called "intrapreneuers"—innovative people who do new things to bring about reform in their industry sector. But they do it from inside existing organizations rather than by starting new ones.

[8]All quotes from Ken Oloo are from his presentation at Mavuno Church, Nairobi, January 22, 2010.

Chapter 13: Pathway 4

[1]This church's story is told in Samuel G. Freedman, *Upon This Rock: The Miracles of a Black Church* (New York: Harper Perennial, 1994).

[2]See Krista Petty, "Calvary Chapel Fort Lauderdale, FL: A Model of Cause-Related Community Involvement," UrbanMinistry.org (2007) <www.urbanministry.org/files/Calvary_Chapel_Florida_FINAL.pdf>.

[3]I've had the privilege of learning of these churches and ministries—New Song Baltimore, Lawndale Community Church, Bethel New Life, Joy of Jesus and FCS Urban Ministries—through my involvement with the Christian Community Development Association. Visit <www.ccda.org>.

[4]Unless otherwise noted, the following quotes from Mike Honeycutt, former senior pastor, Southwood Presbyterian Church, are from a telephone interview with the author, October 15, 2010.

[5]Mike Honeycutt, "Shepherding Change in the Local Congregation," *Leadership: Succeeding in the Private, Public, and Not-for-Profit Sectors*, ed. Ronald R. Sims and Scott A. Quatro (Armonk, N.Y.: M. E. Sharpe, 2005), pp. 143-51.

[6]Unless otherwise noted, this and the following quotes from Mike Stanfield, president, Ducommun, are from a telephone interview with the author, October 7, 2010.

[7]Mark Stearns, director of Mercy Ministries, Southwood Presbyterian Church, quoted in "A Journey to Remember," Lincoln Village Ministry <www.lincoln villageministry.com/Home.html>.

[8]Amy L. Sherman, "Enlarging Worlds: Huntsville's Southwood PCA 'Adopts' Strapped Elementary School—And Its Families," *Equip for Ministry*, November/December 2005, p. 7.

[9]Ibid., p. 8.

[10]Liz Clemons, director, James A. Lane Unit of the Alabama Boys & Girls Club, telephone interview with the author, October 14, 2010.

[11]Yvonne Henry, a teacher at Lincoln Elementary School, quoted in Jennifer Pyron, "Teaching and Learning Better Together," *Working Toward Excellence: The Journal of the Alabama Best Practices Center* 8, no. 1 (Fall 2008): 15.

[12]From Lincoln Elementary's application for the 2010 Panasonic National School Change competition.

[13]Sherman, "Enlarging Worlds," p. 8.

[14]Unless otherwise noted, all quotes from Mark Stearns, director of Mercy Ministries, Southwood Presbyterian Church, are from a telephone interview with the author, September 16, 2010.

[15]Quoted in Kari Hawkins, "Opening doors: Church groups find ways to revitalize community, families," *Huntsville Times*, August 5, 2005.

[16]Ibid.

[17]Sherman, "Enlarging Worlds," p. 8.

[18]All quotes from Frank Six, university affairs officer, Marshall Space Flight Center, are from a telephone interview with the author, October 18, 2010.

[19]"A Journey to Remember," Lincoln Village Ministry (video) <www.lincolnvillage ministry.com/Home.html>.

[20]Sherman, "Enlarging Worlds," p. 9.

[21]All quotes from Margaret Powell, intervention specialist, Martin Luther King Jr. Elementary School, are from a telephone interview with author, October 8, 2010.

[22]Quoted in Pyron, "Lincoln's Powerful Community Partnership," *Working Toward Excellence: The Journal of the Alabama Best Practices Center* 8, no. 1 (Fall 2008): 14.

[23]Derek Simpson, partner, Warren and Simpson PC, telephone interview with the author, October 13, 2010.

[24]"Journey to Remember."

[25]Ibid.

[26]Ibid.

[27]Unnamed female resident of Lincoln Village quoted in "Journey to Remember."

[28]Liz Clemons, telephone interview with the author, October 14, 2010.

[29]Michelle Gilliam Jordan, department head, Department of Community Development, City of Huntsville, telephone interview with the author, October 15, 2010.

[30]Mickey Plott, broker, PLOTT ReGroup, telephone interview with the author, October 14, 2010.

[31]Sam Yeager, founder, Bristol Development Group, telephone interview with the author, October 5, 2010.

[32]Ibid.

[33]"Journey to Remember."

[34]Dale Bowen, housing coordinator, Lincoln Village Preservation Corporation, telephone interview with the author, September 16, 2010.

[35]Data reported by the school in its application for the 2010 Panasonic award.

[36]Ibid.

[37]Quoted in Pyron, "Lincoln's Powerful Community Partnership."

[38]Ibid.

[39]All quotes from Brian Tome, lead pastor, Crossroads, are from a telephone interview with the author, October 5, 2010.

[40]All quotes from Brian Wells, former teaching pastor, Crossroads, are from a telephone interview with the author, October 24, 2009.

[41]Deborah Leydon, partner, Dinsmore & Shohl LLP, interview with the author, Cincinnati, Ohio, October 21, 2009.

[42]All quotes from Andrew Peters, former justice director, Crossroads, are from an interview with the author, Cincinnati, Ohio, October 21, 2009.

[43]Mark Pruden, licensed professional clinical counselor, Mark Pruden and Associates, interview with the author, Cincinnati, Ohio, October 1, 2010.

[44]Jamie Elkins, field office intern, International Justice Mission, telephone interview with the author, September 16, 2010.

[45]David Masys, corporate salesman, GE Health Care, interview with the author, Cincinnati, Ohio, October 1, 2010.

[46]Don Gerred, justice director, Crossroads, interview with the author, Cincinnati, Ohio, October 1, 2010.

[47]Linda Averbeck, senior attorney, IRS Office of Chief Counsel, interview with the author, Cincinnati, Ohio, October 2, 2010.

[48]Ibid.

[49]All quotes from Roberta Teran, associate director, Global Logistics, Procter and Gamble, are from a telephone interview with the author, October 1, 2010.

[50]Rob Seddon, South Africa Partnership Director, Crossroads, telephone interview with the author, October 12, 2010.

[51]Mike Honeycutt, "Shepherding Change in the Local Congregation," pp. 143-51.

[52]Telephone interview with author, October 14, 2010.

[53] Andrew Peters, former justice director, Crossroads, interview with the author, Cincinnati, October 21, 2009.

[54] Dale Bowen, housing coordinator, Lincoln Village Preservation Corporation, telephone interview with the author, September 16, 2010.

[55] Steve Corbett and Brian Fikkert, *When Helping Hurts: How to Alleviate Poverty Without Hurting the Poor and Yourself* (Chicago: Moody Press, 2009), p. 62.

[56] Alan Judge, real estate attorney, telephone interview with the author, October 5, 2010.

Conclusion

[1] Greg Thompson, "By Bringing Us into His Work," sermon delivered at Trinity Presbyterian Church, Charlottesville, Va., October 31, 2010.

[2] Scott Adams, creator of *Dilbert*, quoted in Virginia Postrel, "The *Dilbert* Doctrines: An Interview with Scott Adams," *Reason*, February 1999 <www.reason.com/archives/1999/02/01/the-dilbert-doctrines-an-inter>.

[3] Scott Seaton, "Restoring the City," sermon delivered at Emmanuel Presbyterian Church, Arlington, Va., September 12, 2010 (audio file) <www.emmanuelarlington.org/pages/page.asp?page_id=128989&programId=74889>.

Appendix A

[1] Lesslie Newbigin, *Signs Amid the Rubble: The Purposes of God in Human History* (Grand Rapids: Eerdmans, 2003), p. 47.

[2] John Eldredge, *Waking the Dead: The Glory of a Heart Fully Alive* (Nashville: Thomas Nelson, 2003), p. 14.

[3] John Calvin, *Institutes of the Christian Religion* 2.2.15.

Appendix B

[1] This guide was originally produced by leaders at Emmanuel Presbyterian Church in Arlington, Virginia, and is used and adapted with their permission.

About the Author

Dr. Amy L. Sherman directs the Center on Faith in Communities at the Sagamore Institute and is a Senior Fellow with the Institute for the Study of Religion at Baylor University. She is the founder and former executive director of Charlottesville Abundant Life Ministries in Virginia. Sherman is the author of six books, and her articles have appeared in such periodicals as *Christianity Today, The Christian Century, Books & Culture, World, First Things* and *Prism*. Since 2005 she has served as a Senior Fellow with the International Justice Mission.

To go further with *Kingdom Calling,* visit the website:
www.vocationalstewardship.org